Intertextuality and Comparative Method
Three Essays

Intertextuality and Comparative Method

Three Essays

Charu Sheel Singh

ALTAR

ALTAR PUBLISHING HOUSE
NEW DELHI (INDIA)

Published by

ALTAR PUBLISHING HOUSE
L- 9 A, IInd FLOOR, STREET NO.42
SADATPUR EXTENSION
DELHI-110094 (INDIA)
CELL- 0-9899346553, 0-9868990429

Intertextuality and Comparative Method Three Essays

Edition 2010
ISBN 978-81-910524-0-4

Printed in India
at Tarun Offset Printers, Delhi

For Maya
Who Made The Odd and the
Even Numbers of My Life Click

Foreword

THE THREE essays in this book are an exercise in the way comparative method dissects and disseminates meaning in literature by analysing images, symbols, and ideas in terms of influence, analogy, tradition, reception and communication. Precisely, these are the issues before any study that considers literature either as simply though essentially involving comparison between the texts of one tradition with those of the other, or wishes to theorise about what a possible literary theory could be. The first and third essays put into practice most of the above concepts; the second develops a literary theory, chiefly out of the *mandala* figure, common both to Hindu and Buddhist tantric traditions. The essay also tries to show that Jacques Derrida's method was anticipated by Buddhist thinkers much earlier (Derrida being not unaware of it). The three essays are not merely influence-studies; they document worth-chronicling contexts, combine theory, criticism, history, and establish vital links, not with a view to arrive at external factualism and mechanistic atomism--the "stagnant backwater" as Rene Wellek says—but to get a glimpse of the multifoliate bi-focal and bi-polar segments of meaning that the art-work enfolds within its multi-dimensional repertories, and distinctly, though interpenetratingly, laid functional contrasts of images and symbols.

All comparisons and contrasts, involving the three essays, try to avoid subjective fallacies as far as possible, and do not, in turn, impose objective realities where there are none. Rene Wellek, in his famous article "The Crisis of Comparative Literature", says: "Both a relativistic antiquarianism and an external formalism are mistaken attempts to dehumanize literary study. Criticism cannot and must not be expelled from literary scholarship." In *Discriminations,* Wellek criticises "unreflecting positivism" and the general tendency to find a "cause" in influence-studies: ". . . the whole conception of a 'cause' in literary study is singularly uncritical; nobody has ever been able to show that a work of art was 'caused' by another work of art, even though parallels and similarities can be accumulated. A later work of art may not have been possible without a preceding one, but it cannot have been caused by it."

In both of Wellek's statements criticism is the sole dependable tool for staying clear of all sorts of relativisms, fallacies, and generalisations. Criticism, in a way, is the Buddhist middle path which saves the comparative method degenerating into the irremediably extrinsic and the unspecific. Criticism could well help the comparatist avoid what Damian Grant said in *Times Literary Supplement* (19th March, 1964, p. 235), the "devices of factitious synthesis and the distraction of pointless cross reference". The essays in this book, however, follow a workable hypothesis for comparatiye literary studies as given by Rene Wellek: "An examination of literary texts (including works of literary theory and criticism) in more than one language, through an investigation of contrast, analogy, provenance or influence; or a study of literary relations and communications between two or more groups that speak different languages."

Henry Gifford argues that a comparatist must have a "binocular vision;" for example, in the study of American culture or literature, the critic should have "the mind of Europe" within the layers of his bones and arteries. T.S. Eliot's emphasis upon knowing the texts of more than one tradition is well known though he seems to be a cosmopolitan in crisis of personal identity. Here again, *distinguishing* and *relating* are the two elementary functions (again a task of the critical power) that a comparatist has to perform. It has been Curtius' method to begin with general concepts and then go to the minute particulars. However, an unrelenting preoccupation with *continuities* or for *expressional constants,* results, more often than not, in the loss of the uniqueness of a work of art's identity—a charge also levelled against Northrop Frye (who refuted it). Auerbach, for this reason, has tried to dissuade the comparatist from dwelling unnecessarily upon such general concepts as "the romantic", "the baroque", etc.

Auerbach's method is to consider the text as an interplay of vital social and circumstantial forces that shape, deshape, and reshape it in a continuity that is time (whether historical, psychological, or celestial), which is surely not without its fragmented particularities and separate existences howsoever, minutely interrelated. For this reason Auerbach also devotes a chapter to the concept of time in his book *Mimesis.* However, the contrapuntal dialectic of the general and the particular, with emphasis upon recognising the individual contours and outlines of identity of a work of art (while simultaneously relating it to a certain trans-immediacy) may not lead us very far. The need for a new category has often been felt in the light of new challenges. Henry Gifford rightly says: "Whole continents are becoming articulate—South America yesterday, Africa today. On the other hand, the status of literature, its reception, conceivably its character, are changing. The new electronic media may eventually displace literature." The electronic media will certainly displace literature, it will only change its character notwithstanding Gifford's fears.

The changing situation implies endless discovery and interpretation, and search for values, not necessarily permanent and fixed but relative and acclimatised in relation to the art-work that they consider and out of which they emerge. The need for criticism in comparative literary studies is primary; historical sense, psychological, biographical, social and moral factors can only come under its scrutiny. The problem of identity and difference is perennial both in philosophy and in literature, and unless the two are in some kind of tensional or dialectical relationship, the realization of the art-work's essence (Hegel's Idea) would remain a dream. All syntheses include differences, and all differences do have an identity-element that grows into and permits synthesis.

The first essay studies Eliot's theory of poetry—its main critical and literary concepts—in the light of Hindu-Buddhist philosophy. The burden of the essay is that a good number of studies are available, chiefly by Indian scholars, that view Eliot's poetry and his literary-critical concepts in the light of Hindu thought (Buddhism comes rarely) by way of similarities and differences. There has not been a single study, to my mind, which develops a theory for studying Eliot's literary-critical concepts out of Hindu-Buddhist philosophical texts. My essay on Eliot views Eliot's critical, literary, and philosophical concepts in the light of the *mandala* theory of literature and literary criticism—a theory (which I call a Buddhist poetics drawing on certain key concepts in Buddhism) that I develop in the second essay. The second essay, therefore, could be taken as a prelude to the first.

Throughout the first essay I never deviate from employing "criticism" to whatever I examine in Eliot's literary theory or poetry. The essay also discusses the question of Eliot's tradition and that of value, relative or otherwise, that emerges out of comparative method. Value-judgments are not unnecessarily avoided; they are given, often with a sense of inevitability (with no claim to their absoluteness), and this keeps passionately alive the notion of a subject studying an object. Degrees of interiorization—of subject into the object and vice versa—are at no stage ruled out but deliberately affirmed, especially with reference to F.H. Bradley's "point of view" theory and his notion of the Absolute. This comes in for close comparison with the Buddhist concept of emptiness *(sunya)* and *Bhagavadgita's* "beyond the beyond". The essay brings in close parallels, probably for the first time, between Eliot's creative process and that of a yogi as described in Patanjali's *Yoga-Sutras.*

The focus of attention in the second essay is the contemporary French philosopher and critic, Jacques Derrida, and his method. Derrida obviously had access to Buddhism and Hinduism both from the tradition he inherited (and which he deconstructs) and through, independent sources. I trace the origin of what Derrida calls Western "logocentrism" to Indian influence upon the Western thinkers. I show, in the process, that Derrida's central method, or his deconstructive strategy, is largely derived from Nagarjuna, the Buddhist thinker of the second century A.D., who propounded the propositional way of arguing things in order to show the essential emptiness inherent in all phenomenon. Dinnaga, another Buddhist thinker, anticipates Derrida's method by his theory of the contextual elimination of the terms of a proposition *(Apoha)* in order to arrive at the emptiness of things. This emptiness is both materially void, and ideationally full of content. The third part of this essay goes on to develop what I consider a possible Buddhist poetics could be. No claim is made to follow original Buddhist texts in their linear materiality (in order to escape poverty of ideas). I take full freedom of interpretation, exploit metaphorical possibilities, in order to collocate and discern themes, their pre-figurations and post-figurations, both conscious and unconscious. Time and space concepts are methodically used in order to accommodate Bradleyian "points of view" and degrees of perspectives available from the circumference in order to get a glimpse of the centre.

The final essay is again an exercise, much like the first, in tracing analogies, influences and counter-influences, in the poetry of Blake and Whitman, who, the essay holds, share an identical myth of the primal—Man—the source of all genealogical and mythological configurations. The questions of tradition and emergent values are also closely examined. The essay is an exercise in ideas and structure—how ideas grow out of the cross fertilization of perspectives, and how inter-contextualization gives birth to a new materiality of the text, which, more often than not, is a new emergent value. The identical character and ideational typologies further this sense of value which ultimately grows into an ideologue. This ideologue is not a static monolith of fixed contours; it keeps on changing its cross-referentiality and is open to inter-continental, inter-elemental, and inter-terrestrial influences that co-fabulate and mythologize the secret narrative of human experiences. The essay offers a new kind of trans-traditional synthesis and shows key concepts of comparative literary study working in all their functional delicacy. This book was earlier published under a different title. The present title makes the book more contemporaneous and relevant to our times.

Charu Sheel Singh

Contents

Essay I

Conflagrated City Versus Voids of Eternity

T.S. Eliot's Theory of Poetry in the Light of Hindu-Buddhist Philosophy

FEI-PAI LU holds that "Eliot's earlier doctrines were designed to advocate the poetry of 'concentration' whereas his later doctrines pleaded for the poetry of 'expansion'. Concentration and expansion are terms indicative of the two basic directions of movement involved in a theory of Unity—the centripetal and the centrifugal; meanwhile they are specific enough to render intelligible the nature of Eliot's change in critical doctrines."[1] In terms of the figure of *mandala* I will be arguing that the impulse to create (and even to appreciate) is basically a centripetal impulse, and its outer manifestation is determined, to a large extent, by the artist's creative potency, which, in turn, is determined by the deposits of *Karma* that the artist's consciousness has. This is what Eliot also calls "point of view" which equals F.H. Bradley's concept of the "finite centre". The chapter will, first of all, discover grounds for studying Eliot's poetics in the light of Buddhism, and then, go on to discover Buddhist configurations in Eliot's theory of poetry. It will also consider Eliot's entire poetic output in relation to the Buddhist poetics that I have developed in the second essay. In fact, it will view Eliot's whole poetry in terms of the *mandala* figure that is basic to the exposition of my theory of Buddhist Poetics.

Eliot's accessibility to, and his familiarity with, Hindu and Buddhist texts is well known and is well documented by available scholarship. However, it may not be out of place here to cast a bird's eye-view on what the reaction of the distinguished Western scholars has been to Eliot's use of Hindu and Buddhist sources. Helen Gardner thought about the *Four Quartets* that "to introduce Krishna at this point in 'The Dry Salvages' is an error, and destroys the imaginative harmony of the poem".[2] At other places though, Helen Gardner's attitude is different, for she is content in finding a parallel to Hindu-Buddhist texts in relation to Christian thought. The comment is again on "The Dry Salvages": "Mr. Eliot introduces here, as he had in *The Waste Land,* the scriptures of the East. He finds the same doctrine of response to what is always present in the *Bhagavadgita.* ... Man must not look for the fruits of action; he must live as if there were no future, as if every moment were the moment of death. The New Testament teaches a similar carelessness for the morrow, which is echoed in *The Rock:* 'I have said, take no thought of the harvest, but only of proper sowing.'"[3]

The problem with Helen Gardner's method is (and she is not unaware of it) that it begins and ends with *Four Quartets* in her book *The Art of T.S. Eliot.* Gardner says: "The danger of this critical approach is that we should read the later poetry into the earlier, and appear to suggest that the transformation of experience which gives us *Four Quartets* makes in some way invalid the earlier experience which gave us *The Waste Land.* I can only say that I am aware of the danger and have tried to guard against it, ..."[4] I suggest that had Helen Gardner followed the chronological and sequential method, she would not have discovered the introduction of Krishna in "The Dry Salvages" as leading to the destruction of "imaginative harmony" of the poem. Helen Gardner's method fails to account for the nature of Eliot's consciousness which used to assimilate disparate experiences into a structural whole. Probably, her own lack of imaginative and harmonious appreciation of the *Quartets* she equates with Eliot's incapacity to perceive imaginative franchise.

F.O. Matthiessen's statement that he himself had "not yet read the *Upanishad* from which Eliot borrowed" in *The Waste Land* and that he does not consider it "necessary to read either the particular *Upanishad* or the Buddha's Fire Sermon in order to comprehend Eliot's poem" is simply astounding. That a critic of Mr. Matthiessen's stature should vindicate such facile readings of the poem is perhaps shocking.[5] Matthiessen's following utterance surely does not fulfil the demands of serious scholarship: "The self-consuming burning of sterile passion which is the theme of 'The Fire Sermon' receives added emphasis from the pertinent reminder of the expression of that theme by Buddha and St. Augustine, though no reading of their work is required to understand the poem."[6] Every particular approach to poetic artifact leaves its own gaps, which it is the task of succeeding scholarship to fulfil. Matthiessen says that "my approach to Eliot's poetry, and to poetry generally, is through close attention to its technique".[7] He laments that "The romantic critic is generally not interested in the poet's work, but in finding the man behind it. The humanistic critic and the sociological critic have in common that both tend to ignore the evaluation of specific poems in their preoccupation with the ideological background from which the poems spring".[8] It might, on the contrary, be said that technique is not totally independent of the ideas used in a poem, and an exclusive preoccupation with technique will definitely not do justice to the ideas used. The context, therefore, of Matthiessen saying that neither a reading of Buddha's Fire Sermon nor that of the *Upanishad* is needed, is established. The bane of most of the critical approaches turns out to be that one approach claims relatively more competence at the *expanse* of another, though, very often, it only fulfils the gaps left out in earlier approaches.

Philip Wheelwright is forthright in his approach to Eliot's literary and philosophical borrowings. He freely quotes from the *Bhagavadgita* to show parallels between Eliot's use of the death, the sea, the *karma*, rebirth, and other ideas and symbols, and as these occur in the *Gīta*. Occasionally, Philip Wheelwright claims the translation by Eliot from the *Gīta* as almost literal.[9] Harold E. McCarthy laments, in his seminal article on "T.S. Eliot and Buddhism", that the symposium compilation on Eliot by Richard March and Tambimuttu does not contain a single article "written exclusively from the point of view of Indian philosophy".[10] The nature of my own lament is not precisely this as there are a number of works available now which view Eliot in the light of Hindu-Buddhist philosophy. No Indian or foreign scholar has so far come out with a Hindu-Buddhist literary theory which is implicit in the poetic output of T.S. Eliot and which is waiting to yield interpretation on the basis of the outlines of that theory. In other words, scholarship which merely compares and contrasts Hindu-Buddhist parallels with the poetry of T.S. Eliot has failed to invent categories of criticism which could give Eliot's poetry window to an interpretation closely allied to the accompanying literary theory. This chapter is precisely aiming to do that.

McCarthy also laments those who only casually mention parallels from Indian thought. Instances he cites are: Montgomery Belgion in his essay "Irving Babbitt and the Continent", F.F.C. Ludowyk in his essay "T.S. Eliot in Ceylon", among others. Among systematic studies of Eliot, important critics like Elizabeth Drew *(T.S. Eliot: The Design of His Poetry)*, William Blissett ("The Argument of T.S. Eliot's *Four Quartets*")[11] and H.H. Waggoner, in his chapter on Eliot in *The Heel of Elohim*,[12] argue negatively about Indian thought. Except Elizabeth Drew, most of these scholars think that the use of Indian thought by Eliot comes to the poems in the form of an intrusion and is not part of Eliot's structural framework of poems. This could be called nothing other than the genetic fallacy. Even a distinguished critic like B. Rajan claims: "Section three begins badly. Mr. Eliot is never happy in 'the maze of Oriental metaphysics' and his wanderings this time are' uncomfortably sinuous...."[13] All that could be said of Mr. B. Rajan's remark is that he seems to suffer from his own problems of acculturation, and is, therefore, not able to effect the synthesis of cultures which the poet's consciousness virtually is. To read the part as part of the whole and to read the part as part only are two distinct readings. Eliot effected the first and critics having negative ideas on Eliot's incorporation of Indian thought seem to effect the second.

A few examples from Eliot's life should confirm the nature of interest that Eliot had in Indian philosophy and religion. At Harvard, Eliot came under the influence of Irving Babbitt. Babbitt was not only an anti-romantic, Eliot said of his teacher: "Professor Babbitt knows too much; and by that I do not mean merely erudition or information or scholarship. I mean that he knows too many religions and philosophies, has assimilated their spirit too thoroughly (there is probably no one in England or America who understands early Buddhism better than he) to be able to give himself to any".[14] It must be said that Eliot was trying to arrive at the same kind of synthesis of various religions and philosophies which Babbitt had done earlier. Buddhism, I have been holding, is a meta-religion and meta-philosophy because, unlike most of the other religions, it does not talk of rituals or dogma; it talks of stages of consciousness, points and levels of synthesis, and the relation of the individual entity to the absolute whole. Some of these concerns meet us again in the philosophy of F.H. Bradley. Eliot was engaged in a serious study of philosophy and logic at Harvard from 1909 to 1915. In 1911 Eliot was working under the guidance of Josiah Royce and exploring the epistemological systems of Meinong and Bradley. It was at this time that Eliot was learning Sanskrit. About Babbitt's lectures Eliot had already said: "The lectures which I attended were, I believe, concerned with French literary criticism; but they had a great deal to do with Aristotle, Longinus and Dionysius of Halicarnassus; they touched frequently upon Buddhism, Confucius, Rousseau and contemporary political and religious movements."[15]

After Eliot returned from Paris where he spent one year under Alain-Fournier and had the opportunity to attend

Bergson's lectures, in the autumn of 1911, simultaneously reading Meinong and Bradley at Harvard, Eliot joined three courses in ancient Indian languages and literature. Hugh Kenner informs us that from 1911 to 1914 Eliot devoted himself to a study of "metaphysics, logic, psychology, philosophy, Sanskrit and Pali, and wrote no more poems for three years".[16] Incentive to study Pali and Sanskrit also came from Babbitt and Lanman. At Harvard, Eliot also had the opportunity to study with James Haughton Woods and Paul Elmer More the intricacies of Indian philosophy. Through Herbert Howarth we know that: "America had been hankering for ancient India for three-quarters of a century ... The New England Transcendentalists pursued the literature of the Orient and exulted in a mode of thought which devalued the material progress around them... The craving for esoteric knowledge involving the rummaging among the few available texts from India, spread rapidly among persons uninformed or half-informed but very eager. . . The hybrid movement exasperated opposition. One form it took was pragmatism, patient or impatient. Another was Pound's rejection of India as formless, 'obnubilated', . . . Another was the serious, hard study of the subjects which the movement had appropriated. This was Lanman's kind."[17]

It was to the last category that Eliot's Indic studies belonged and those of his teachers. Charles Rockwell Lanman was, editing the Journal and Proceedings of the American Oriental Society and Harvard Oriental Series. Lanman's famous book *Sanskrit Reader,* Eliot kept in his library for a long time. Obviously, Eliot's courses in Pali and Sanskrit were done with a view that they might help him in reading the texts of Indian philosophy in the original. Eliot read Patanjali under Professor James Haughton Woods and his statement that Hindu philosophy left him in a state of "enlightened mystification"[18] has been negatively interpreted by critics. I incline to the view that Eliot underwent some kind of mystical experience after reading the *Upanishads,* the *Gita* and Patanjali's *Yoga-Sūtras* – an experience which surpasseth understanding and language. Those who interpret "mystification" as chaos are not doing justice to T.S. Eliot's sensitive areas of belief. McCarthy is one critic who has pointed out that Eliot's readings of Indian philosophy are not just wayward and done for the sake of mere interest. He says that "Eliot's enlightened mystification is something more than one would derive from a quick and superficial reading of the *Gita* or an attendance at a course of lectures delivered by a travelling swami".[19]

On Eliot's negative approach to Indian thought, it must be remarked that Eliot made no secrets of his feeling that he did not like eastern or Indian philosophy to be incorporated into the structure of Western civilization. This, of course, in spite of his unquestionable interest in Hindu and Buddhist philosophy, and, though, for the same reason, Babbitt is lavished praises for his erudition and knowledge, he is disapproved by Eliot for attempting to bring Eastern philosophy into Western thinking habits. It is significant to note that Eliot becomes a catholic, a high-priest of the established Church in a very special sense after starting as an universalist, a cosmopolitan, and even as an orientalist. The opposite is true of Babbitt. This is what Eliot says of Babbitt: "A good half of the effort of understanding what the Indian philosophers were after—and their subtleties make most of the great European philosophers look like schoolboys—lay in trying to erase from my mind all the categories and kinds of distinction common to European philosophy from the time of the Greeks. My previous and concomitant study of European philosophy was hardly better than an Obstacle. And I came to the conclusion seeing also that the 'influence' of Brahmin and Buddhist thought upon Europe, as in Schopenhauer, Hartmann, and Deussen, had largely been through romantic misunderstanding—that my only hope of really penetrating to the heart of the mystery would lie in forgetting how to think and feel as an American or a European: which, for practical as well as sentimental reasons, I did not wish to do . . . And I cannot but feel that in some respects Irving Babbitt, with the noblest intentions, has merely made matters worse instead of better." [20]

The reasons for leaving the study of Indian thought, Eliot says, were both sentimental and practical. This only proves that Indian thought had entered into Eliot's sensibility like a contagion and the time had come, he felt, when he must choose to be either a European or an Indian. This is at least how Eliot saw himself. The respects in which Babbitt made the matters worse for a European, according to Eliot, were the respects in which Indian ideas were gradually powering through the European sensibility, and coming to overthrow European modes of thinking altogether. This obviously led to the crisis of identity and the swerving of the branch from the root and plantation in a different soil. It would be wrong to say that later Eliot lost a taste for Indian ideas; he, however, carried on with those which had become part of his poetic sensibility and creative imagination.

One of the other reasons for Eliot disapproving the influx of Indian ideas into Europe was that most of these ideas did not come from the original sources; the intellectuals in Europe could get them only through secondary means. As an example, see how Eliot and Babbitt judge Schopenhauer's reading of Buddhism: "They (many persons) have also inclined. . . to interpret Buddha subrationally. The. . . tendency is probably best exemplified in Schopenhauer who founds ethics upon a distinctly subrational type of sympathy (or pity) and then proceedes to associate this type of sympathy with Buddha and with the wisdom of the East in general. Schopenhauer knew little about the authentic teaching of Buddha, but his error is so fundamental that it is doubtful whether he would have corrected it even if he had been more adequately informed."[21] Since the original is not available, versions of the story change; but it must be remarked that they are the versions of the "original" which is not an insignificant aspect of the problem in itself by any means. On Eliot's negative use of Indian sources Damayanti Ghosh goes a bit too far when she says that Yeats made a liberal use of the *Upanishads,* the theosophy, the *Gita* and Indian mysticism, "Eliot disapproved of theosophy, of which, too, the source is ultimately Indian mysticism".[22] It must be clarified that a creative writer can use his sources or exploit them for the creative purpose to the extent his temperament would permit him to do. Eliot of course disapproved only of certain aspects of mysticism which were beyond the comprehension of European sensibility. In fact, the concept of still point amid a moving world encountered in the *Quartets* is common both to Buddhism and to the *Gīta's* mysticism. Damayanti Ghosh, however, seems correct when she says that "both the positive and negative influences on Eliot were specifically Indian, and not Oriental".[23]

Eliot knew Pali and read Buddhist sources in the original. Henry Clarke Warren's *Buddhism in Translations* was, however, available to him in English translation, and it was first published in 1896 as Volume Three of the Harvard Oriental Series. Warren's teacher was also Charles R. Lanman as he was of Eliot's. Warren's book is a very competent introduction to the Theravada or Southern School of Buddhism. As this chapter will have occasion to show, Eliot made a highly competent use of Warren's book and other Buddhist sources in his extremely subtle poetic formulations or frameworks. A great deal of Eliot's familiarity with Indian sources also came from his editing the *Criterion* for sixteen years—from 1922 to 1939. It would be worth our pains to glance over the articles and reviews of books published on Indian philosophy and religion in the *Criterion.* I give a chronological account:

(1) Stanley Rice, "Alcestis and Savitri: A Suggestion", Vol. I, No. 4, July 1923, pp. 385-401; (2) May Sinclair, "Jones's Karma", Vol. II, No.5, Oct. 1923, pp. 43-56; (3) E.M. Forster, *Passage to India,* reviewed by J.P. Fassett, Vol. III, No.9, Oct. 1924, pp. 137-39; (4) Stanley Rice, "Hindu Music", Vol. IV, No.3, June 1926, pp. 538-51; (5) Katherine Mayo, *Mother India* and Arthur Mayhew, *The Education of India,* reviewed by K. de B. Codrington, Vol. VI, No.6, Dec. 1927, pp. 559-64; (6) Khub Dekhta Age, *India Tomorrow,* an unsigned book review in Vol. VIII, No.3, March 1928, p. 285; (7) John Gould Fletcher, "East and West", Vol. VII, No.4; June 1928, pp. 295-305; (8) Sirdar Ikbal Ali Shah, "The Meeting of the East and the

West", Vol. VIII, No. 4, June 1928, pp. 306-24; (9) Saval Himand, *Living India,* Earnest F. Neve, *A Crusader in Kashmir,* Robert Smith Wilson, *The Indirect Effects of Christian Missions in India,* and Arthur Mayhew's, *Christianity and the Government of India,* reviewed by K. de B. Codrington, Vol. VIII, No. 33, July 1929, pp. 356-58; (10) Mahatma Gandhi, *Mahatma Gandhi: His Own Story,* Edward J. Thompson, *The Reconstruction of India,* and Sir John Simon's two broadcast talks to India, reviewed by K. de B. Codrington, Vol. X, No. 39, Jan. 1931, pp. 356-58; (11) R.K. Yajnik, *The Indian Theatre, Its Origins and its Later Developments* (sic) *under European Influence* reviewed by K. de B. Codrington, Vol. XIII, No. 52, April 1934, pp. 523-25; (12) W.B. Yeats, "Mandookya Upanishad", Vol. XIV, No. 57, July 1935, pp. 547-59; (13) Irving Babbitt, *The Dhammapada* (translated from the Pali with an essay on Buddha and the Occident), reviewed by Philip S. Richards, Vol. XVI, No. 62, Oct. 1936, pp. 123-28; (14) Betty Heimann, *Indian and Western Philosophy, A Study of Contrasts,* reviewed by T.W., Vol. XVII, No. 68, April 1938, pp. 588-91; (15) H.G. Rawlinson, *India,* reviewed by Ronald Duncan, Vol. XVII, No. 69, July 1938, pp. 775-77.

The list is by no means exhaustive and references to India lie scattered in other articles, books and reviews published in the *Criterion.* All the articles and books listed above singularly go on to show Eliot's sentimental and ideational involvement in the myth, philosophy and religion of India. I shall make use of the relevant articles at an appropriate stage of my discussion. This must, however, be mentioned that Eliot's readings in Indian religion and philosophy have evoked quite an enthusiastic lot of response from India. Many of such responses lack a sense of balance and often tend to overdo the cause and nature of influence. M.S. Ramaiah's bibliography of Indian scholarship on Eliot[24] contains no less than 445 articles, 110 dissertations and 73 books. As the number of studies done appears inspiring, it also leads to a remarkably despondent contemplation as most of these studies are influence-studies relying heavily upon the method of parallelism including comparison and contrast. While there is nothing inherently wrong with this method there is a great danger of certain points of emphasis being misplaced at inappropriate junctures. Moreover, another unhealthy aspect of such Indian studies of T.S. Eliot has been that none of them, to my mind, offers a critical or literary theory (other than those offered by Sanskrit literary theoreticians) which could either emanate from an analysis of Eliot's work or could view Eliot's work in the light of that theory.

If one could begin with a theoretical framework which Eliot's poetics and poetry implicitly further, and create new categories out of the whole corpus of Eliot's indological readings, Eliot's poetry is bound to get some refreshing insights and a fresh outlook. In an unpublished article R.S. Sharma suggests that "It would be interesting to pursue Eliot's journey through the realm of *rasa* from *Karuna* through *bhayanaka* and *vibhatsa* to *santa*".[25] Prof. Sharma's suggestion is a step in the right direction. An ingenious critic, however, should not take categories as given; he should rather invent them in the light of the entire poetic output of the poet and his readings in various sources. Prof. Sharma also cites Eliot's cases of misreading his Indian sources—sources which have also been read and mis-read by Indian scholars in relation to Eliot. To such controversies I can only suggest that it is not easy to judge, much less pass a judgement upon, an author's creative use of his sources and other material including language. Most of such judgements are nothing more than cases of intentionalist fallacy which do not, from any standpoint, throw valuable light upon an author's achievement. The tendency to read *one's* own self into the author's work can only be negatived by an enlightened critic. This is particularly important in relation to Eliot who, throughout his life, practised *Bhagavadgīta's* detachment, *Upanishadic* negation and Buddhist *Sūnya* (void) and negation both.

In recent times, the most important work to emerge on Eliot is Eliose Knapp Hay's *T.S. Eliot's Negative Way.*[26] "The way up and the way down", "attachment", "detachment" and "indifference" are the key terms of E.K. Hay, to find access to the meaning in Eliot's poetry. In Eliot's unpublished Clark Lectures of 1926 she discovers, agreeing with Edward Lobb *(Thomas Sterns Eliot, Poet* and *T.S. Eliot and the Romantic Critical Tradition),* that these lectures brought about a turning point in Eliot's career from "one kind of negativity (skepticism) to another – the Christian *via negativa.* Lobb, with equal justice, sees them as the culmination of Eliot's longstanding rejection of Western epistemology, or 'psychologism', as Eliot called it".[27] Eliot's rejection of Western epistemology is in fact a key to the understanding of the structure of many of his poems. E.K. Hay brings important parallels from Buddhism but she basically tries to suggest that it is the Christian *via negativa* that Eliot effects. I will, on the contrary, try to show how Eliot made a creative use of certain Buddhist epistemological models, which shaped, to a large extent, the structure and frame-work of his major poems.

Among many Indian studies of Eliot, the layout of the Chapters of Professor J. Birje-Patil's book[28] is most promising; however, he fails to correlate his categories with a system or mythological framework, and that is where the value of his book is diminished. Patil studies Eliot's poetry under the categories: (i) Inviolate Self (love song of Prufrock); (ii) The Jaded Self ("Gerontion"); (iii) The Fragmented Self ("The Waste Land"); (iv) The Redeeming Self ("Ash Wednesday") and (v) The Self-Redeemed ("Four Quartets"). Elizabeth Drew alone, among many Eliot critics, considers the symbol of *mandala* as basic to the structure of *Four Quartets.* In this, she has, time and again, recourse to the writings of C.G. Jung who has extensively written on *mandala* in his seminal work *Psychology and Alchemy.* Elizabeth Drew says: "In the *mandala* pattern, the circle suggests the imagined wholeness of being, and the centre the point at which the resolution of opposites occurs which makes such a sense of wholeness possible".[29] Prof. Elizabeth Drew's analysis, though brilliant, is not adequately developed to the extent where *mandala* could emerge in the form of a general theory of literature significantly related to vital metaphors and symbols, which could be part of both the human body-system and the system of a multiplicity of linguistic codes that a great work of art generates. The present chapter will serve as the ground for the explication of my theory.

Northrop Frye's conception of literature as an order of words and the word as the circumference of reality comes closer to my own theory though Frye has already felt the need for a *mandala* theory of literature which I have quoted at an appropriate stage in my argument. Since Northrop Frye's literary theory, as developed in his *Anatomy of Criticism,* revolves round the nature-cycle, he sees in Eliot's poetry, and justifiably, the cyclical movement of nature. "Winter, death or old age, night ruins and the sea have ready-made associations with each other and so have spring, youth or birth, dawn, the city, and rain or fountains. Eliot's fondness for cyclical imagery meets us at every turn".[30] Frye is very much aware that the cycle is no smooth flow but a force generated by opposing forces often forming a dialectic "These groups of images make up not only a cycle but an opposition".[31]

While giving a clue to the understanding of the *Four Quartets,* which I take to be true of whole of Eliot's Poetry, Frye says: "Draw a horizontal line on a page, then a vertical line of the same length cutting it in two and forming a cross, then a circle of which these lines are diameters, then a smaller circle inside the same centre. The horizontal line is clock time, the Heraclitean flux, the river into which no one steps twice. The vertical line is the presence of God descending into time, and crossing it the Incarnation, forming the 'still point of the turning world'. The top and bollom of the vertical line represent the goals of the way up and the way down, though we cannot show that they are the same point in two dimensions. The top and bottom halves of the larger circle arc the visions of plenitude and of vacancy respectively. The top and bottom half of the smaller circle are the world of the rose-garden and (not unnaturally for an inner circle) of the subway, innocence and experience."[32] Northrop Frye's chartering of the geometrical design that Eliot's *Four Quartets* evokes and inspires, could be taken as a close variation upon the *mandala* symbol which I give below. This must, however, be mentioned at the outset that though there is a general uniformity about the figure of *mandala,* there are always individual variations keeping in view the object to be evoked and the objective to be gained.

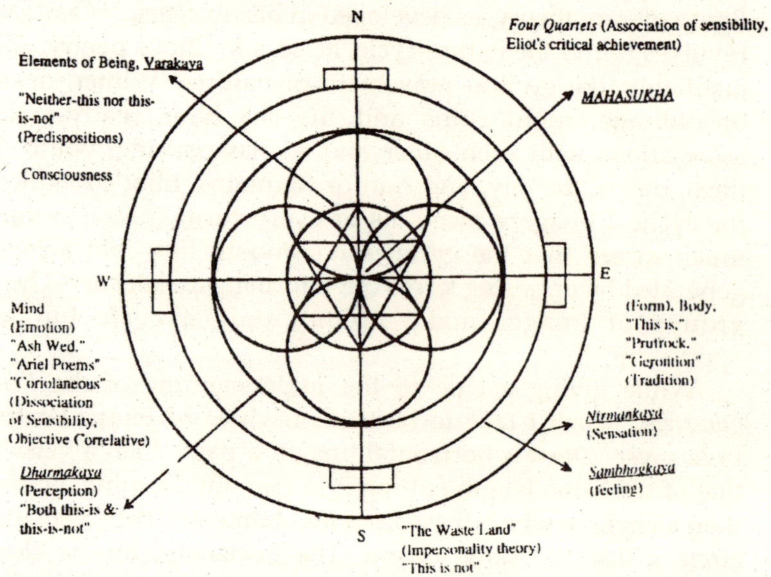

Along with what Frye calls the clock time (the horizontal line), I shall try to decipher and collocate the level and degree of the descent of God (vertical line) in Eliot's work. In other words, I shall see the chronological ordering of Eliot's poems as sequences and moments in Eliot's inner enlightenment which led him to see the world not outside and apart from himself but within the localised compartments of his being. While Eliot undertook the courses at Harvard under Prof. Josiah Royce and C.R. Lanman, he developed a certain mystical tendency in himself, which, much to his own surprise, he disliked very often. Especially when Eliot was busy writing *The Waste Land* as Spender tells us, "he almost became a Buddhist—or so I once heard him tell the Chilean poet Gabriele Mistral, who was herself a Buddhist".[33]

Eliot had been highly interested in charting the volume and intensity of the movement in his poems. In fact, the cycle of poems that Eliot has written do form a movement as my *mandala* figure shows. This was mainly because Eliot got interested in the classical art's virtue of "emotion through motion." His criticism did not lag behind either, and followed as it did, the movement and the cycle of his poems as my *mandala* figure shows it again. In a letter to Stephan Spender in May, 1935, Eliot, while commenting upon Spender's *The Destructive Element*, said: "You don't really criticise any author to whom you have never surrendered yourself. . . . Even just the bewildering minute counts; you have to give yourself up, and then recover yourself, and the third moment is having something to say, before you have wholly forgotten both surrender and recovery. Of course the self recovered is never the same as the self before it was given".[34]

The moments Eliot is talking about here, I see basic to his poetry and criticism. These moments are also movements and they parallel, very closely, the four-tier method of propositions propounded by Buddha and largely expanded by the Buddhist Nāgārjuna. Nāgārjuna propounded four forms of apprehending the world in order to arrive at the reality of the *Sūnya* (void). These forms are: This is; This is not; both this-is and this-is-not; and neither-this nor this-is-not. All four forms could be taken as forms of relative negativization. Eliot's first moment, that of giving oneself up, is the moment of surrender, where everything is "affirmed" (This is) in the understanding process; the second moment of Eliot, that of recovering oneself, is the moment of negation ("This is not") where part or whole is negated of what is apprehended in the first stage in order to recover the sense of lost identity. Eliot's third moment, "having something to say", is as paradoxical an affirmation as Nāgārjuna's "both this and this-is-not". The fourth moment of Eliot is again a form of positive denial which parallels Nāgārjuna's "Neither this nor this-is-not". The ultimate aim in both Eliot and Nāgārjuna, by this form of propositional argument, is to arrive at the void of things—the void in itself being not a category.

This four-tier logic Eliot assimilates into the fivefold Buddhist epistemological model to which we shall come shortly. Warren's translation discusses dependent-origination *(Prātitya samutpāda)* as an endless chain, chiefly a manifestation of desire, which goes on multiplying itself, engrossing the individual and virtually killing him spiritually. Buddha tells Ananda, his dearest disciple, that old age and death depend on birth; birth is there because existence is there. Existence arouses attachment, attachment is because of desire. Desire realizes itself through sensation, sensation depends upon contact. Contact is there because name and form are there, and name and form are there because consciousness is there. Consciousness, in turn, depends upon name and form. Each entity realizes the dependence of its existence upon the other.[35]

Since the root cause of misery and ignorance is desire, desire is said to manifest itself in a fourfold manner. Desire is actually the Buddhist equivalent of "clinging" *(tanhāpaccayā upādānam, Majjhima Nikāya,* I. 261). The fourfold clinging is to sense-pleasures *(kāmupādānam),* to rituals *(sīlabbatupādānam),* to metaphysical beliefs *(ditthupādānam)* and to soul (or substance) theories *(attavādupādānam).* Buddha tells Ananda: "Ananda, here we have in attachment the cause, the occasion, the origin, and the dependence of existence".[36] In order that the subject knows that he is not the one who believes in the gratification of senses *(kamā-tanhā, Majjhima Nikāya,* I. 48, 299, III. 250), or the one who believes in the desire for immortality *(bhava-tanha, loc.cit),* or even the one who aspires for annihilation or the desire for power *(vibhāva-tanhā, loc.cit.),* he must expunge this desire from his consciousness. Buddha asks Ananda: "If there were nowhere any desire, pray, on the cessation of desire would there be any attachment?"[37] Pat comes Ananda's reply: "Nay, verily, Reverend Sir".[38]

Stephen Spender quotes his friend Richard Wollheim on

Bradley to emphasize the, latter's relation to Eliot in his poetry: "Bradley's philosophy may—at any rate from one point of view—be seen as centrally concerned with the relation of consciousness to reality. As such it tries to answer such questions as: Is my consciousness a consciousness of the external world or is it simply confined to private internal sensation? Is there in the universe any consciousness other than mine, or do all experiences belong to me? If there are other consciousnesses than mine, how are these related or are they the centres of quite independent realities?"[39] The relation of consciousness to reality is what Buddhist epistemology is all about. Buddha taught four intent contemplations to his monks which raise Bradley's problem in a different terminology. I shall quote relevant portions from Warren's translation as the problem is basic to Eliot's poems and to the categories through which I want to view Eliot's poetry and criticism.

Buddha's four intent contemplations are with respect to the body, sensations, mind and elements of being. These parallel *Bhagavadgīta's* categories: Higher than the sense *(Indriya)* is the mind *(manas);* higher than the mind is the soul *(Buddhi);* what is higher than the soul is "he" (used for *Atman)* (G. 3.42). In each of the four kinds of observances in Buddhism, the priest or the practitioner is required to be strenuous, conscious and contemplative. We could express it by the following diagram.

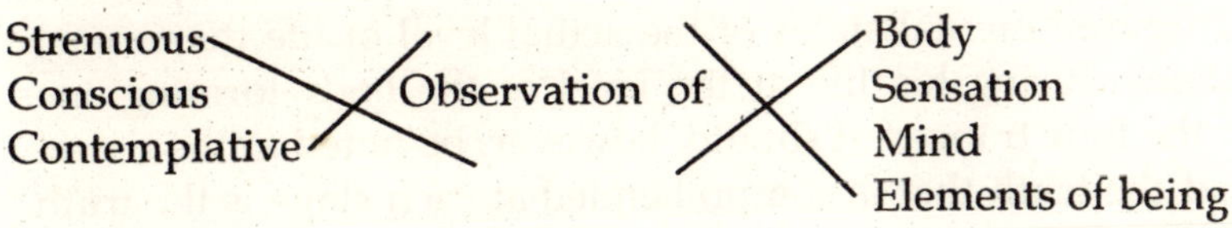

These four categories could also be said to have a fallen aspect in which they become poor inverted reflections of their former glorious selves. Eliot uses poetic variations of both of these categories to highlight the sense of drama that is taking place both within the individual and also in society. These four categories also form a circle. Elizabeth Drew quotes

Jung: "Jung asserts that the *mandala* dream image always combines the elements of a circular rotation (frequently of rotating light), some element of 'fourness', and the all-important centre."[40]

About the first phase of the contemplation *(i.e.,* contemplation on the body) Buddha says that a priest "trains himself to be conscious of all his expirations, and trains himself to be conscious of all his inspirations, and trains himself to quiet his expirations, and trains himself to quiet his inspirations (In thus training himself, he obtains the four trances through the reflex of his respirations. And rising, from his trance he investigates either his expirations and inspirations, or else the members of his trances. . . He who makes use of his trance determines name and form in the following manner: 'On what are the members of my trance based? They are based on matter, and matter is the material body, . . . then he searches for the dependence of name and form, and perceives ignorance, etc., or the formula of dependence, and thinking', . . .) . . . Thus he lives, either in his own person, as respects the body, observant of the body, or in other persons, as respects the body, observant of the body, or both in his own person and in other persons, as respects the body, observant of the body, either observant of origination in the body, or observant of destruction in the body, or observant of both origination and destruction in the body. . ."[41]

As we shall see, Prufrock and Gerontion represent disfigured mental states of the actual level of life that a yogi attains during his life at the level of the body-forming one of the four trances. It should, however, be noted at the outset that the truth that is comprehended at each stage is the truth of the Dependent Origination. About life at the level of sensation Buddha tells priests: "Whenever, O priests, a priest, in experiencing a pleasant sensation thoroughly comprehends the pleasant sensation he is experiencing, and in experiencing an unpleasant sensation. . . an indifferent sensation. . . an interested and pleasant sensation. . . a disinterested and pleasant sensation. . . an interested and unpleasant sensation

. . . a disinterested and unpleasant sensation . . . an interested and indifferent sensation. . . a disinterested and indifferent sensation thoroughly comprehends the disinterested and indifferent sensation he is experiencing.

"Thus he lives, either in his own person, as respects sensations, observant of sensations, or in other persons, as respects sensations, observant of sensations, or both in his own person or in other persons, as respects sensations, observant of sensations; either observant of origination in the sensations, or observant of destruction in the sensations, or observant of both origination and destruction in the sensations; . . ."[42]

It must be noted that realization at each level draws the same conclusion in relation to the seeker: "and the recognition of the sensations by his intent contemplation is merely to the extent of this knowledge, merely to the extent of this contemplation, and he lives unattached, nor clings to anything in this world".[43] It is also significant that each stage and level of realization exhausts propositional possibilities of language and lets the subject free itself of latest emotional, sensational or other *karmic* deposits. In our formulation of the study of Eliot's poetry and criticism, Eliot wrote *The Waste Land* where the subject passes from ignorance to knowledge through transformations of his myriad selves, and finally attempts to attain truth beyond categories. Whereas in the first stage the subject was enmeshed in itself, fighting with its own ego and alter-ego, in the second stage, the subject is able to detach himself from himself, and is able to visualize what the transformed life would be like.

About life at the level of mind Buddha says: "Whenever, O priests, a priest, in having a passionate mind thoroughly comprehends that passionate mind, or in having a mind free from passion. . . a mind full of hatred. . . a mind free from hatred. . . an infatuated mind. . . a mind free from infatuation . . . an intent mind. . . a wandering mind. . . an exalted mind. . . an unexalted mind. . . an inferior mind. ..a superior mind. . . a concentrated mind. . . an unconcentrated mind.... an emancipated mind. . . an unemancipated mind thoroughly comprehends that unemancipated mind.

"Thus he lives, either in his own person, as respects the

mind, observant of the mind, or in other persons, as respects the mind, observant of the mind, or both in his own person and in other persons, as respects the mind, observant of the mind; either observant of origination in the mind, or observant of destruction in the mind; . . ."[44]

Eliot possibly learnt the technique of poetic equation and presenting his theme in a counter and counter-point manner from these sermons of Buddha. Moreover, Nāgārjuna's four *Mahāvākyās* or Great Sentences also employ the same technique: This is, this is not, Both this-is and this-is-not and Neither this nor this-is-not. One sentence is countering the other, and in the process, forming a dialectic. Nāgārjuna said: "There are only four conditions, namely, primary condition, and objectively supporting condition, immediately contiguous condition, and dominant condition. A fifth condition does not exist".[45] The struggle in Eliot comes to the level of mind from the sense. The subject realizes in no uncertain manner that his sensibility has not only been dissociated in its relation to the past, it feels that it has also *to* overcome this dissociation. This we shall see in *Ash Wednesday* and other poems written round about the same period.

The Four Quartets is a metaphysical or even a religious poem as many critics have called it. The life at the fourth level is called in Buddhism the life of elements of being. One who lives at this level has to encounter an obstacle of five attachment groups. These groups are constituted of form, sensation, perception, predispositions, and consciousness. In order that one gets beyond these obstacles, one has to know the cause of the birth of these five groups as well as the rationale behind their destruction. Once a seeker attains this 'his condition is described by Buddha thus: "Thus he lives, either in his own person, as respects the elements of being, observant of the elements of being, or in other persons, as respects the elements of being, observant of the elements of being, or both in his own person and in other persons, as respects the elements of being, observant of the elements of being; either observant of origination in the elements of being, or observant of destruction in the elements of being, or observant of both origination and destruction in the elements of being; and the recognition of the elements of being by his intent contemplation is merely to the extent of this knowledge, merely to the extent of this contemplation, and he lives unattached, nor clings to anything in the world."[46]

Eliot's poetry is a journey through these five attachment groups. Such groups give five different kinds of consciousnesses, each peculiar to its own level, and offering, at that level, its own mode of synthesis and differential operation. What is basic at each level is the knowledge of the birth and death of characteristics that emerge. It is this knowledge which segregates the subject from the happenings around him – a mental state which Krishna describes so aptly in the *Bhagavadgīta:* "Raise self by self, let not the self droop down; for self's friend is self indeed, so too is self self's enemy. Self is the friend to the self of him whose self is by the self subdued; but for the man bereft of self self will act as an enemy indeed".[47] It must be recalled that Eliot had described *Bhagavadgīta* as the "second greatest philosophical poem",[48] next only to Dante's *The Divine Comedy,* and claimed that his writings are tinged by an Indian influence.[49] Eliot further said, at another place, that the "forest philosophers of India"[50] satisfied his need for philosophical poetry more than he needed. The reference is obviously to the *Upanishads* and the *Gīta.* Eliot emphasized the marriage of philosophy and religion with poetry because he knew that "Philosophy is essential to the structure and that the structure is essential to the poetic beauty of the parts; and we must show that the philosophy is employed in a different form from that which it takes in admittedly unsuccessful philosophical poems".[51]

The above statement is significant for us to realize the full implications of Eliot's belief that *Bhagavadgīta* is the second greatest philosophical poem in the world. That in *Bhagavadgīta* (it must be emphasized) Eliot saw philosophy shaping a structure and contributing to its development is very important because in his essay on Blake, Eliot had disparagingly said that "what his (Blake's) genius required, and what it sadly lacked, was a framework of accepted and traditional ideas which would have prevented him from indulging in a philosophy of his own, and concentrated his attention upon the problems of the poet".[52] Eliot concludes in the same essay: "The concentration resulting from a framework of mythology and theology and philosophy is one of the reasons why Dante is a classic, and Blake only a poet of genius".[53] Eliot's criteria of judging the greatness or smallness of a poet are best seen at work here though it is a different matter altogether when we hear N. Frye saying that the days of Eliot's type of criticism are gone and that the above statements of Eliot are based on an erroneous reading. Reading Blake with Northrop Frye in *The Fearful Symmetry* will tell the reader what it means to read Blake as a formal and philosophical poet.

The reasons for Eliot calling *Bhagavadgīta* the second greatest poem (on the basis of the rationale discussed above) should now be explicated. I have already related phases of Eliot's writing poetry and criticism in terms of five Buddhist categories. Parallel from verse 42, chapter 3, of the *Gīta* was given to emphasize similar categorical thinking in Hindu-Buddhist traditions. Eliot's five categories in terms of Buddhism are the latter's five attachment groups: form, sensation, perception, predispositions and consciousness. These are also related to five consciousness groups as is already seen. These categories in the *Bhagavadgīta* appear as follows:[54]

Person

Primal Matter

Nature developed in life = great self = individual self

Soul = Contemplative Intellect

Mind

Senses

Bhagagavadgīta's sense, mind, soul, primal-matter and person or *purusha* correspond with the Buddhist categories: Form, sensation, perception, predisposition and consciousness. *Purusha* is pure consciousness, self-refulgent and self-existent.

While in the *Gīta* a recourse is had to the first cause (though it is transcended) Buddha denies a first cause believing in the dependentally-originated nature of objects. Buddhism and *Bhagavadgīta* (or *Upanishads)* meet in that Krishna deconstructs. His latest theoretical postulates by telling Arjuna that he is beyond words and whatever he has told him is mere words and words only. *Upanishads* also visualize soul's journey as a flight from beyond to beyond. When Ānanda asked Buddha about God, Buddha chose to remain quiet, for the moment God is *described,* God is no more. In Eliot too, this is what the "Still Point" comes to mean. Eloise Knapp Hay also says that *The Waste Land* "presented the conclusion that nothing could be known of this Absolute (a conclusion reached both by the Buddha and by Eliot's skeptical thesis on F.H. Bradley, as its last two chapters show) . . ."[55]

That five attachment groups in Buddhism are five concentration groups also has been indicated already.[56] Concentration holds a very important place in Eliot's poetry and criticism. Concentration itself is a kind of consciousness which further leads to ever-widening areas of consciousness. Fei-Pai Lu observes: "The act of concentration, which yields a complex of feeling which Eliot variously designates as experience, finite centre, and point of view, is an act of transmutation, organization, and resolution. The configuration of feelings which is experience may be called the 'finite centre', for, although embedded in the whole of feeling, each configuration is a local concentration; it may be called 'point of view', for although, prefigured in the vast unconsciousness, each configuration is a centre of consciousness."[57] Transmutation, organization and resolution are the three categories that Fei-Pai Lu gives us and which the finite centre or the local consciousness effects within itself in order to multiply and lose itself in the "whole of feeling". This way again we get the five categories or the five movements as Eliot used to call them. Elizabeth Drew says: "in the *Mandala* pattern, the circle suggests the imagined wholeness of being and the centre the point at which the resolution of opposites occurs which makes such a sense of wholeness possible."[58]

The logic behind five consciousness groups in Buddhism, based on form, sensation, perception, predisposition and consciousness, is a logic based on karmic compulsions and generally unavoidable inevitabilities which are necessitated by the subject's passing through a mode of particular consciousness at a particular time on a never-ending chain of undying impressions which is also the flux. Buddhism recognises two kinds of karmas: those depending on ignorance and other karmas. Henry Clarke Warren says: "There are six karmas depending on ignorance; namely, the triplet consisting of meritorious karma, demeritorious karma, and karma leading to immovability; and the triplet consisting of bodily karma, vocal karma, and mental karma. All these are nothing but worldly meritorious and demeritorious thoughts. The other karmas are four in number; namely, static karma, constituent karma, active karma, and strenuous karma."[59]

As per the nature of karma, meritorious or demeritorious consciousnesses are formed. They may, likewise, result in form-fruition or non-fruition formlessness (Prufrock or Gerontion's struggle being confined tothese two limits) which also corresponds to psychological heaven and hell in Buddhism. We are told that "The consciousnesses are in all eighty-nine in number and occur on fourteen different occasions; in conception, existence-substratum, attention, seeing, hearing, smelling, tasting, touching noticing, cognizing, defining, the swift-nesses, identical object, and passing away."[60] This descriptien gives us the basic Buddhist epistemological model. Consciousness is visualised as a chain in the first instance. The desire to do some karma or the other (but of which consciousness arises) is born with human beings—the reason being ignorance. An example of how conception and existence-substratum consciousness in human consciousness is produced is given below from Warren's *Buddhism in Translation.* The same logic holds true of all succeeding stages of consciousness enumerated above. "When, through the power of the meritorious consciousnesses belonging to the realms of form and formlessness, these beings are born in the realms of form and formlessness, then, at the moment of conception occur nine fruition-consciousnesses of the realms of form and formlessness" having as their object any karma-reflex that might have been present at the time of death. . . . But when conception-consciousness ceases, then, close cn its heels, occurs the precisely similar existence-substratum-consciousness, being the fruition of the same karma and having the same object. This repeats itself, as does the stream of a river, as long as no other thought arises to interrupt the series. . .".[61]

If one views Eliot's poetry as a journey of the subject through different stages of consciousness, one will not be easily able to discount the close similarity between Buddhist epistemological model and the cycle of Eliot's poems—especially as I am studying them here. We know that in Buddhism eighty-nine consciousnesses occur at fourteen different occasions (chapter fourteen of *Visuddhi Magga).* These fourteen occasions are variations upon five categories that I have enumerated. In terms of five categories, fourteen variations will be assimilated as follows: 1. Conception (Form); 2. Existence-Substratum (Sensation); 3. Attention, seeing, hearing, smelling, tasting, touching, noticing, cognising, defining, the swiftnesses (Perception); 4. Identical object (predisposition); and Passing away (consciousness). The passing away is subject's disappearance from the chain of impressions into pure consciousness, out of which, depending upon the nature of his karmas, he emerges again on the chain of karmic deposits. ". . . the series of thoughts of beings in their rounds of rebirth through modes of existence, destinies, halting places, and abodes, is without interruption. But in the case of one who has attained saintship it ceases as soon as passing away consciousness ceases."[62] It will be seen that *The Four Quartets,* which completes Eliot's cycle of poems, gives us the belief that Eliot achieved *Nirvana* by neutralising himself from the chain and then passing into emptiness which is without categories.

There is a key verse in Patanjali's *Yoga-Sutras:* "The recognition of the permanent, of the pure, of pleasure, and of a self in what is impermanent, impure, pain, and not-self is undifferentiated consciousness."[63] This verse could very well be taken to form Eliot's poetic cycle consisting mainly of the love song of Prufrock, *The Waste Land, Ash Wednesday* and *The Four Quartets.* All these poems are poems of double reflexes, and while they expose one level of reality (impermanence, ignorance, etc.), they incline towards, and get subsumed in, permanence and pure consciousness. It is the self of the protagonist in Eliot's poetry which passes through these various stages in its struggle to be itself.

Tradition in Eliot comes both as a "burden" of the past in a very special sense as well as the responsibility of the present. Karmic deposits, which are always there in human consciousness, inevitably bring in fruition of karmas or works. "And this fruition is of three kinds, birth and length-of-life and kind-of-experience".[64] The level at which the subject lives in the poems of Eliot is the level that is, by and large, determined by the nature and kind of karma. In terms of *Bhagavadgīta,* this would come to mean the preponderance of one *guna* (quality) over the other; or the *sattva* (goodness), the *rajas* (passion) and the *tamas* (darkness) combining in different formal combinations and producing coincidences of determinate or indeterminate character. The logic that is being followed in the *Gita,* Buddhism, and Patanjali's *Yoga-Sutras,* is the logic of meritorious or demeritorious consciousness which, in turn, depends upon the meritorious or demeritorious works. But the fruitions are of two kinds—those within time and those outside it. "Of these two (orders), the limitation (in time) *(niyama),* (in so far as it has its limits in one existence), belongs only to the fruition which is to be felt in a birth of (this) seen (life) and which is limited (in time); whereas the fruition which is not to be felt in (this) seen (life) and which is without limit (of time) does not (have the limit in time which has its limit in a single existence)".[65]

Eliot's consciousness, I feel, combined the two fruitions into the life present; he not only followed tradition. (Patanjali's "memory"), he also regenerated it. As we shall see *The Four Quartets* is the fruition of this as well as of next life. We further know from Patanjali that particularised forms are forms of *(ahamkara)* or personality-substance. Such particularised forms are again dissolved into the Great Being about whom all that could be said is that it exists. The key verse is: "The particularised and the unparticularised (forms) and the resoluble only (into primary matter) and irresoluble primary matter are the divisions of the aspects *(guna)*".[66] Haughton-Woods' commentary runs: "Of these four the elements air and wind and fire and water and earth are the particularised (forms) of the unparticularised fine elements *(Tanmātra)* sound and touch and colour and taste and smell. Similarly the organs of the thinking substance are ear and skin and eye and tongue and nose, and the organs of action voice and hands and feet and organ-of-excretion and organ-of-generation. And as the eleventh the central organ which has all kinds of things as its intended object. These are the particularised (forms) of the unparticularised (personality substance) which is characterised as having the feeling of personality".[67] The technique of double-reflexes—the particularised or the gross forms emanating out of the subtle elements—is used by Eliot as a technique of poetic equivocation. Moreover, such poetic equations are the soul of Eliot's poems, for it is in them that the clue to Eliot's method and ideas lies. This is how Eliot's poetry is highly metaphysical and highly stylistic at the same time, "For Eliot's method again and again is to deprive of its context some perfectly natural statement, or else some quotation, and leave the words to echo by themselves, often in a new context, where the echoes multiply",[68] feels Hugh Kenner. In fact Eliot Was as much conscious of the possibilities as the limits of language and his method amounted to the exposure and exhaustion of words beyond which they indicated their helplessness to go.

Eliot's own statement that strange coincidences come to acquire a new depth of meaning when used in a context not able to contextualize those strange coincidences in a proper way is to be taken to mean that language is fissured at its very root. Eliot said: "Why for all of us, out of all that we have heard, seen, felt, in a life-time, do certain images recur, charged with emotion, rather than others? The song of one bird, the leap of one fish, at a particular place and time, the scent of one flower, an old woman on a German mountain path, six ruffians seen through an open window playing cards at night at a small French railway junction where there was a watermill; such memories may have symbolic value, but of what we cannot tell, for they come to represent the depths of feeling into which we cannot peer".[69] The incapacity of language to carry feeling along with itself to its own depth is highlighted by Eliot again and again. There is a strong suggestion of iterability in Eliot's use of language which brings him very close to Derrida. There is a strong suggestion, too, of Eliot having read Buddhist Dignaga's important treatise *Pramānasamuccaya.*

Dignaga rejected both *Mīmansaka* and *Naiyāyika* schools in that both held the belief that words have direct reference to objective realities. This, by analogue, rejects Ferdinand de Saussure and Husserl's claim that there is an arbitrary relationship between the signifier and the signified, and that the sign is the exteriorization of meaning which is somewhere in the interior. Dignaga, Eliot and Derrida meet in their belief that the referent is essentially negative. In Eliot, most of the referents are shirking back from the task that has been assigned to them. They expose the poverty of meaning instead of carrying its fullness. Dinnaga's theory, as that of Derrida's, is a theory of "contextual elimination" —one term cancelling the other out in an endless substitutionary process. Our meaning notions are based on *Vikalpās* or conceptual images whose existence as well as essence is based on a constant negation of all its counter-correlates *(anyapoha).*[70] This is what most of the dialectical situations in Eliot are coming to.

Eliot's method was shaped, to a large extent, by his deep and analytical studies of Miss Weston, Sir J.G. Frazer, Dante, Santayana, Bergson, Russell, Bradley, Josiah Royce, C.R. Lanman and James Haughton-Woods, among others. Bertrand Russell was at Harvard during the spring of 1914 as a Lowell lecturer. He gave a seminar on symbolic logic and singled out T.S. Eliot and Raphael Demos for being exceptional.[71] Josiah Royce's seminar on "A Comparative Study of Various Types of Method" was also held in 1914 for which Eliot produced four papers. "Description and Explanation" Eliot read on February 24, 1914, while another paper on Causality was read for Eliot by one Sen Gupta on March 17, Sen Gupta was a fellow graduate. Of the two more substantial papers that Eliot contributed one was on the role of interpretation in the social sciences.

Eliot's range covers Durkheim, Levy-Bruhl, Frazer, Jane Harrison, Max Müller, Tyler and Lang.[72] I quote Richard Wollheim for an assessment of Eliot's paper, though he, in turn, relies upon Costello: "His (Eliot's) problem is this: if we study primitive ritual, it is not enough to attend to the mere outward behaviour of those who participate in it. We must also attend to the interpretation they put upon it. But in doing so we have to rely upon our interpretation of what this is. So instead of the Classical view, according to which scientific advance is always an increasing approximation to the truth—a view championed by Royce, who spoke of interpretation as 'a self-correcting process'—Eliot maintained that each new interpretation merely adds to the facts by introducing a new point of view: and he chose to see here support for the Bradleian thesis that no judgement is 'more than more or less true"'.[73] Eliot believed in an identical reference arousing several points of view. He agreed with Bradley on the relativity of perception which could only be relational. Eliot said in his thesis on F.H. Bradley that "In the theory which I outline, the distinction of objective and subjec-tive, external reality and mental, is unnecessary. Whatever is gathered together in consciousness equally is, and is real or unreal only in relation".[74] This view again comes very close to the Buddhist idea of flux where everything is to everything else only in some sort of relation and nothing else. In fact, Nāgārjuna's propositional way of arguing and he theory of Dependent-Origination as developed in *Mūlmādhyamak-Kārika* and *Vigrah-Vyāvartani* are strongest cases in point possible to establish relationality and relativity of objects.

The last paper that Eliot contributed was on the topic of psychology presented on May 5 of the year 1914. Eliot advanced the thesis that if immediate experience is allowed to bifurcate itself into the subject and the object, is there anything still left for the mind to think over? Richard Woolheim competently contextualizes the problem by telling us that throughout the nineteenth century it was felt that everything could not be analysed in terms of ideas—especially the totality that is the mind. "To make good this deficiency what was required was to substitute an account in which the mind stands in a certain relation to things other than itself for one in where there is a mere contemplation of its own ideas".[75] The question of the extent and limit of substitutions, however, persisted. Eliot, however, believed that Bradley underestimated the problems arising out of finite centre's peculiar, even idiosyncratic, way of apprehending outside reality, and that he (Bradley) appeared somewhat reluctant to emphasize the whole at the cost of the parts.

In his paper Eliot outlined three confusions. The first confusion is that all feelings are assimilated into the mind by an analogous process. Eliot says some feelings are objective, and to be known and observed in the same way as any other object in the world. When this does not happen "the objectivity of feelings in this sense can get denied, because we tend to confuse them with the feeling of Immediate Experience, which has nothing objective to it".[76] The second confusion pertains to the confusion on two points of view in the light of which an individual's life can be seen or an event in the world. There are two kinds of laws operative on standpoint theory: the first is the law of the "connections of the real world" in terms of which a psychological event could be explained. About the second law Eliot says: "The idea as you try to grasp it as an object, either identifies itself with the reality or melts back in the other direction into a different reality, the reality of its physiological basis".[77] Eliot's criticism of the two-standpoint theory is that in the transition from one to the other there is a great possibility of the observer combining the elements of the two into a single description, thus, producing confusion. "As a result we then postulate something that is at once experienced (as such events are seen from the subject's point of view) and also subjective (as they are seen from the observer's point of view)";[78] The third confusion concerns mistaken notions about referentiality of words as signs. There are many aspects of the problem involved here. There is idea, mental content, image, concept and identical reference, says Eliot and any competent meaning theory has to answer them satisfactorily.

Bradley, too, attacked empiricists and psychologists, who believed, in some sense or the other, that a referent equals a mental image. While Bradley apparantly denied such one to one relationship, he still held the belief that the mental imagery has some role to play in the production of meaning. Eliot's objection to the above is that it is very difficult to recognise a sign in the first place—even if it is recognised it is difficult to believe that the sign assimilates the ideas, for one can identify that which is signified independently of the sign. Richard Wollheim says that how Eliot would make us arrive at meaning is not very clear. "A man could not think without knowing what he was thinking of, or, for that matter, that he was thinking at all, nor could he identify what he was thinking of without thinking of it."[79]

Eliot has, time and again, in his thesis on Bradley, made it abundantly clear that the whole is not analysable into parts, it can only be perceived from our individual standpoints, and therefore, the perceptions would vary. Hence Eliot's belief in the multiple meaning-capacity of a single sign. Writing in the chapter "On the Distinction of 'Real' and 'Ideal,'" and expounding the birth of meaning as a means of communication, Eliot says: "The first point to be made is that the difference between real and ideal is in a sense an ideal difference. It is created within a limited sphere of meaning and recognizable only within that sphere."[80] It is this small sphere which creates erroneous notions of meaning with reference to the whole or Ideal. The fallacy of this position leads one to believe that the intended reality is different from the meaning-reality. Eliot dismisses the "difficult prejudice"[81] of the realistic school that the real and the ideal are different. Ideal is that which has a reality of its meaning apart from itself. Once this is recognized then it will be known that the ideal contains the real and that no reality is without an ideality. The ideal qualifies reality and reality finds fulfilment in an ideal. "It will be said, I know, that the externality of the idea is implied in its internality. But this implication exists only for a point of view which contains both points of view."[82]

Concept and idea play a significant role in the production of meaning. Eliot says that the "idea is the total content which we mean about reality in any particular presentation."[83] Making clear the nature of relationship between the concept and the idea Eliot says: "And it is true that reality exists only through its appearances. It is only in some sense in ideas that concepts exist..."[84] But the concept could only be called real in order not to be confounded with the ideality of the ideal. The issues involved in the production of meaning are: 1. The relation of idea to mental content; 2. The relation of idea to image; 3. The relation of idea to content and speech; 4. The relation of idea to identical reference. Eliot distinguishes the idea from 3 and 4 and disagrees with the fixity of reference which is not exactly the fixity of meaning. Eliot quotes Bradley (*Logic*, p. 12): "We may say... that all (judgments) have but one (idea). We take an ideal content, a complex totality of qualities and relations, and we then introduce divisions and distinctions, and we call these products separate ideas with relations between them. And this is quite unobjectionable. But what is objectionable, is our then proceeding to deny that the whole before our mind is a single idea... The relations between the ideas are themselves ideal... and the whole in which they subsist is ideal, and so one idea."[85]

This is the mistake the empiricists and realists commit—those who believe in the exact equivalence of the image or idea and its representation in language. Eliot clarifies that the idea and its predication of reality may exist prior to their articulation in language. The word as idea and the word as concept are two different ways of feeling the whole, though degrees of ideality and conceptuality are very much there.

Eliot also grants higher ideas and lower ideas, the former being relatively ideal and less prone to predication, while the latter more frequently predicated. Such levels of ideas and experiences in Eliot correspond with levels of judgement too. When an idea becomes ideal, it can only be felt and not judged. In the four-tier hierarchy that Eliot postulates of idea in relation to mental content, image, concept and the idea itself, he gives a very prominent place to the mind, and somewhat radically, as Richard Wollheim says. Eliot says that "There is, in this sense, nothing mental, and there is certainly no such thing as consciousness if consciousness is to be an object or something independent of the objects which it has. There are simply 'points of view,' objects, and half-objects."[86] Eliot is very close to Berkeley's stand who believed in *ise ist percipi,* to be is to be perceived, in opposition to Locke who thought mind a *tabula rasa.* We shall shortly see how close Eliot is, in his conception of the mind, to *Bhagavadgīta* and the middle path in Buddhism. Richard Wollheim thus concludes his argument on Eliot's concept of the idea: ". . . for Eliot the idea is *almost* identical with its reference. What seems to prevent Eliot from totally identifying the two is a difference of aspects or function between them. For an idea is active, in that it has inherently an ostensive, or 'pointing towards' character. It points towards its reference.

"But this way of putting the matter could itself easily be misunderstood, for it might mislead us into thinking that an idea points to something outside itself, which is its reference. But it doesn't. Every idea means' itself *(KE,* p. 56). The conclusion that Eliot draws from this discussion he expresses by saying, 'ultimately... ideality and reality turn out to be the same' *(KE.* p. 57)".[87]

Krishna is an ideal whose reality is hidden in His creative power which is *māyā.* Krishna's reality can, however, be recognised only by a person who has attained a certain degree of enlightenment that sees beyond the appearance. Krishna declares: "Who sees Me everywhere, who sees the All in Me, for him I am not lost, nor is he lost to me" *(Gīta,* 6.30). It is here that the reality and the ideality become one. Krishna is a major point of cross-referentiality who signifies so many things, both simultaneously and at particular intervals of time, on the basis of the relation of the part to the whole and *vice-versa*. Krishna, however, also transgresses all nominalism, all nomenclature of understanding, all categories; in other words He self-deconstructs Himself telling Arjuna that all doctrine is mere words. Eliot, too, aligns himself with such thinking. Idea, Eliot holds, is ideal though ideas can never exhaust meaning. "The idea, and its predication of reality, may exist previous to the articulation of language" (*KE,* p. 44). Just as Krishna disappears in the unmanifest (*Gīta* 8.20-21), so does Eliot say that "The goal of language is in this sense unattainable, for it is simply that of a complete vocabulary of concepts, each independent of the rest; and all of which, by their various combinations, would give complete and final knowledge—which would, of course, be knowledge without a knower" (*KE,* p. 46).

Eliot also postulates degrees of perception: "Every perception involves some degree of recognition and the operation of a universal" (*KE,* p. 46). Krishna is the universal principle, and He declares: "Higher than I there is nothing whatsoever: on Me this universe is strung like clustered pearls upon a thread" (*Gīta,* 7.7). He further declares: ". . . my Self sustains (all) beings, it does not subsist in them; it causes them to be-and-grow. As in (wide) space subsists the mighty wind blowing (at will) ever and everywhere so do all contingent beings subsist in Me" (*Gīta,* 9. 5-6). Eliot says that the process of the genesis of selves is unknowable (*KE,* p. 151), and that the subject is continuous with the object. Object is defined by Eliot as a point of attention (*KE,* p. 99), and as Richard Wollheim says: ". . . for Eliot presumably as for Bradley (and, for that matter, for Hulme), the relation of contrarity is something that we observe to hold between terms only on the basis of our experience: there are, in Bradley's words, 'no native contraries'."[88] Whereas Nāgārjuna drives home the same point by exposing the interdependence of one term over the other which results in emptiness, Krishna says: "By these three states of being inhering in the constituents this whole universe is led astray and does not understand that I am far beyond them and that I neither change nor pass away" (*Gīta*, 7.13).

Eliot says that "There may be, in a sense, degrees of ideality and conceptuality" (*KE*, p. 45). Krishna's assertion that "know too that all states of being, whether they be of (Nature's constituent) Goodness, Passion, or Darkness, proceed from Me; but I am not in them, they are in Me" (*Gīta*, 7.12) leads us to Eliot's statement above. The three categories of beings detailed in chapters sixteen, seventeen and eighteen of the *Bhagavadgīta* give us an account of what Eliot's "degrees of the ideality and conceptuality" mean. Eliot also says that higher order of ideas proceeds from the lower order which implies the continuity of the subject into the object. In fact *Gīta's* entire force of argument depends upon leading Arjuna from ignorance to knowledge for which Krishna instructs Arjuna into five causes by which all works attain fruition: "Material basis, agent, material causes of various kinds, the vast variety of motions, and fate, the fifth and last. These are the five causes of whatever work a man may undertake,—of body, speech, or mind—no matter whether right or wrong" (*Gīta*, 18. 14-15). Material basis is the body, while material causes are the sense-organs. When both are combined we get the agent.

In my classification of Eliot's work the circle is to mean the material body, and each of the four cardinal points is to signify the agent in its sense-dominated, mind-dominated, soul-dominated capacities. The fourth stage is the manifestation of self-in-itself stage where one faculty does not dominate over the other but is in harmony with all the rest. The centre is the result of such harmony—the complete absorbing point out of which all manifest objects in the circle, the four cardinal points, again come into existence. Krishna says that "subduing my own material Nature ever again I emanate this whole host of beings, . . ." (*Gīta*, 9.8). In Eliot, too, there is a whole of feeling and categoriless experience: "Feeling is more than either object or subject, since in a way it includes both" (*KE*, p. 28). Eliot advances towards the argument that there is an agent in all of us who creates and levels all distinctions. The relational nature of experience and understanding gives us a world only half-open at a particular stage, and particular is all that the feeling and experiencing agent can have at distinct moments of time. For this reason Eliot is taking elaborate pains in his thesis on Bradley to pass beyond categories into the Buddhist emptiness or the *Upanishadic* silence.

"The unconscious, in short, denotes something within experience, as the conscious does, and neither of these terms will represent the whole" *(KE,* p. 29). The five stages referred to in the verse from the *Gīta* are in fact five distinct levels of awareness generating five different phases of language. The cardinal point in the east is a spring and rising sun stage, the material body in its lyric intensity, where the sign is accompanied by the simile and the symbol, forming different combinations of meaning. The cardinal point in the south is a stage of growing sun where language becomes basically metaphorical in the formal phase. Whereas the first stage is sense-dominated the second stage is mind-dominated which gives the material body the impression that it is also an agent. The cardinal point in the west is the mythical phase of language where the dialectic is fully formed. The ruling trope of language is metonymy. The dialectic at this stage makes the agent aware of the world in terms of the receptivity of his own sense-organs. The fourth stage completes the sun-cycle; it is a stage of a variety of motions being reconciled, a stage where language passes through the anagogic phase, and the trope at work is synecdoche.

Eliot agrees with James *(Radical Empiricism,* p. 23) that there comes a stage when the knower cannot be separated from the known: "We grant that no division can be found between an awareness and that of which it is aware" *(KE,* p. 29). Eliot has already said that "everything is real as experience and as thing everything is ideal" *(KE,* p. 167). This gives us a continuous dialectic which ultimately resolves into a self that is beyond categories and distinctions. Eliot is combining in his thesis on Bradley, *Gīta's* macrocosmic and microcosmic model with the propositional logic of Nāgārjuna advanced in *Mūlmādhyamākkarika.* I have already said that each of the four cardinal points represents one propositional stand of Nāgārjuna with one of Eliot's poems corresponding to that stage. Krishna declares in the *Gīta:* ". . . Who so shall put his trust in Me alone, shall pass beyond this (my) uncanny power *(māyā)" (Gīta,* 7.14). And further: "Faith is connatural to the soul of every man: man is instinct with faith: as is his faith, so too he must be" *(Gīta,* 17.3). Eliot's following statement, too, combines Nāgārjuna *and Bhagavadgīta:* "Inasmuch as objectification is the creation of a new world, and the assertion that the two worlds are the same is an act of faith, only to be contrasted with another act of faith to the effect that the two are not the same" *(KE,* p. 160).

This gives us Eliot's dialectical model as well as his vision of the whole, which, self-deconstructing (like *Gīta's* God), goes on transcending itself to the utmost limits of the deposits of karma in human mind and consciousness. This is where Eliot aligns himself with the Indian tradition. Eliot comes very close to Samkhya philosophy at one place in his thesis on Bradley. He says that "As we develop subject and object side, they seem to approximate independence, for the object is certainly independent of this knower, and the knower independent of any particular object: On the one side we get souls or selves, on the other the physical universe" *(KE,* p. 29). In fact, the field of knowledge in the *Gīta* is called *Kṣētra,* and its knower *Kṣētra-jna:* "The body is called the 'field' and he who knows it is the 'knower of the field', or so it has been said by those who know it" *(Gīta,* 13.1). The imagery of the field and the knower of the field also occurs in *Maitri Upanishad* (2.5) and *Svetāsvatara Upanishad* (6.16). However, the dialectical counterpart of the knower of the field also occurs in *Chandogya Upanishad* (8.31) where the term is "one who does *nol* know the field". In consonance with the above statement of Eliot, we find this statement of Krishna in the *Gīta:* "Eightfold divided is my Nature—thus: earth, water, fire and air, space, mind, and also soul,—and the ego. This is the lower: but other than this I have a higher

Nature; This too must you know. (And this is Nature) developed into life by which this world is kept in being. To all beings these (two Natures) are (as) a womb; be very sure of this. Of this whole universe the origin and the dissolution too am I". *(Gīta,* 7. 4-6).

Elsewhere Krishna has already said that "It is material Nature's (three) constituents that do all works wherever (works are done); but he whose self is by the ego fooled thinks, 'It is I who do'" *(Gīta,* 3.27). Eliot also makes a very important statement on two selves: "We perceive an object, we will say, and then perceive it in a special relation to our body. In our practical relations with objects we find it convenient and even essential to consider the object's relation to ourselves as itself an object; in many cases this is what is important. This self may be primarily the body, but the body is in felt continuity with the spiritual self. And in cases where the presence of the self is an important part in the meaning of the knowledge a sort of theory of knowledge is at work. It is this sort of knowing, I presume, that induces us to think of knowing as a relation. There is a relation between the object and the self: a relation which is theoretical and not merely actual, in the sense that the self as a term capable of relation with other terms is a construction. And this self which is objectified and related is continuous and felt to be continuous with the self which is subject and not an element in that which is known *(Knowledge and Experience)"*. (p. 155).

Eliot's postulation of the bodily-self and the spiritual self is to be specifically noted. Moreover, Eliot's idea that when the spiritual-self conjoins to the bodily-self and the latter encounters objects in Nature, knowledge is produced, is very much akin to what Krishna says in the *Gīta.* Notice, too, the idea of the two selves: "Finite they say, are these (our) bodies (indwelt) by an eternal embodied (self),- (for this self is) indestructible, incommensurable. . . .who thinks this (self) can be a slayer, who thinks that it can be slain, both these have no right knowledge. .." *(Gīta,* 2.18-19). Eliot's idea of the continuity ofthe self is to be read in the light of this verse from the *Gīta:* "With self integrated by spiritual exercise (now) he sees the self in all beings standing, all beings in the self: the same in everything he sees" *(Gīta,* 6.29). The continuity of the bodily and the spiritual selves is further established by this verse: "In the world of living things a minute part of Me, eternal (still), becomes a living (self), drawing to itself the five senses and the mind which have their roots in Nature" *(Gīta,* 15.7). The key verses round which I feel the entire range of Eliot's poetry revolves and on which his epistemology is centred, are following: "Raise self by self, let not the self droop down; for self's friend is self indeed, so too is self self's enemy. Self is the friend to the self of him whose self is by the self subdued; but for the man bereft of self self will act as an enemy indeed" *(Gīta,* 6. 5-6). This will expalin Eliot's relations, categories as well as his idea of meaning-surplus and the flight from beyond to beyond. Richard Wollheim also says: ". . . Eliot expressly rejects the equation of self with point of view: one self will contain many points of view."[89]

However (and this should again be seen), Eliot also seems to follow the Buddhist middle path. Commenting upon Leibniz's "pluralism", Eliot says that it "is only a step to the 'absolute zero' of Bradley, and that Bradley's Absolute dissolves at a touch into its constituents" *(KE,* p. 200). Here, Eliot's concept of the Absolute parallels the *sūnyata* of Buddhism and the Absolute ofthe *Bhagavadgīta* – Krishna, who is the formal as well as the formless limit of all thinking and conceptualization. This dialectic of silence and articulation, so basic to Buddhism, occurs in Eliot's poetry, criticism, and thesis at several places. At one place Eliot says in *Knowledge and Experience:* "... And the thing, in order to be a thing even, must be capable of entering into a kind of existence in which it is not a thing" (pp. 99-100). The concept of emptiness in Buddhism is a valid method of seeing the emergent thing as different both from its source of origination as well as its point of culmination. This is existence "in-between" the two extremes of life and death, the middle path. Krishna tells Arjuna that beginnings and ends of the world are not known, what is known is the middle. In Buddhism the world itself is visualized as "becoming" which, in turn, is taken to be emptiness. As Streng says: ". . . emptiness does not destroy everyday life but simply perceives its nature as being empty. Thus the ideal is not dissolution of the structures of existence, but the awareness that these structures are empty, . . ."[90] Eliot's emphasis upon relative nature of things amounts to Buddhist emptiness. The following statement should be noted: "The fact that we can think only in terms of things does not compel us to the conclusion, that reality consists of things. We have found from the first that a thing is thoroughly relative, that it exists only in a context of experience, of experience with which it is continuous" *(KE,* p. 165).

This continuity is Buddhist "flux" too—an endless series of inter-related and interdependent animate and inanimate objects which are part of the universal activity of becoming. Eliot's "indifference" is also a variation upon *Bhagavadgīta's* disattachment and Buddhist emptiness. Buddha avoided concepts of permanence either with reference to language or with reference to metaphysics. "Thus, linguistic expressions that imply permanence and annihilation would be 'meaningless' *(an-atthā)* in that they do not communicate anything that is given in experience *(dhammā),* where experience is understood in terms of the felt results *(atthā)* rather than in terms of an indefinable ultimate reality".[91] Buddha, likewise, though having given most of his sermons in a dialectical form, did not preach that the dialectic is ultimate or even that it is useless—*janapada-niruttim nābhiniveseyya Samannam natidhvaveyya.*[92] He simply chalked out a middle way between eternalists and annihilationists in the Indian tradition.

Eliot's belief in the dependently-originated nature of things is highlighted at several places in his thesis. At one place he says: "For it is not as if the isolated individuals had contributed each a share and entered into partnership to provide a public world. The selves, on the contrary, find themselves from the start in common dependence upon one indifferent Nature" *(KE,* pp. 144-45). Eliot's footnote on this should also be taken a serious note of. Eliot quotes Bosanquet and obviously approves of it: "... the foundation of it all is this, that no phase in a particular consciousness is merely a phase of the apparent subject, but it is always and essentially a member of a further whole of experience, which passes through and unites the states of many consciousnesses, but is not exhausted in any, nor in all of them, as states, taken together. It is true that my state of mind is mine, and yours is yours; but not only do I experience in mine what you experience in yours—that would be consistent with the total independence of the two minds—but I experience it differently from you, in such a way that there is a systematic relation between the two contents experienced, and neither is intelligible or complete without the other". *(KE,* f.n. pp. 144-45).

Buddha believed that the action and the agent are dependently arisen. Eliot also says: "I am very far from meaning that it is the act of naming which makes the object, for the activity does not proceed from one side more than from another. Objects cannot arise without names, and. names never spring up without, objects, . . ." *(KE,* p. 133). Nagarjuna's four causations, "Everything is such, not such, both such and not such, and neither such and not such: this is the Buddha's admonition",[93] is thus commented upon by Kalupahana: "Along with the negation of a permanent and eternal self, Nagarjuna also rejected absolute 'otherness' *(parā-bhāva).* Existence and non-existence, in this metaphysical sense, were rejected by him. . . if absolute arising and absolute ceasing were to be accepted, these would negate empirical arising and ceasing which is the basis of 'dependent arising' *(pratī-tyasamutpāda)*".[94] For this reason, even emptiness in Buddhist thought is relative. Both in Eliot and in Buddhism there is an absolute negative reference, which goes on postponing the activity of final meaning, which, in actuality, there is none. The principle of dependent-origination is not a cause-effect process. "Nothing arises from another thing, nor from itself. The same analysis holds true for the relation of consciousness of something and the object of consciousness."[95]

Eliot, likewise, says: "That objects are dependent upon consciousness, or consciousness, upon objects, we most resolutely deny. Consciousness we shall find, is reducible to relations between objects, and objects we shall find to be reducible to relations between different states of consciousness; and neither point of view is more nearly ultimate than the other. . . . We cannot create experience out of entities which are independent of experience" *(KE,* pp. 29-30). Eliot's method is as empirical as that of Nāgārjuna's but the idea in both is not to limit reality or its apprehension but to see it delimited beyond finite centres' points of view. In the gradual progress of Eliot's philosophy, we learn that increasingly he became concerned with such concepts as void, silence, and harmony.

All that Nāgārjuna wanted to accomplish by his empirical method was to show the limits of rational and empirical thinking in relation to the Absolute. Both Eliot and Nāgārjuna are singularly concerned with release. Streng's clarification will further enlighten us on Eliot's statement above. "The terms *nirvānā* (lit. 'blowing out', *i.e.* elimination of attachment) and *tathāgatha* (lit. 'thus gone' = the buddha) are useful for indicating complete spiritual release, Nāgārjuna maintains, only if they do not refer to entities which become objects for 'grasping"'.[96] Eliot's separation of consciousness from objects is a step in the direction of release from all mental fabrication. Eliot, like Buddha, has already denied any arbitrary relationship between the signifier and the signified. This is quite unlike Saussure and very much like Derrida who has brought in the concept of "floating signifiers". In Chapter XVI, verse 9 of *Mūlmādhyamak-Kārika,* Nāgārjuna dwells upon the phenomena of release: "I will be released without any 'acquisition'. 'Nirvānā will be mine'. Those who understand thus hold too much to 'a holding on' *(i.e.,* both to the acquisition of *Karmas,* and to a view-point)".[97]

In a letter to Paul Elmer More, himself a student of the *Gīta* and the *Upanishads,* in 1928, Eliot contrasted himself to most people "who are unconscious of any void" and said that for him the void existed "in the middle of all human happiness and all human relations".[98] The words "void" and "middle" are to be noted for their Buddhist ring. Nāgārjuna did not believe in a one-to-one relationship between concepts and their referents which produce an endless chain of inferences that never lead to release. All that ultimate release or Truth in Buddhism means is this that one should be released from attachment to phantom reality—what the *Gīta* and Eliot would say as the Self-in-itself. Emptiness in Nāgārjuna, Streng tells us, is used with a "soteriol-ogical purpose, *i.e.*, 'emptiness' is used as 'a means of ultimate transformation"'.[99] In fact, the middle path in Buddhism is emptiness only. In Chapter XXIV, in Streng's translation, of *Mūlmādhyamak-Kārika,* verses 18 and 19 say: "The 'originating dependently' we call 'emptiness'. This apprehension, *i.e.,* taking into account (all other things), is the understanding of the middle way. Since there is no *dharma* whatever originating independently, No *dharma* whatever exists which is not empty". What is basic to Eliot's notion of reality (flux) though it may be, is that it is also an ideality, and ideality is ideality by the fact that it transcends our formulable schemes.

Agreeing with Bradley on the "continual *va-et-vient* of ideas in the process of realization" *(KE,* p. 125), which is what the Buddhist flux is, Eliot says: "But the 'imaginary object' has all these relations and in fact *is* these relations" *(Ibid., KE).* Eloise Knapp Hay says on Eliot's involvement with Buddhism via his teacher Babbitt: "The self without system pointed in every direction to the annihilation of self, since every particular becomes meaningless alone. Exactly here Eliot found himself situated by his dissertation on F.H. Bradley, and it was just here that he began to move resolutely toward representation of the dilemma in poetry, rather than to continue with analysis of the dilemma in philosophy". [100] We, however, do know from our previous discourse that Eliot did analyse the self in relation to the Absolute, though it is an Absolute which is an Absolute by virtue of its incomprehensibility and our incapacity to imagine about it. ". . . *The Waste Land* presented the conclusion that nothing could be known of this Absolute (a conclusion reached both by the Buddha and by Eliot's skeptical thesis on F.H. Bradley, as its last two chapters show) . . ."[101]

For the same reason Eliot says: "The process of the genesis of the self and of other selves is ultimately perhaps unknowable, since there is no 'because' which we can assign". *(KE,* p. 151). Krishna tells Arjuna in the *Gīta:* "Among emanations the beginning and the end and the middle too am I . . ."(10.32). Arjuna exclaims, seeing Krishna's world-body, *virāt-rūpa,:* ". . . End, Middle, or again beginning I cannot see in You, O Monarch Universal, (manifest) in every form!" (11.19). And: "Unmanifest are the beginnings of contingent beings, manifest their middle course, unmanifest again their ends. . ." (2.28). In Buddhism, the Absolute is realized through four negations. David J. Kalupahana quotes Prof. Inada on the translation and interpretation of verse 9 of *Mūlmādhyamak-Kārika:* "Non-conditionally related to any entity, quiscent, non-conceptualized by conceptual play, non-discriminative and non-differentiated. These are the characteristics of reality *(i.e.;* descriptive of one who has gained the Buddhist truth)".[102] What is to be significantly seen here is the non-conditionality of relations which is necessary to realize the Absolute, howsoever partially (and not to formulate the unformulable). Eliot's whole theory of points of view and relations and interdependence of relations is based on the defective perception of conditionality which binds instead of releasing.

Buddha preached the middle path between self-mortification (language in its literal phase) and self-indulgence (language in its metaphoric aspect being indulged to for the sake of pseudo-creativity). The middle way chalks out the language of identity, an idea which carries a "felt-whole" at a particular instant of time. Eliot's statement that there is no difference between awareness and that which it is aware of, is basically a statement implying Buddhist middle path. Speaking on identity and reference in relation to memory Eliot has already said: "The relation found to obtain between an experience and our recollection of it was not a relation of mere resemblance,[103] but involved a common[104] reference to a Third reality,[105] which was known simply as *The* reality which both intended. A reference to an identity, it was laid down, *is* the identity, in the sense in which a word *is* that which it denotes" *(KE,* p.143). The intention *intends* the identity because it is there. Eliot is obviously very close to Husserl whose eidetic and transcendental reductions are negative tools which make it possible for the intention to *intend* the identity and identify itself with it. As Eliot says that in metaphysical argument there is no addition or deletion of inferences, only an "'inner development, so that the starting point itself is altered, . . ." *(KE,* p. 117), so in Buddhism too Buddha used emptiness as "a means of ultimate transformation."[106] Eliot's monism is almost identical with *Bhagavadgīta's:* "The self, we find, seems to depend upon a world which in turn depends upon it, and nowhere, I repeat, can we find anything original or ultimate" *(KE,* p. 146).

In an important discourse to Kaccayāna which Buddha gave on the middle way, the middle way is thus expounded: "'Everything exists',—this, Kaccayāna, is one extreme. 'Everything does not exist', — this, Kaccayana, is the second extreme. Kaccayāna, without approaching either extreme, the *Tathagata* teaches you a doctrine by the middle.

"Dependent upon ignorance arise dispositions; dependent upon dispositions arise consciousness; dependent upon consciousness arises the psychophysical personality; dependent upon the psychophysical personality arise the six senses; dependent upon the six senses arises contact; dependent upon contact arises feeling; dependent upon feeling arises craving; dependent upon craving arises grasping; dependent upon grasping arises becoming; dependent upon becoming arises birth; dependent upon birth arise old age and death grief, lamentation, suffering, dejection and despair. Thus arises the entire mass of suffering. However, from the utter fading away and ceasing of ignorance, there is ceasing of dispositions; from the ceasing of dispositions, there is ceasing of consciousness; from the ceasing of consciousness, there is ceasing of the psychophysical personality; from the ceasing of the psychophysical personality, there is ceasing of the six senses; from the ceasing of the six senses, there is ceasing of the contact; from the ceasing of the contact, there is ceasing of feeling; from the ceasing of feeling, there is ceasing of craving; from the ceasing of craving, there is ceasing of grasping; . . . And thus there is the ceasing of this entire mass of suffering".[107]

Eliot too regards the "rise and decay of objects" *(KE,* p. 156) as basic to any theory of knowledge. This will explain Eliot's basic metaphysical as well as epistemological position. This is his basic method too. We have given a great deal of evidence for making the above statement. Babbitt himself tells us that from 1911 to 1914 emphasis of Eliot's studies fell upon Sanskrit and Pali scriptures. Eliot's Harvard Lectures' notes show, as E.K. Hay tells us, that: ". . . he (Eliot) did more than scratch the surface of Indian thought. He studied the *Pancha-Tantra* and *Bhagavadgīta,* as well as the sacred books of Buddhism – the *Jātākas,* Buddhaghosa's commentary on the *Anguttara Nikāya* (Legends of the Buddhist Saints), selected dialogues of the Buddha, Patanjali's *Sūtras* with the *Bhāshya* and the *Varttika,* and the Commentary of Vachaspati Mishra – all in the original languages. In the last year he took meticulous notes on a full-year course given by one of the world's leading Buddhist philosophers – Masaharu Anesaki".[108]

To William Chase Greene, Eliot appeared as "a smiling and quizzical Buddha",[109] while to Stephen Spender, Eliot seemed committed to Buddhism: "Buddhism remained a lifelong influence in his work", and further, that "at the time when (Eliot) was writing *The Waste Land,* he almost became a Buddhist – or so) once heard him tell the Chilean poet Gabriele Mistral, who was herself a Buddhist",[110] I have full agreement with E.K. Hay when she says that Eliot's Buddhist studies gave him a religious position that was compatible both with his personal experience and with his philosophical skepticism. . ."[111] Eliot also confessed in a 1946 talk: "Long ago I studied the ancient Indian languages, and while I was chiefly interested in philosophy, I read a little poetry too;

and I know that my own poetry shows the influence of Indian thought and sensibility".[112] In our *mandala* figure, the cardinal point "east" gives birth to T.S. Eliot's idea of tradition whereas his poetry produces poems like "The Love Song of J. Alfred Prufrock", Prufrock being a subject full of passion, as the sun is in the east when it rises. The weight of tradition, however, fails to fulfil Prufrock's desire, and the dialectic is already born. It has been remarked that the four cardinal points, each one of them, are associated with one key critical concept and one of T.S. Eliot's major poems. The cycle is realized in the form of desire as frustration to desire as fulfilment and beyond. This change and transformation in the subject of Eliot's poetry corresponds to my poetic categories of the lyric (east), the longer poem (south), the dialectical poem (west) and the epic (north). It has also been said that the one category is into the other and their existence makes a simultaneous order of experience. My discussions of Eliot's critical concepts, therefore, should be read in the light of the explanation of categories in terms of philosophy, epistemology, *Bhagavadgīta,* and Buddhism, which I have already given. The attempt at understanding a critical concept will be accompanied, as far as possible, by a corresponding recourse to the poem.

Richard Wollheim feels that Josiah Royce influenced Eliot in his assertion that "a community of souls" was necessary because it was upon this that "the individual was dependent for his existence".[113] This, Wollheim feels, is the ground for Eliot's idea of tradition. There is no better place to begin a discussion of tradition than Eliot's essay "Tradition and the Individual Talent" (1919). Eliot says of tradition: "It cannot be inherited, and if you want it you must obtain it by great labour. It involves, in the first place, the historical sense, which we may call nearly indispensable to anyone who would continue to be a poet beyond his twenty-fifth year; and the historical sense involves a perception, not only of the pastness of the past, but of its presence; the historical sense compels a man to write not merely with his own generation in his bones, but with a feeling that the whole of the literature of

Europe from Homer and within it the whole of the literature of his own country has a simultaneous existence and composes a simultaneous order. This historical sense, which is a sense of the timeless as well as of the temporal and of the timeless and of the temporal together, is what makes a writer traditional:'[114] This oft-quoted statement of Eliot on tradition has been very widely understood. Like Richard Wollheim, Maxwell also feels that "A sense of community is essential to a mature authoritative art, capable of revealing the hidden significances in, and the connexions between, the disparate elements of reality".[115] F.O. Matthiessen feels that writers and critics prior to Eliot, like Saintsbury or W.P. Ker, had a historical rather than critical sense, for their studies involved description and categorisation on the basis of the outlines traced by Arnold. ". . . there was no detailed intensive re-examination of the quality and function of poetry until the publication of *The Sacred Wood* in 1920".[116]

Maxwell is in fact right in saying that Eliot means the *sense of* tradition when he says the tradition cannot be inherited. Northrop Frye makes a vital point when he says that "Eliot starts from Burke's view that society is prior to the individual".[117] Frye further says: "The particular continuum into which an individual is born, Eliot calls his culture or tradition. By culture Eliot means 'that which makes life worth living'. One's total way of life, including art and education, but also cooking and sports. By tradition also, Eliot means both a conscious and an unconscious life in a social continuum. 'What I mean by tradition involves all those habitual actions, habits and customs. . . which represent the blood kinship of the same people living in the same place'",[118] "Blood kinship" is a very significant phrase used by Eliot, and this has been noticed by Frye. Expounding the metaphysics of births and deaths Krishna says in the *Gīta:* "The worlds of doers of good works he'll win and dwell there countless years: and then will he be born again, this man who failed in spiritual exercise, in the house of holy men by fortune blest. Or else he will be born in a family of men well-advanced-in-spiritual-exercise, possessed by insight; but such a birth as this on earth is yet harder to obtain. There is he united with the soul as it had matured in his former body; and once again he strives to win perfection's prize. By (the force of) that same struggle he had waged in former times he is carried away though helpless (of himself); for even he who only wants to know what integration is, transcends that 'Brahman' which is (no more than) wordy rites" *(Gīta,* 6. 41-44).

In the detailed quotation from the *Gīta* above, and the quotation from T.S. Eliot on tradition, the common point is more than one. The sense of continuity emphasised both in the *Gīta* and in Eliot is identically described. When Eliot says that the tradition cannot be inherited but acquired by great labour, and with a consciousness of the past that is able to see its relevance in terms of the present, he is merely saying what Krishna says, "the struggle he had waged in former times", which means the protagonist of history "wills" (Eliot's labour) certain things. Such things form the subject's *samskaras* or impressions, and the chain of such impressions spreads many births and deaths. The journey on this continuum is a journey from disintegration (Eliot's "point of view" theory) to integration (Eliot's Absolute). Moreover, in Eliot's statement on tradition there is a certain sense of emptiness which the creative artist has to effect in his personality in order to bring in the feelers, tones and nuances of other traditions in his bones. This fact is well noted by M.C. Bradbrook when she says that "The fullest statement of this need for Negative Capability, and Mr. Eliot's nearest approach to a manifesto is 'The Function of Criticism:' which is complemented rather than superseded by such a corrective as 'Religion and Literature"'.[119]

Bradbrook draws attention to what happens when a single crystal is seeded into a non-crystalline mass of the same substance: "All the patterned molecules, irregularly diffused, fall into the beautiful and intricate crystalline harmony of that single ordered unit, but the chemical constitution of either is in no way changed. Mr. Eliot's criticism seeds the crystallization of the reader's existing knowledge and sensibility. In a sense nothing is added"[120] I suggest that Miss Bradbrook's comparison is not very appropriate, for tradition involves not only a process of selection and rejection but also the transformation of the subject. Bradbrook's statement does not hint at this; moreover it only talks of "nothing is added" without talking of vital deletions. In fact the individual personality is a magnet, Leibniz's monad, which has certain character-traits and characteristics peculiar to itself.

It is in relation to this fact that it views tradition and absorbs what it is capable of absorbing on the basis of its receptivity, perception, and state of consciousness, the blood-relationship as Eliot would call it. In the Preface to *The Sacred Wood,* Eliot made the vital statement on the subject of the book: "the relation of poetry to the spiritual and social life of its time". It is here that the question of belief, tradition and poetry crops up. Eliot had accepted Richards' essay on Poetry and Belief in 1925 for publication in the *Criterion.* The whole debate arose out of the following statement which Richards made in the paper: "A sense of desolation, of uncertainty, of futility, of the baselessness of aspirations, of the vanity of endeavour, and a thirst for a life-giving water which seems suddenly to have failed, are the signs in consciousness of this necessary reorganisation of our lives".[121] To the above Richards attached the following footnote: "To those familiar with Mr. Eliot's *The Waste Land,* my indebtedness to it at this point will be evident. He seems to me, by this poem, to have performed two considerable services for this generation. He has given a perfect emotive description of a state of mind which is probably inevitable for a while to all those who most matter. Secondly, by effecting a complete severance between his poetry and *all* beliefs" and this without any I weakening of the poetry. . . ".[122]

Before coming to how Eliot responded to Richards' criticism of *The Waste Land,* let the following statement of Eliot be noted which he made concluding his "preface" to the 1928 Edition: "We can only say that a poem, in some sense, has its own life; that its parts form something quite different from a body of neatly ordered biographical data

. . . . on the other hand, poetry as certainly has something to do with morals, and with religion, and even with Politics perhaps, though we cannot say what.. ."[123] From the statement of Eliot above, it must be emphasized, that he is insisting upon the role of transformation in the areas of belief. Socially accepted beliefs do pass through the burning cauldron that is the artist's mind, and the order of reality that emerges in the art-work is not the same as that of real life. Moreover, one can believe as much in an integrated world-view as in a disintegrated, depending again on Eliot's acceptance of Bradley's "finite centres" theory.

Religion and morals have been playing a large part in the formation of beliefs in diverse human societies and Eliot is quite aware of it. This must be pointed out that when Eliot, like Arnold before him, was asking for a study of more than one literature and religion, he was simultaneously attacking provincialism and the development of a pseudo-taste and sensibility among people. In 1927, shortly before his conversion, Eliot chose to reply to Richards: "As for the poem of my own in question, I cannot for the life of me see the 'complete separation' from all belief. . . A 'sense of desolation', etc. (if it is there) is not a separation from belief; it is nothing so pleasant. In fact, no doubt, uncertainty, futility, etc., would seem to me to prove anything except this agreeable partition; for doubt and uncertainty are merely a variety of belief".[124] The problem of Richards is that he has taken religious belief as given and does not want that what was accepted at one time should be rejected at some other time.

Eliot wrote in the same "Note" which replied Richards: "Mr. Richards seems to me to be slightly under the sentimental influence of Matthew Arnold." Richards accepted Arnold who had said that in future, poetry will take the place of religion. For Richards it probably meant that poetry will accept all those beliefs which, for centuries, had been part of religion or the Church. What this would mean in the long run, Eliot says, is this that it is only in "an ideal state of society" that "one might imagine the good New growing naturally out of the good Old, without the need for polemic and theory; this would be a society with a living tradition. In a sluggish society, as actual societies are, tradition is ever lapsing into superstition, and the violent stimulus of novelty is required".[125] The artist, likewise, cannot impose a system of beliefs upon his creative sensibility; he can only enquire, dissect, analyse and transform them in relation to his creative requirements. One of the reasons for Arnold being somewhat *un*critical of tradition—both literary and religious—could be that "Matthew Arnold distinguishes far too bluntly, it seems to me, between the two activities: he overlooks the capital importance of criticism in the work of creation itself. Probably, indeed, the larger part of the labour of an author in composing his work is critical labour—the labour of sifting, combining, constructing, expunging, correcting, testing: this frightful toil is as much critical as creative".[126]

Eliot's concept of tradition, based as it is in the continuity of the subject's relation to what he perceives, subscribes to the Buddhist view of change in continuity.

> The being of a past moment of thought has
> lived, but does not live, nor will it live.
> The being of a future moment of thought will
> live, but has not lived, nor does it live.
> The being of the present moment of thought does
> live, but has not lived, nor will it live.[127]

What is important in the quotation from *Visuddhi Maggā* is that the present is enclosed by the past and the future, the one has lived, and the other will live; but it is only in relation to the present, which alone "does live", that the past and the future also live.

Emphasizing at several places in his prose-writings the dynamics of tradition, Eliot says at one place with his characteristic assertion under creative impulse: "The majority of critics can be expected only to parrot the opinions of the last master of criticism; among more independent minds a period of destruction, of preposterous overestimation, and of successive fashions takes place, until a new authority comes to introduce some order. And it is not merely the passage of time and accumulation of new artistic experience, nor the ineradicable tendency of the great majority of men to repeat the opinions of those few who have taken the trouble to think, nor the tendency of a nimble but myopic minority to progenerate heterodoxies, that makes new assessments necessary. It is that no generation is interested in Art in quite the same way as any other; each generation, like each individual, brings to the contemplation of art its own categories of appreciation, makes its own demands upon art, and has its own uses for art".[128] Eliot comes, in fact, very close to Heidegger's concept of tradition who effects its re-creation only after its destruction. The process of nega-tion is at work in both: Eloise Knapp Hay says: ". . . a striking parallel can be found between his work and that of at least one of his contemporaries trained in this tradition, Martin Heidegger, born in Germany in 1899, believed that German Idealism was the only modern philosophy (1) to see Being as always a Transcendental and (2) to dare thinking of negation as comprehended in Being".[129]

This obviously implies the *Upanishadic* method of *neti neti*, "not this", "not this" (both Heidegger and Eliot being serious students of Indian philosophy and religion), which goes on self-negating itself till the moment of silence when language exhausts its voluptuousness, so to say, and the moment of unformulable Absolute dawns. Eliot's tradition, likewise, is a means to reach the Absolute, as my cycle of Eliot's critical journey and poetry will show. Elsewhere too, Eliot has vindicated a consistent monitoring of tradition: "We look to institutions of education to maintain a knowledge and understanding of the past. And the past has to be re-interpreted for each generation, for each generation brings its own prejudices and fresh misunderstandings".[130] Tradition for Eliot comes in the form of a whole, an absolute reference point, in relation to which all finite centres manifest their individ-ual point of view. Those who repeat the opinions of others, as Eliot says, without making use of their inborn talent (this is where emphasis in the *Gīta* falls) deserve a continuity of endless rounds without a vision of the centre. Krishna says: "Birth after birth in this revolving round, these vilest among men, strangers to (all) good, . . . I ever hurl into devilish wombs" (16.19). Here tradition assumes the form of self-torture and death in place of creativity. Whereas in the *Gīta* this whole is Krishna Himself, in Buddhism it is the silence *ad infinitum* which Eliot's whole approximates and symbolizes.

Fei-Pai Lu feels that "tradition admits experiment, yet it is a movement of destiny"'.[131] In the *Gīta,* this point of destiny is Krishna who claims the origination as well as the dissolution of the world from His own and into His own being. In the Indian tradition, as for example, in the *Purush-Sūkta* of the *Rig Vēda,* we come across this whole, only a small portion of which is visible, the rest being invisible, unknowable. In psychological terms we could call it the unconscious. We know that Eliot was advocating for an unconscious Christian literature and simultaneously arguing for the knowledge and interiorising of adaptable aspects of other traditions. This is how Eliot explicates his concept of the whole: "The existing monuments form an ideal order among themselves, which is modified by the introduction of the new (the really new) work of art among them. The existing order is complete before the new work arrives; for order to persist after the supervention of novelty the *whole* existing order must be, if ever so slightly, altered; and so the relations, proportions, values of each work of art toward the whole are readjusted; . . .".[132]

Eliot's *whole,* which is tradition in its extreme depth and magnitude imaginable, is what I have been calling the *mandala. Mandalas* are basically tools of worship, and they are made to evoke different gods and goddesses as per the seeker's inclination. In other words *mandalas* also evoke traditions, which, when they meet individual consciousness, regenerate it. Elizabeth Drew says that "it will be clear to those familiar with *Four Quartets* that Eliot's imagined circle and 'still point' have what Jung calls the *mandala* form, though any materials supplied by the unconscious would only confirm what Eliot had already accepted intellectually: psychology is the handmaid and not the housekeeper of the theology."[133]

I, too, have argued that the "still point" is the seed which Krishna puts into the womb of Nature, His female consort, in order to bring to life the fruition of the seed, *i.e.,* the world. "Great Brahman is to Me a womb, in it I plant the seed: from this derives the origin of all contingent beings. In whatever womb whatever form arises—and grows--together, of (all) those (forms) Great Brahman is the womb, I the father, giver of the seed" *(Gīta,* 14.3-4). Any form depends upon its seed, and the seed is the composite accumulation of ideas and impressions *(sanskaras).* As the seed, so the sprout. Now, all such seeds which inhabit the globe which, in itself, is a *mandala,* occupy different positions in its circumferential ambience. From their own vantage points, such parts, which manifest tradition (centre) as per their individual traits, try to approach and apprehend the centre with a process of selection and rejection that is necessitated by the inner compulsions of the part to be in tune with the demands of the centre. Just as Fei-Pai Lu says[134] that Eliot's tradition is both a determinant, and at some stage, limits the possibilities of growth, so also does it give opportunity for the seeker to receive, modulate, aspects of it in the light of the magnitude, the individual talent as Eliot says, that is in him. Since Eliot's slant of meaning is always becoming theological, all that the logic of circumference and the centre comes to mean is this that the individual has to realize God within himself. Just as the word is the circumference of the idea, so our bodies are the circumferences of the soul or mind. In Eliot all words are not only part of the Word—a concept common to both the Christian and the Indian *(Rig Vēdic Vāch)* traditions, they are also part of the continuum, the Buddhist flux in which the Word as essence cannot manifest itself fully. This again gives us the logic of the *Gīta* ("By Me, Unmanifest in form, all this universe was spun", 9.4, and "Subduing My own material Nature ever again I emanate this whole host of beings", - 9.8) and that of the *Purush-Sūkta,* that the whole is not all visible. Buddhism, of course, subscribes to the belief in the whole only, in silence, for all of us are relative as our points of view are in relation to the whole. But the fact that there is an Unmanifest part of the whole can only be known by the man who is in full consciousness of himself.

Eliot also says: "But the difference between the present and the past is that the conscious present is an awareness of the past in a way and to an extent which the past's awareness of itself cannot Show".[135] The sources of Eliot's concept of tradition are traced to various authors and critics, from his immediate teachers at Harvard to Arnold, Hulme, Pound, among others. Rajnath considers Arnold, Babbitt, Hulme and Pound as four major influences upon the formation of Eliot's concept of tradition.[136] The points that are commonly emphasised, even by scholars like Sean Lucy, are the similarity between Arnold and Eliot's idea of tradition and culture, and Arnold and Eliot's emphasis upon the study of a literature and tradition that is other than the native. Eliot, like Arnold, attacked provincialism. In an article in 1922 entitled "The three Provincialities" Eliot says that the Irish, the American and the English literatures should try to excel not in terms of nationalities but in terms of language. The Postscript that Eliot wrote in 1950 to the same essay said: "True literature has in it something which can be appreciated by intelligent foreigners who have a reading knowledge of the language, and also something which can only be understood by the particular people living in the same place as the author".[137]

Rajnath, however, says that Eliot could as well have got his idea of tradition from Babbitt and Pound. Moreover, the difference in Arnold and Eliot's concept of tradition is this, Rajnath says, "First, the relation between Arnold's authority and individual is one-sided; that is to say, it is the authority that effects the individual and not the other way round. Conversely, Eliot's theory of tradition centres on an interaction between tradition and the individual talent. Secondly, Arnold lays his emphasis on the repudiation of provinciality through the influence of academy. . . . But with Eliot, on the other hand, provinciality is not discarded but only transfused into universality".[138] It is quite possible to agree with the turns of emphasis that Rajnath lays; what is worrying is that most of Eliot scholars tend to emphasize only the apparent and the empirical aspect of tradition. Denis Donoghue is worried about the practical bearability of Eliot's concept of tradition. He says: "Eliot's particular notion of tradition is vulnerable not in principle but in practice, not because its constituents, when he chooses to produce them, are eccentric and ignoble they are not—but because he failed to bring them to bear upon any matter in hand. The mind of Europe and the mind of Britain are negotiable ideas, but Eliot deployed them as parallel lines of force, one superior to the other, and they never meet."[139]

Eliot is well known to have said that the European tradition is mainly constituted of Greek and Latin civilization, for the main categories of criticism and the basic concepts of literature come only from them. If, however, Eliot's statement is considered in greater detail and with full implications, categories and concepts, normally attributed to Greece and Italy, may have, many of them, their source in other cultures. In spite of saying that Britain serves as a bridge between Latin culture and Germanic culture both of which she shares, much has not been emphasized by Eliot scholars in what role did Indian thought play in the formation of Eliot's idea of tradition. Eliot said, for example, that "I am not a Buddhist, but some of the early Buddhist scriptures affect me as parts of the Old Testament do; I can still enjoy Fitzgerald's *Omar,* though I do not hold that rather smart and shallow view of life".[140] This is the kind of statement that makes it clear that Eliot was the sort of consciousness in whom certain of his readings were forming very important combinations, and acquiring a shape, at the articulated level, where it was very difficult to locate the exact source of a particular idea or image.

The above statement of Eliot is a pointer in that direction where the Old Testament and Buddhism can exercise the same amount of influence. Eliot, relating tradition as a journey from relative disunity or ignorance to knowledge or the discovery of the city of God as Sean Lucy says, is strongly reminiscent of the Buddhist idea: "Work out your own salvation with diligence"—a key phrase in *The Cocktail Party.* Herbert Howarth tells us that "before he had met that sentence in Lanman's class or Warren's book, Eliot had met it in Babbitt on whose mind it was engraved".[141] Such indeed is the nature of Eliot's concept and application of tradition in his prose and poetry. Emphasising the role of the mind in forming tradition, Maxwell says: "His (Poet's, Critic's) exploration depends on the working of his mind and a new personality. The journey will end where it began, in the mind".[142] In Patanjali we read: "This (mind-stuff), although diversified by countless subconscious impressions, exists for the sake of another, because its nature is to produce (things as) combinations".[143] Eliot's familiarity with Patanjali's *Yoga-Sūtras* is elsewhere documented. In Patanjali the mind performs the basic transformatory role not only in the development of human personality, but also in the re-formulation of tradition constituted of past *samskārās* or impressions. This mind, related with the senses below and the intellect and the self above, is also a "Whole" which is never fully manifest. We remember Eliot saying, "What I want is a literature which should be unconsciously, rather than deliberately and defiantly, Christian; . . ."[144]

Eliot's reference is to Chesterton's propagandist Christian fiction like *Mall Who Was Thursday* or his *Father Brown,* which he does not want. Eliot's concept of the unconscious in tradition we shall explore shortly. An example of the individual talent reacting upon tradition is well provided by Eliot and his teacher (Babbitt). Eliot clearly gives an example of the transformatory power of the mind which yet believes in the continuity of the past with the present. In Babbitt, this continuity gets a different emphasis to the extent of exclusion of one major aspect of tradition altogether. Eliot makes his position clear in no uncertain terms: "Mr. Babbitt is a stout upholder of tradition and continuity, and he knows, with his immense and encyclopaedic information, that the Christian religion is an essential part of the history of our race. Humanism and religion are thus, as historical facts, by no means parallel; humanism has been sporadic, but Christianity continuous. ...

"It is a little difficult to define humanism in Mr. Babbitt's terms, for he is very apt to line it up in battle order *with* religion *against* humanitarianism and naturalism, and what I am trying to do is to contrast it with religion. . . .

"I should say that he (Babbitt) regarded Confucius, Buddha, Socrates, and Erasmus as humanists (I do not know whether he would include Montaigne). It may surprise some to see Confucius and Buddha, who are popularly regarded as founders of religions, in this list. But it is always the human reason, not the revelation of the supernatural, upon which Mr. Babbitt insists. Confucius and Buddha are not in the same boat, to begin with. . . . Confucianism endured by fitting in with popular religion, and that Buddhism endured by becoming (I wrote becoming, but to me it seems that Buddhism is as truly a religion from the *beginning* as is Christianity) as distinctly a *religion* as Christianity—recognising a dependence of the human upon the divine."[145]

It is this dependence of the human upon the divine which brings Eliot again close to the *whole* that is the divine and the *part* that is the human. In the quotation above, Babbitt is shown as mixing up issues incompatible with each other as per Eliot, though with Eliot's statement that he is a Royalist in politics, many of us will not agree. Eliot insists that "we must *use* our heredity, instead of denying it".[146] I feel that Eliot, going in for as many traditions as possible, and simultaneously asking for their unconscious formation in the artist's creative consciousness with Christian element dominating, puts a great emphasis upon the role of *memory* in relation to tradition. This aspect has not been worked out in detail by Eliot scholarship, especially memory and mind, as they occur in Patanjali's Yoga-System and in Eliot's critical hypothesis about tradition. Patanjali says: "Memory *(Ṣmrti)* is not-adding-surreptitiously *(asampramasa)* to a once experienced object. The restriction of them is by (means of) practice and passionlessness. Practice *(abhyāsa)* is (repeated) exertion to the end that (the mind stuff) shall have permanence in this (restricted state)."[147]

James Haughton-Woods' commentary upon the above[148] will make clear the mechanism of Eliot's tradition: "The presented idea, if affected by the object-known *(grāhya)*, shines forth in consciousness *(nirbhasa)* in a form of both kinds, both of the object-known and of the process-of-knowing *(grāhya)*, and gives a start to the corresponding subliminal-impression. This subliminal impression (of these two kinds changes into) its phenomenal (form) by the operation of the conditions-which-phenomenalise *(vyañjaka)* it *(sva)* that is to say, the subliminal impression, and brings forth (in its turn) a memory which (also) consists of the object known and of the process of knowing. With regard to these two *(tatra)*, – in the case of the idea *(buddhi)*, the form of the process-of-knowing is predominant; and in the case of memory, the form of the object-known is predominant."[149] This quotation from Patanjali catches the basic nerve of Eliot's idea of tradition. It is the memory which keeps the tradition alive by remembering events that are past. Memory puts into its storehouse many subliminal impressions. These subliminal impressions, when they come into contact with a living organism, are phenomenalised into newer forms. The quality and the character of phenomenalization depends upon the conditions in which the agent of phenomenalization happens to be at a particular time.

The mind, as remarked earlier, is open to two formative in fluences—one from the side of intellect which is thinking-substance and the other from the side of the Self whose reflection and form the thinking substance is. This is what Eliot's statement implies when he says that tradition is not only a consciousness of the past, it is a consciousness of the past into the present. There are two kinds of forms—the form of the process-of-knowing and the form of the object known. In terms of Eliot the former points to the continuity of tradition, while the latter points to tradition-manifestation at a particular juncture of time. What is vital in Eliot and Patanjali is the fact that the agent who is reacting upon the past is not an inert entity. When Eliot says that "the conscious present is an awareness of the past in a way and to an extent which the past's awareness of itself cannot show",[150] he means that the agent who receives subliminal impressions, since he himself is a magnet, transforms them, too, to the extent to which the conditions which phenomenalize him, permit. Further, Eliot says that "What is to be insisted upon is that the poet must develop or procure the consciousness of the past and that he should continue to develop this consciousness throughout his career".[151] Patanjali also emphasizes the role of practice in striking a balance between the past and the present in aphorism 13, Book I, already quoted: "Practice is (repeated) exertion to the end. . ." Eliot's past and Patanjali's memory come in the form of fluctuations, mutations in time. Just as Eliot emphasizes the process of selection and rejection, so does Patanjali say that "Memory is on-adding-surreptitiously to a once experienced object"—(aphorism 11). The primary element of memory, Haughton-Woods elucidates "is the configuration of the object known".[152] Memory is of two kinds: one that makes live *images* of the past into the present, and the other that does not imagine. Haughton-Woods says: "All memories arise; out of an experience either of source-of-valid ideas or of misconceptions or of predicate-relations or of sleep or of memory. And all these fluctuations have as their being pleasure and pain and infatuation... All these fluctuations must be restricted. Because it is (only) upon their restriction that there comes concentration whether conscious or not conscious (of objccts)".[153]

Concentration is what Eliot's tradition aims at, and concentration can be achieved only when, from the point of view of a particular consciousness, there is a sense of the equilibrium between fluctuations that are stabilized and the consciousness that is encountering such a process of stabilization. It is these equilibrated states, which are also states of consciousness during the life-course of an artist as well as a nation, that determine notions of greatness or smallness. The centre of moulding course of historical events, in Patanjali and Eliot, is not history or memory overwhelming the individual; it is the individual who *imprints* his being upon the material of his reception. Memory, "In so far as it directs itself towards the object-known (the subliminal impression), is affected by the object-known. But, strictly speaking, it makes-to-shine-forth-in consciousness, (that is), it illumines, not only the object-known but also the process-of-knowing, that is, the form of both kinds, the nature of the two. This (subliminal impression) is thus described as one which has the manifestation *(añjana)* or form *(ākāra)* of the manifester *(vyanjaka)* or cause *(kārana)* or itself, in other words, which has the form of the cause of itself".[154]

Expounding variety in combining different images and ideas Eliot says: "If you compare several representative passages of the greatest poetry you see how great is the variety of types of combinations. . . For it is not the 'greatness', the intensity, of the emotions, the components, but the intensity of the artistic process the pressure, so to speak, under which the fusion takes place, that counts".[155] Attention is already focussed to aphorism 24 of Book IV in Patanjali's *Yoga-Sūtras:* "This (mind-stuff), although diversified by countless subconscious impressions, exists for the sake of another, because its nature is to produce (things as) combinations". Eliot emphasizes the actual state of equilibrium between the medium that is the artist and the process that is the history or memory or tradition. Numerous examples could be given of Eliot's concern as much with tradition as with the talent in the individual. One, however, notices with pain Eliot's extremely rigid stand against many of his teacher's beliefs. For example, one could agree with Eliot when he says that the civilization cannot be "willed" as Babbitt would have us believe. But Eliot's almost fanatic recourse to having an establishment of the Church and an organised religion, which alone could foster a union of intellectual and spiritual coordination, is highly understandable: "For us, religion is Christianity; and Christianity implies, I think, the conception of the Church. It would be not only interesting but invaluable if Professor Babbitt, with his learning, his great ability, his influence, and his interest in the most important questions of the time, could reach this point".[156]

One might reasonably ask Eliot here, why new

combinations of ideas are being attacked and why are they being asked to conform to one norm? What surprises is Eliot's wholesale vindication of authority in spite of all that talk of individual talent. While it could be granted that individual talent cannot mean chaos and disorder, an honest difference of opinion could not be labelled as blasphemy. This is all the more surprising because Eliot was a student of Yoga and Indian philosophy which do not form part of any organisation or Establishment. Eliot confuses the process of free and liberal thinking with the autonomy of the Church as if man could not think, feel and create without a label. All that it implies is that memory could also come in the form of oppression by the authority. While Eliot is reluctant to make a statement upon Babbitt's kind of humanism: ". . . my purpose has been, not to predict a bad end for Mr. Babbitt's philosophy, but to point out the direction which I think it should follow if the obscurities of 'humanism' were cleared up. It should lead, I think, to the conclusion that the humanistic point of view is auxiliary to and dependent upon religious point of view",[157] he does not forecast the future of his own authority-centred stand which has already resulted in the over-throw of so many empires and theocracies in history. Disagreeing with Middleton Murry's views on Romanticism and Classicism, Eliot fervently approves in him the idea of Catholicism and the concept of the "inner voice". However, Eliot would not understand Murry's simultaneous need for outer principles along with inner voice. Especially since inner voice, Eliot points out, is full of certain psychological hazards.

I feel Eliot is raising certain undesirable points which Murry did not intend. Here again, one version of tradition and the individual talent is coming in conflict with another. And we discover that it is in such variations in approach to the self-identity that Eliot's theories of tradition, impersonality and dissociation of sensibility occur. Patanjali tells us that "The fluctuations are of five kinds and are hindered or unhindered".[158] In my formulation of theory to study Eliot's poetry and criticism, four are the four cardinal points and the fifth is the centre. Woods explicates: "The hindered *(Klista)* are those which are caused by the hindrances *(Kleca)* (undifferentiated-consciousness, &c.) and are the field for growth of the accumulation of the latent-deposits of *Karma;* the unhindered have discriminative discernment as their object and thus obstruct the task *(adhikāra)* of the aspects *(guna).* These are still unhindered even when they occur in the stream of the hindered. . . . In this wise, the wheel of fluctuations and subliminal impressions ceaselessly rolls on (until the highest concentration is attained)".[159] This gives a clue to Eliot's idea of the still centre amid a universe in motion. The universe begins with the Love Song of Prufrock and ends with the *Quartets,* and it could be seen that Eliot's achievement lies in uniting into harmony the compartmentalised portions of human personality. Woods says that "Operating in this wise, this mind-stuff, having finished its task, abides in its own likeness, or (rather) becomes resolved (into primary substance)".[160]

In his essay on Charles Whibley, Eliot says that there are four ways of thinking: talking to others, to one another, to oneself, and to God. Related are Eliot's three voices of poetry: the poet talking to himself, to others and through a character. All these are instances of depersonalization which we shall consider shortly. For the present, the similarity between the vital typologies that Eliot chooses and the typologies that we encounter in the *Gīta,* the *Yoga-Sūtras* and Buddhism should be noted. The similarity is all the more remarkable in terms of the identity of meaning-implications that are generated out of Eliot's poetry and Hindu-Buddhist philosophical texts. Eliot's four ways of thinking, for example, are a variation upon Nagarjuna's four propositions: "This is" (Eliot's "talking to oneself"); "This is not" (Eliot's "talking to one another"); "Neither-this nor this-is-not" (Eliot's "talking to others"); and "Both-this and this-is-not" (Eliot's "talking to God" who includes all affirmations and negations). Moreover, the aim of Nagarjuna, by advancing such logic, is to show the emptiness of objects as already indicated, thereby implying liberation from word-construction habit, and, achieving this way, original unity; the aim of Eliot, likewise, is to show how one stage leads to the other, finally making way for original harmony, deep concentration, which is *samādhi* in Patanjali and *Mahā-sukha* in Buddhism. Patanjali says: "of these (five perfections) that which proceeds from contemplation leaves no latent deposit".[161] Eliot's four ways of thinking are, by implication, Patanjali's four perfections (fifth being the centre to which the four lead), which, in their fallen states are imperfections indeed.

Northrop Frye says that Eliot's literary polemic derives from a myth of decline. I believe that Oswald Spengler's great book is the source of both Mr. Frye's critical formulations (via Blake of course), and Eliot's journey from disintegration to integration. And Oswald Spengler was no mean scholar of Indian mythology and religion as he was of other cultures. Expounding Eliot's historical dialectic, Northrop Frye says that Eliot agrees with Arnold and shares the view that Romantic poets were immature and lacked "centrality" as Babbitt said. This is all the more painful because the post-Romantic residue survived till the time of Eliot and as Eliot said in "Imperfect Critics", this "leads its disciples only back upon themselves". Frye says that "Romanticism, then, as a creative process emanating from and returning to (Eliot's "The poet talking to oneself' and Nāgārjuna's "this is" where the Romantic poet felt that the universal reality is talking to him only and not to others) the ego, occupies the foreground of Eliot's historical dialectic, . . ."[162] Here again, Eliot's application of his categories to understand tradition is to be noted. Frye tells us how Eliot applies these categories upon his poetry which again give us the logic of the cycle, the dialectical opposition and the centre as resolution: "In 'Portrait of a Lady' there is a sequence of four encounters carefully dated December, April, August, and October. The opening page of *The Waste Land* starts with April and goes through the coming of summer to the word 'winter'. The five little lyrics called 'Landscapes' are arranged in the order of the seasons, and the sea-gull in the last poem has a special association with the end of the cycle, reappearing in 'Gerontion' and the fourth section of *The Waste Land*. These groups of images make up not only a cycle but an opposition."[163]

The above confirms that Eliot's approach to history and tradition is cyclic, not only like Arnold Toyanbee and Oswald Spengler, but also like *Purush-sūkta* in the *Rig Veda*, the *Upanishads*, the *Gīta*, and of course Buddhism. We could not equate Eliot's world-view and vision as much with Spengler or Frazer as with his Indian sources and Miss Weston's *From Ritual to Romance*, where a great portion is devoted to the *Rig Veda* and the Grail legend.[164] Moreover, there is a remarkable equanimity between Eliot's religious imagination and the world-view propounded in Eliot's Indian sources. Eliot had said of Blake that he indulged in a philosophy of his "own", for both the lack of any formal training and of a framework of accepted ideas compelled him to do so. Frye, however, remarks that ". . . When we read, *Four Quartets*, whatever influences there may be from Bradley and Patanjali or St. John of the Cross or Heraclitus, we darkly suspect Eliot too of indulging in a philosophy of his own."[165] I do not think it is possible to agree with Frye's remark as it was not possible for me to agree with Eliot's remark on Blake.[166]

The *Upanishads* with which Eliot was familiar through Harvard Oriental Series translation and through Robert Ernest Hume's translation[167] propound the view of a tradition that enjoys the freedom of open discussion as evidenced by dialogues between a Guru and a disciple. It was not always that the disciple took his Guru's words for marble pieces. Intense discussions used to follow which often took the form of a dialectic. Buddha's method, I have said, is deconstructive. He deconstructs the entire philosophical, religious, and even literary tradition that precedes him and Eliot would not have got a better example of the individual talent trying to live, against and for, the continuance of tradition. That the individual is a medium, is a concept common to Buddha, Eliot and the *Gīta*. The concept of emptiness is what Buddha's system is founded upon, as is the concept of negativity, and as Eliose Knapp Hay says, Eliot would not have talked of both had he not undergone some kind of Buddhist realization, which is quite true. ". . .if Eliot had not first steeped himself in the negative way of Buddhism, he would not have found his bearings towards the negative way of Christianity".[168] This parallels the *neti neti*, "not this", "not this" of the *Upanishads* practised to destroy latent-deposits of action or thought that continue to take form in the human mind.

All this happened to Eliot because of Irving Babbitt, for it was Babbitt who had directed Eliot first to study Sanskrit and Pali.[169] Babbitt's own interests in Buddhism had originated because of his marriage to the daughter of Peking's first American consul. Babbitt translated the *Dhammapāda* with a long essay entitled "Buddha and the Occident". E.K. Hay, to whom I owe these details, says: "The essay stresses the mystical and supernatural aspects of Buddhism and then goes on to describe other characteristics which must have had a powerful appeal for Eliot, especially the Buddha's critical and experimental approaches to ultimate reality. Throughout his essay, Babbitt contrasts Buddhism to Christianity, always to the advantage of the Buddhists."[170] On Buddha's approach to the tradition preceding him, Miss Hay quotes from Babbitt's book: "Buddha also differs from the religious teachers with whom we are familiar by his positive temper. The idea of experiment and the idea of the supernatural have come to seem to us mutually exclusive. Yet Buddha may perhaps be best defined as a critical and experimental supernaturalist".[171] This statement of Babbitt gives a lot of weight to my conclusion that Eliot's belief in the supernatural, the divine or the Absolute, which could not be fully known, and his concept of the individual talent experimenting with tradition, derive basically from Buddhism. Eliot's honest disagreements with his teacher are cases in point of Eliot's own method.

The corresponding poem with tradition is the Love Song of J. Alfred Prufrock which I associate with my own theory's lyric stage. This is the stage of the lyric when the dialogue and the dialectic of the protagonist of history remain, for a major part, unconscious. The cardinal point is the east, the direction wherefrom rises the sun, full of passion and promise and inspiration and desire, all of whom, in their fallen state, may never be fulfilled or realised. That is to say, the function of images, symbols and the other vocables of language is operative at two levels: the level of the utterance and the level of the implication of what is uttered. The three circles in my *mandala* figure come to signify Buddhist *Nirmānkāya, Sambhogkāya* and *Dharmakāya.* The lyric, in my theory, corresponds to the *Nirmankāya,* the longer poem to the *Sambhogkāya,* and the epic to the *Dharmakāya.* The circles are also associated, beginning from the outside, with *Bhagavadgīta's tamas* (darkness), *rajas* (passion) and *sattva* (goodness). In the first stage, the *tamas* subordinates the other two; in the second state, the *rajas* subordinates the *tamas* and the *sattva,* whereas in the third stage, the *rajas* and the *tamas* are subordinated by *sattva.* When a seeker crosses these states of consciousness, these categories are consumed in his burning energy for liberation, and a primeval stage is reached of male and female principles, living in their ancient glory. But the realization of the androgynous nature of man is not the ultimate realization of the seeker. In a final effort he has to transcend it as well in order to *become* the potency of the centre, the seed, the *tāntric Parābindu,* and the *Upanishadic* "beyond the beyond".

This *Parābindu* assimilates many centres in itself; in fact the entire effort of the seeker's journey involves to see this *Parābindu* not from many subjective points of view that are there round the circle, but to see the centre in itself as it really is. This is what we know as the total realization of the emptiness of all objects. All *bindus* are seeds with creative potencies; they are, however, *bindus* in relation to the *Parābindu* which gives us the logic of a still centre amid a world in motion. "The Love Song of J. Alfred Prufrock" and "Gerontion" cover the first stage of the journey of Eliot's protagonist of poems to the centre. Frye already discovers the dialectic: "The two kingdoms are also contrasted in the minds of Prufrock and Gerontion, who exemplify a theme, running through all of Eliot's work, of assuring a double part. In addressing 'you' who is also themselves, they follow a dialectic which separates the world they are in, and have committed themselves to, from a paradisal world set over against it, which they contemplate until they feel finally separated from it. In 'Prufrock' this latter world is a wish-fulfilment world symbolised by the sea, it is the sea of the mermaids, as opposed to the sea of ordinary experience in which Prufrock awakens and 'drowns', the latter being the sea in which he is a pair of ragged claws, and which in the apocalypse, according to the Bible, will disappear, taking Prufrock with it. Gerontion, as his name indicates, is an old man at the point of death, his reverie a parody of Newman's *The Dream of Gerontius.* All the images surrounding him are of the end of the natural cycle: the decaying house which is a symbol of his dying body, the gull, the sea, and the winter. . . . Both poems move towards a self-recognition scene, a scene which is parody because it is the ego, the illusory self capable only of death, that is recognised."[172]

Prufrock and Gerontion's sensibilities are fissured; the former, however, is not very conscious of the bifurcation of his being, and so the dialectic in Prufrock is a bit more unconscious than conscious. The lyric, which is the first stage of my literary theory, realizes the dialectic in a character or situation only in an unconscious manner; and it will be seen, as my categories, along with Eliot's poetry, proceed that the journey is from a state of the subject's unconsciousness to his coming into a conscious realization of the situation he is in, to his attempt to separate himself from the situation either by transforming it or by forgetting that he is a part of it (the consdous dialectic). The journey finally ends in the resolution of the dialectical opposition and in the fulfilment of the dream of harmony which still points to the journey beyond. Prufrock's is a tragic lyric which celebrates his attempted success at articulating his ideas with a continuously suppressed, though consistently emerging, idea of his insalubrious defeat. The lyric intensity is provided by the ovewhelming question which is always there on the surface of Prufrock's mind but never quite coming out. The contraction of time into tiny figments of unsatisfied desire leads into reptiles of thought that multiply and engross the protagonist into a combination of unresolvable ideas. The highly industrialized images of the fog, the chimneys, the smoke, enter into the nerves and the arteries and into the vital filaments of Prufrock's being and eat his mind and body.

In terms of my categories where the study of Prufrock, Gerontion, and the concept of tradition go together, I feel that the dead weight of tradition, which fails to find a match in Prufrock's meagre or little individual talent, leads him into indecision, lack of grasping, perception and articulation, and even the loss of speech and the distortion of syntax. Matthiessen says that "in any age the thing of highest importance for the poet is to 'express with individual differences the general state of mind, not as a *duty*, but simply because'..if he possesses that rare, unyielding honesty which alone will give his work depth—'he cannot help participating in it"'.[173] Prufrock then, in terms of my critical formulation, represents the above stage of consciousness; his problem is basically the problem of articulation. He is born out of a tradition that knows of no lyrical songs, only of lyrical failures. Prufrock represents the lowest stage of creativity too, a combination of *tamas/rajas* and *sattva* (the *tamas* dominating) and the unmanifest energy at the spinal column trying to seek formal fulfilment without success. Philip Wheelwright, describing the complete barrenness of hollow men, Prufrock, and Gerontion, says that they cannot maintain the vision of an island of hope in despair. The hollow men, he says, are "the neurotic courtesan of *The Waste Land,* Gerontion huddled in a decayed house with his senseless scraps of memory, Prufrock with his hypochondriac hesitations. Separation for them is only negative, a duty lingering death".[174]

Wheelwright goes on comparing this death-wish with the death-principle in Freud. I feel that Prufrock, Gerontion and even "Hollow Men" represent various stages of the Absolute negative reference that manifests itself so predominantly throughout Eliot's poetry and criticism from the beginning to the end. The stage of consciousness of Eliot's protagonist, when he passes through the hollow men, Prufrock and

Gerontion stages is absolutely negative, implying Nagarjuna's fourth category, "Neither-this-nor-this-is-not", without any sense of the corresponding *elan vital* or affirmation absolute. Prufrock and Gerontion, both of whom are at the lowest ebb of the cycle, their mental state in terms of the *Gīta* could be: "But that (kind of knowledge) which sticks to one effect as if it were all,—irrational, not bothering about the Real as the (True) object (of all knowledge, thinking of it as) finite,—this (knowledge) belongs to Darkness (18.22). The work embarked on by a man deluded who has no thought of consequence, nor (cares at all) for the loss and hurt (he causes others) or for the human part (he plays himself), is called (a work) of Darkness (18.25). The agent, inept and vulgar, stiff-and-proud, a cheat, low-spoken, slothful, who is subject to depression, who procrastinates, is called (an agent) in Darkness' way (18.28)."[175]

Many words from the *Gīta* exactly fit into the character of Prufrock and Gerontion. For example, the last verse quoted from the *Gīta* talks of low-spokenness, depression, procrastination, which exactly describe Prufrock's character. The example of procrastination is the oft-repeated "There will be time, there will be time". The example of low-spokenness is:

> "(They will say: 'But how his arms and legs are thin!'
> Do I dare
> Disturb the universe?
> In a minute there is time
> For decisions and revisions which a minute will reverse".

The example of depression is:

> "For I have known them all already, known them all—
> Have known the evenings, mornings, afternoons,
> I have measured out my life with coffee spoons";

Compare also these lines spoken by Gerontion with the verses quoted from the *Gīta*. The lines show a total loss of attempt at self-understanding, sloth, torpor and inhibition:

"I have lost my passion: why should I need to keep it
Since what is kept must be adulterated?
I have lost my sight, smell, hearing, taste and touch:
How should I use them for your closer contact?"

Prufrock and Gerontion's (and *The Hollow Men)* mental states are all the more important as they are juxtaposed with the rising of the sun in my own theory. The rising sun is a symbol of passion, glory, energy and promise. Such qualities only have their negative aspects in poems under discussion. This also highlights Eliot's basic technique.

Harold E. McCarthy considers suffering and impermanence as basic to Eliot and Buddhism. He quotes the following from Henry Clarke Warren:

> "Whether Buddhas arise, O priests, or whether Buddhas do not arise, it remains a fact and the fixed and necessary constitution of being, that all its constituents are transitory.
>
> "Whether Buddhas arise, O priests, or whether Buddhas do not arise, it remains a fact and the fixed and necessary constitution of being, that all its constituents are misery".
>
> "Whether Buddhas arise, O priests, or whether Buddhas do not arise, it remains a fact and the fixed and necessary constitution of being, that all its elements are lacking in an Ego."[176]

Harold McCarthy's comment runs: "This key intuition of Buddhism is precisely the intuition which underlies the poetry of T.S. Eliot. It is the progressive expression of this intuition which has led the superficial reader to speak of Eliot as basically pessimistic,... (and Buddhism itself has often been spoken of as profoundly pessimistic), there is no doubt at all that in Eliot's poetry the intuition of impermanence and suffering plays a dominant role. Sometimes it is impermanence, flux, or change which is stressed; sometimes suffering is stressed. But in the end, the two join hands and are clearly seen as two sides of the same situation."[177]

An agreement with Harold McCarthy's views would be quite understandable. Prufrock, Gerontion, or the rest of the poems in Eliot, are basically poems of suffering. I would incline to the view that the impermanence is subordinated to, and emerges through and from, suffering and not *vice versa.* Lines such as the following spoken by Gerontion,

"I was neither at the hot gates
Nor fought in the warm rain
Nor knee deep in the salt marsh, heaving a cutlass,
Bitten by flies, fought.
My house is a decayed house,"

are the lines of pain, anguish and suffering which give birth to a total sense of nihilism. Grover Smith says: "Eliot's Prufrock is a tragic figure. Negligible to others, he suffers in a hell of defeated idealism, tortured by unappeasable desires."[178] Of "Gerontion", Grover Smith says: " 'Gerontion' describes only 'the unstilled world,' the turning wheel, the hollow passages—not 'the Garden/where all love ends,' the ending of lust and the goal of love."[179]

Bhagavadgīta already says that lust, desire and greed lead to the door of death and destruction. In Buddhism desire, whether satisfied or not, is the fire of passion which consumes man. In the earlier part of my discussion I deliberated upon the four contemplations in Buddhism. The first contemplation is on the body and sensations, the *Nirmān-kāya,* body in the process of building itself and transforming through a process of developing indifference and disinterestedness. Body itself is the form of the mind or soul acquiring meaning through sense. But, as said before, each stage of my theory is doubly operative, both at a level really its own, and at a level that it falls into out of some error. Prufrock, Gerontion, in this sense, are poems of the fallen states, both of mind and body, and represent a total breakdown in the sense of grasping. The form fails to become formal, refuses to articulate itself as per the demands of a sensible body into a sensible mind.

Prof. Dasgupta says: "The lowest *cakra* of the body (whether the *Nirmān-cakra* of the Hindus) is the material plane and *Mahāsukha* of the Buddhists or the *Mulādhāra-Cakra* of the Hindus) is the material plane and *Mahāṣukha (Parabindu)* remains here in its grossly physical form—. . ."[180] This stage could also be called the stage of the manifestation of tradition as imbroglio, neither conscious of its own directionality nor effected by the individual talent.

Ceaseless suffering and desire's ungratified spurs lead from the self as imbroglio to the self as divided. The desire to escape suffering multiplies the self into many minute selves, Bradley's finite centres, that posit their own positionality in relation to the centre, and own and disown their identity in a process that is continuous and ever forward-moving. The dialectic in the second stage of my literary theory is more conscious of itself. The subject raises preliminary notes of dissent against all that *undoes* it, though the subject is yet unable to win over them. As a result, the subject is aware, howsoever unconsciously, of the bifurcation of his being, and as Gerontion says, after such knowledge what forgiveness; so the subject's bewildering search to find his roots creates in him multiple points of view (itself a mark of confusion since no cohesive principle is discovered), which, though being the soul of the artifice of literature, is in itself not quite liberating as the unitive principle is missing still. The *Sambhōg-kāya,* or the body that breeds itself into the phenomenal experience, signifies the undiscriminative state of consciousness at this stage in the cycle.

The inbreeding instinct descends into experience, and since the mind is not highly discriminating at this stage, the instinct tends to merge itself into experience and feels *dukkha* or suffering. The critical concept that will involve us here are those of impersonality and objective correlative, and the corresponding poems of this stage would be *The Waste Land* and *The Hollow Men.* Grover Smith, seeing the continuity of the chain of suffering, remarks: " 'The Hollow Men' corresponds to the last lines of 'Gerontion,' with the sufferers turning in the wheel whose centre holds for them neither the Word, the eyes, the star, nor the rose;..."[181] Grover Smith also made a very vital statement on "The Hollow Men": "Eliot, during his graduate studies at Harvard, applied himself for two years to Charles Lanman's course in Sanskrit and spent a year, as he has remarked, in the mazes of Patanjali's metaphysics under James Wood. The experience, though it left him 'in a state of enlightened mystification,' may possibly have percolated through to 'The Hollow Men.' The Hindu *Trimurti*, Śiva, Brahma, and Vishnu, who respectively embody the powers of reproduction and destruction, of creation and of preservation or salvation, might almost be the patrons of the three ideals. The power of Siva is the power in sex and in the cycle of death and rebirth; that of Brahma, God the creator of the world, is the power in mind;" that of Vishnu, incarnate as Saviour, is the power in the descending Spirit that preserves men from evil. Vishnu, in Hindu mythology, is described as having assumed nine incarnations to deliver mankind and as being destined, in his tenth and final incarnation of the white horse, to destroy the earth. His *ātman* is his essence; his *avatāra*, his descent. In every *avatar* essential *ātman* takes on flesh, and the supreme *Avatār* is the descent of Vishnu to unite the divine and the created."[182]

Grover Smith has, in a way, outlined the whole metaphysical design of Eliot's poetry from imprisonment, suffering to liberation. In particular, his description of the Hindu *Trimurti* is an advance by an important Eliot Scholar of the West to make the point that Eliot was deeply influenced by various typologies and categories of Hindu-Buddhist religion and philosophy. Brahma, Vishnu and Shiva would correspond to the *Nirmānkāya* (Brahma as creator), the *Sambhōg-kāya* (Vishnu as preserver of created forms) and *Vajrakāya* (Shiva in His supreme concentration *(Samādhi)*, uniting all thinkable proportions of the visible and the invisible universe, truly embodying *Sat-Chit-Ānanda* – truth consciousness, joy (which is the true nature of existence and creation). Shiva or Buddha at the centre of the *mandala* are all potencies in the concentrated form of a seed. Shiva or Buddha, in their one aspect, provide the supreme experience of unity to created beings; in their other aspect, they also destroy it. Shiva as Brahma brings to fruition potencies inherent in the primal seed; Shiva as Vishnu preserves them in a world of time, while Shiva, in His destructive aspect, assimilates all creation into His own being.

Assiduously following Patanjali's *Yoga-Sūtras* and the Buddhist concept of suffering in his theory of impersonality and objective-correlative, Eliot says that "the progress of an artist is a continual self-sacrifice, a continual extinction of personality".[183] Dr. Mool Chand Shastri, in, a somewhat anxiously written book on the *Buddhist Contribution to Sanskrit Poetics,*[184] says that the "Existence or non-existence of soul can be regarded as demarcation criteria in the examination of Buddhist and non-Buddhist works available on poetics".[185] This statement could be said to be as naive as it is true. The concept of personality as preached by Buddha and the one that we meet in Eliot coincide and even merge. The following passage is a dialogue between one Bhantē Nāgasēna and the king:

"'Bhante Nagasena', said the king, 'is a person when just born that person himself, or is he someone else?'

'He is neither that person', said the elder, 'nor is he someone else'. 'Give an illustration.'

'What do you say to this, your majesty? When you were a young, tender, weakly infant lying on your back, was that your Said the elder, 'It was I, your majesty, who was a young, tender, weakly infant lying on my back, and it is I who am now grown up. It is through their connection with the embryonic body that all these different periods are unified'. . . .

'. . . The elements of being join one another in serial succession: one element perishes, another arises succeeding each other as it were instantaneously. Therefore neither as the same nor as a different person do you arrive at your latest aggregation of consciousness.'"[186]

The dialogue will make it clear that there are two kinds of sacrifice. One sacrifice involves the extinction of personality at each moment by time; the other sacrifice involves a stroke of individual will to *feel* suffering and consequently suffer it. One level of sacrifice may either sublimate or degenerate—may result in the growth or decay of human personality. This is also the doctrine of *Pratītya-samutpāda*, dependent-origination. Each moment being a moment of death as well as of creation is a tremendous concept, but it surely requires the greatest of an artist to involve himself in such a process. The mind, for this reason, is a less permanent entity than the body in Buddhism. It is mind which is undergoing continual changes. Eliot says: "The mind of the poet is the shred of platinum. It may partly or exclusively operate upon the experience of the man himself; but the more perfect the artist, the more completely separate in him will be the man who suffers and the mind which creates; the more perfectly will the mind digest and transmute the passions which are its material."[187]

Buddha tells priests: ". . . O priests, that this body which is composed of the four elements lasts one year, lasts two years, lasts three years, lasts four years, lasts five years, lasts ten years, lasts twenty years, lasts thirty years, lasts forty years, lasts fifty years, lasts a hundred years, and even more. But that, O priests, which is called mind, intellect, consciousness, keeps up an incessant round by day and by night of perishing as one thing and springing up as another."[188] In his thesis on Bradley Eliot had said that in metaphysics "there is no concatenation of inferences, but there is a starting-point which expands itself and can neither be arrested nor analysed, for the process is not one simply of addition, but of inner development, so that the starting point itself is altered, and you cannot say absolutely what the starting-point was."[189]

This is Eliot's clear statement of his version of the Buddhist dependent-origination. In the beginning, Eliot did say that there is a starting-point (which in Buddhism or *Bhagavadgīta* is not) but he modified it by saying that in the continuous chain, viewpoints change to the extent that the senses of beginning, middle and end, go on adjusting and readjusting themselves, changing their velocities, volumes and intensities in the eternal continuum. This is Eliot's and Buddhist "mind". Prufrock's "overwhelming question" which he never puts, and his incessant dialation and indecision are part of the Buddhist belief, and Eliot's, that the chain, which is ever-changing, would not allow for a conclusive question or answer to be framed. E.K. Hay rightly regards Buddhism, along with Judeo-Christianity, to be the two most important theological bearings upon Eliot. E.K. Hay so rightly points out: "Like Emerson feeling the oppression of other man's systems, Eliot was disinclined to make a system of his own (as Blake, for instance, decided he must do in self-defense). It was Emersonian of Eliot to reject Emerson, of course. The idealist Emerson wanted a constant writing of new 'scriptures' on the *tabula rasa*. He wanted a continuous news report on the findings of the 'transparent eyeball', meaning human vision without medium or system. By 1914 Eliot recognized that this too was a system, blocked at an impasse, and even Irving Babbitt's recourse to a systemless but affirmative Buddhism, which Eliot as his student accepted to some extent, seemed merely therapeutic. The self without system pointed in every direction to the annihilation of self, since every particular becomes meaningless, alone. Exactly here Eliot found himself situated by his dissertation on F.H. Bradley; and it was just here that he began to move resolutely toward representation of the dilemma in poetry, rather than to continue with analysis of the dilemma in philosophy."[190]

This shows Eliot to be a deconstructor of tradition utilizing his individual talents. Buddha also deconstructed the centrist or the logo-centric tradition preceding him in the form of the *Vēdas,* the *Upanishads,* and the *Bhagavadgīta.* Nāgārjuna too, likewise, rejects *satkār-vādins* and *sarvastvādinā.* The former believe in the identity of effect with cause while the latter posited a permanent entity. Another Buddhist thinker, Dinnaga, who propounded the theory of *Apoha,* also rejected the *Mīmansaka* and the *Naiyāyika* school theorists who believed that words have direct reference to objective realities.

There is a discussion here between Nagsena and King Milinda on what constitutes or does not constitute an ego. The topic is the chariot and the question asked by Nagasena is what is a chariot? King Milinda says:

> "Bhante Nagasena, I speak no lie: the word 'Chariot' is but a way of counting, term, appellation, convenient designation, and name for pole, axle, wheels, chariot-body and banner-staff."
>
> Nagasena replies:
>
> "Thoroughly well, your majesty, do you understand a chariot. In exactly the same way, your majesty, in respect of me, Nagasena is but a way of counting, term, appellation, convenient designation, mere name for the hair of my head, hair of my body. . . brain of the head, form, sensation, perception, the predispositions, and consciousness. But in the absolute sense. there is no Ego here to be found."[191]

The same is true of the living entities and the ego, which are mere modes of expression for the presence of five attachment groups. The statements like "The living entity persists" or that "It is annihilated" fall short of the truth. Buddha says:

> "There are two heresies, O priests, which possess both gods and men, by which some fall short of the truth, and some overturn the truth; but the intelligent know the truth.
>
> And how, O priests, do some fall short of the truth? O priests, gods and men delight in existence, take pleasure in existence, rejoice in existence, so that when the Doctrine for the cessation of existence is preached to them, their minds do not leap toward it, are not favourably disposed toward it, do not rest in it, do not adopt it.
>
> Thus, O priests, do some fall short of the truth.
>
> And how, O priests, do some outrun the truth?
>
> Some are distressed at, ashamed of,. and loathe existence, and welcome the thought of non-existence, saying, 'See here! When they say that on the dissolution of the body this Ego is annihilated, perishes, and does not exist after death, that is good, that is excellent, that is as it should be'.

Thus, O priests, do some outrun the truth.
And how, O priests, do the intelligent know the truth? We may have, O priests, a priest who knows things as they really are, and knowing things as they really are, he is on the road to aversion for things, to absence of passion for them, and to cessation from them."[192]

The Buddhist belief in an ego that is relative to the undeterminable absolute and which keeps on changing its composite character as per the availability of resources (Eliot's unconscious) from the side of the absolute. Because Eliot subscribed to this Buddhist view of the self as fragmentary and available in moments, many Eliot scholars have found Eliot's concept of personality and impersonality as somewhat confusing.

F.R. Leavis talks of the untenability of Eliot's impersonal theory.[193] John Casey says that "Eliot's remarks about the impersonality of art form perhaps the most confusing part of his critical theory".[194] Such problems arise because of some scholars' inability to read carefully Eliot's statement like the one where he says that the poet's "center of interest (is) not the visible world but in the ceaseless question and answer of the tortured mind".[195] How close is Eliot to the Buddhist concept of ceaseless craving, *tanha,* which keeps the subject moving from one standpoint to the other. That is one reason mind in Buddhism is regarded as less permanent than the body. Eliot conforms to the notion of the Absolute, much in the sense that *Bagavadgīta* does, where Krishna is the source of the visible and the invisible phenomena, but He is Himself beyond the beyond. Notice the following statement of Eliot that he made in his essay, "Four Elizabethan Dramatists": "That a work of art should be self-consistent, that an artist should consciously or unconsciously draw a circle beyond which he does not trespass: on the one hand, actual life is always the material, and on the other hand, an abstraction from life is a necessary condition to the creation of the work of art."[196]

The circle that the artist draws at a particular stage of his consciousness of life and of its perception, is peculiar to that stage. This circle is not absolute for its centre goes on effecting changes in diameter, volume and intensity, that are necessary to get a vision of the Absolute howsoever beyond the beyond. The process of abstraction is precisely the deconstructive process at work which annuls the latent notions that arise because of the deposits of *karma* that are always there in the consciousness of the individual. This is where Eliot's method comes close to Nāgārjuna as well. Spender tells us that Eliot was too profoundly ironic to stick to any pose like Yeats and Pound who had assumed aggressive and flamboyant poses. Spender says: "It had seemed to the poets of the end of the last century that a poet, as such, had come to be regarded by his contemporaries as an oddity. He must resist this by creating a role—variously called mask or persona—for himself. Most poets adopted, as Oscar Wilde had done, and as Yeats and Ezra Pound later did, aggressive and flamboyant poses. But Eliot was too profoundly ironic to do this. His pose was that of a poet who has nothing of the poet about his appearance and behaviour and who is very deliberately, but a bit discomfitingly, an ordinary man—even a bit more ordinary perhaps than others. Laforgue provided him with a wonderful model, for in his poetry the poet's role of ironic correctness blends into a moonlit, somnambulist one—Harlequin, Scara-mouche, correct but faintly sinister, shadow among the shadows of the city street."[197]

What Laforgue provided Eliot, according to Spender, is again an ego that assumes differential velocities of texture and structure, which, in all their substantiality, are temporary and ever-changing. In fact, Eliot kept on changing his own poses, and the poses of his poetry in order to drive home the endless supplementarity and substitutionary process that precedes the vision of transcendental harmony which the *Quartets* signifies. The theory of "Pose" is a variation upon the Indian theory of *mudra. Mudras* are body-postures which are not instantly made but perfected through endless penance and suffering. There is an *internal telos* established between a particular *mudrā* and its presiding deity. In a way, the *mudra* could be called an enlightened body-posture which communicates with certain elemental bodies in order to sing the music of spheres.

Eliot's poetry is basically a poetry of incantation and what Eliot is trying to achieve by having the concept of an ever-changing ego is to emphasize the different roles that the personality assumes, an endless chain of incarnations and re-incarnations, all of which attempt to produce a personality that is just right to have the maximum vision of the Absolute. A depersonalized personality is not merely an artistic device, impersonalization (which is not *mere* impersonalization) is a search for the unity and harmony of existence, both in life and among 'words, howsoever relative. For this reason Buddha talks of three unities—of mind, action, and body. Man also depersonalizes in these three directions in order to purify and bring in unison each one to the other. Moreover, even when an individual unites these three he has to further dissolve the sense of an omniscient ego by substituting it to the *Samgha,* the group, which is not only a meeting point of various egos, but also the Buddhist *whole,* though only relatively. Talking of the "Burnt Norton", Spender says: "It cannot, I think, be taken as symbolist poetry in which experience and subject are treated only as starting points on a journey which leads into a world created purely from language, though there are symbolist passages in it. The poet appeals to the reader on the grounds of shared experience of living within time. This experience of being both bound to time and also outside it, is religious."[198]

Buddhist *samgha,* likewise, is the collectivity of egos as well as of time, but the Buddhist trio of *dharma, samgha* and *Buddha* is outside time *through* time. It is for this reason that whenever queried on the Ultimate Reality by Ānanda, Buddha remained silent. Eliot's concept of personality and impersonality again takes us to the basic symbolism of the centre and the circumference. Impersonality cannot exist without a personality and when Eliot says that only the artist knows how to correlate the two and effect their separation, he is coming very close indeed to Patanjali's *Yoga-sūtras.* Fei-

Pai Lu says that "Since higher poetry consists in the synthetic activity of the soul in the formation of a selfhood, it is essential for the poet of the better kind to effect a personal integration of materials available to him and to forge a personal form of expression".[199] The poet's personality in Eliot is a form of magnet, his mind a shred of platinum. By analogy we will understand that there are so many stars in the sky that stand at particular distances from each other because of gravitational force, or by a process of repulsion and impulsion. The sense of loss of extinction of personality is solely effected on the basis of who has the strength to attract whom in the ether. In the same way the surrender of an artist's personality, whether the surrender is whole or part, depends upon the kind of universe of ideas, of emotions and sentiments, he is surrendering himself to. The surrender to tradition, more specifically, depends solely upon the artist's version of it. The artist's personality is a centre of diverse experiences from past and present which accumulate in him and are transformed and shaped into new figments of realities that are impersonal only *through* being personal.

J. Birje-Patil says that "The concepts were further modified through the perspectives offered by Laforgue, Remy de Gourmont, T.E. Hulme and Ezra Pound".[200] Like Patil, other Eliot scholars, too, have not considered the role of Patanjali in framing his ideas of personality and impersonality. I referred to the concept of personality and impersonality in Buddhism already. Patanjali says that the personality is open to sensations and perceptions of various kinds. Not all of them can transform personality in terms of either the creative idea or any particular emotion or sentiment. Therefore, the need for practice: "Practice *(abhyāsa)* is (repeated) exertion to the end that (the mind stuff) shall have permanence in this (restricted state)".[201] Eliot has already talked of the abstraction that the artist effects within the ambient dimensionality of his mind. Abstraction is an essential tool to separate mind from the body, form from the idea. When the artist internalises a particular form he forgets those aspects of it which constitute form and concentrates on those because of which the form has come into being. "This (passionlessness) is highest when discernment of the Self results in thirstlessness for qualities (and not merely for objects)".[202]

The method at work is that of continuous abstraction which equals the *upanishadic neti neti* and the Buddhist negation. Once the artist is through this process of continuous detachment to the point of extreme abstraction, one self of him identifies itself with the idea on which he has been concentrating. This is how we would explain both the objective correlative and impersonality. The intense process of concentration and continuous annulment results in the transformation of the object which was, early, localised into certain immediate reference-points. This local inhabitant and temper of the object is not destroyed by abstraction; it is transcended. Two types of concentration are there in Patanjali: "(Concentration becomes) conscious (of its object) by assuming forms either of deliberation (upon coarse objects) or of reflection (upon subtile objects) or of joy or of the sense-of-personality.[203] The other (concentration which is not conscious of objects) consists of subliminal impressions only (after objects have merged), and follows upon that practice which effects the cessation (of fluctuations)."[204]

The artist is obviously concerned with the first kind of concentration, for his worry is not the cessation of fluctuations but their continuous transformation. Eliot, quoting Pound, says: "The only kind of emotion worthy of a poet is the inspirational emotion which energises and strengthens, and which is very remote from the everyday emotion of sloppiness and sentiment."[205] Eliot further said: "Every precise emotion tends towards intellectual formulation."[206] Patanjali says: "(Concentration not conscious of objects), which follows upon belief (and) energy (and) mindfulness (and) concentration (and) insight, is that to which the others (the Yogins) attain."[207] The inspirational emotion is the emotion which leads to a certain equanimity of other emotions and the mind as such. Belief is the belief about the idea or the emotion the artist practises on.

Ideas and emotions may have their own roots in particular

cultures. Eliot's emphasis upon Christian beliefs and Eliot proclaiming himself as a Christian critic are part of the argument in Patanjali where belief plays a very central role. James Haughton-Woods says: "(That concentration, not conscious of objccts), which is caused by (spiritual) means[208] is that to which yogins attain. Belief is the mental approval (of concentration); for, like a good mother, it protects the yogin. For him (thus) believing and setting discrimination[209] (before him) as his goal there is the further *(upa)* attainment of energy for him who has reached the further attainment of energy mindfulness is at hand. And when mindfulness is at hand the mind-stuff is self-possessed and becomes concentrated."[210] This will make clear that the process of impersonalizing emotion in art can only come from a personality that itself had become impersonal. "The impersonality achieved and maintained by the writer then links his work to the timeless order to which it adjusts itself, and so doing, transmits what is personal into what is universal."[211] The mind of the artist bcing self-possessed implies the artist's transmutation of reality for himself and his particular vision of the world and objects. Eliot's version of this idea is that "When the great poet is also a great classic poet, he exhausts, not a form only, but the language of his time, and the language of his time, as used by him, will be the language in its perfection."[212]

The journey from personality to impersonality implies a certain archetypalising and gradual universalizing of the human instinct that feels the sensations, and human mind that discriminates them. In his Introduction to Pound's poems, Eliot said of experience that: "The development of experience is largely unconscious subterranean so that we cannot gauge its progress except once in every five or ten years; . . . a poet's work may proceed along two lines on an imaginary graph; one of the lines being his conscious and continuous effort in technical excellence. . . ." Eliot's experience could be equated with the undiscriminating consciousness in Patanjali: "Undifferentiated-consciousness *(avidya)* and the feeling-of-personality and passion and aversion and the will-to-live are the five hindrances".[213] Here is a consciousness which is largely unnconscious because there is no pressure of individual talent. It is for this reason that Eliot says that technique involves effort, labour and methodical excellence The undifferentiation in Patanjali is used with reference to a mind which perceives impermanence in per-manence and *vice versa.* Woods comments: "It is this four-fold undif-ferentiated-consciousness which becomes the root of that unbroken-series *(santāna)* of hindrances and of latent-impressions of karma together with its fruition. . . Precisely so, undifferentiated consciousness is not a source-of-valid ideas nor the negation of a source-of-valid-ideas, but another kind of thinking the reverse of knowledge."[214]

The unconscious experience in Eliot, as undifferentiated consciousness in Patanjali, ask for articulation and conscious differentiation respectively. Rajnath is right when he says that C.K. Stead is wrong in regarding emotion (experience) as conscious and images and phrases – (technique) as unconscious.[215] The reverse is true in fact. In an unpublished address on "The Idea of a European Society" (1949) Eliot had made it very clear that: "In writing a poem of any length—a poem which requires *labour*—I find in retrospect that I cannot wholly distinguish, in the result, what was calculated from what was spontaneous, what was conscious from what was unconscious, what was growth from what was construction. I know that the unexpected arrives, and I know that I have given many hours of conscious toil."[216] It is the writer's internal communication with certain ethered bodies that establishes a point of equanimity between the conscious and the unconscious. Octavio Paz also holds that the instance of rhyme in Poetry, whether in-between the lines or at the end, comes unpredictably. It is destiny so to say which mediates between silence and the written character of language.

Eliot once said that "in the man of scientific or artistic temper the personality is distilled into the work, it loses its incidents, it becomes, as with Montaigne, a permanent point of view, a phase in the history of mind".[217] The humanist, the artist, and the scientist are not designations imposed from above; they are distinct temperaments, body organisms, developing into different areas of perception and consciousness, which come to acquire their own point of view in course of time. As said before, the ego in human personality, both in Buddhism and *Bhagavadgīta,* is the centre of physical energy of the mind, the sense and the intellect. As opposed to this centre, there is a centre in man of spiritual energy which draws to itself the energies of the soul, or the transformed energies of the ego. When one centre works in unison with the other, a permanent *point of view* results. It is only then that the sense of personality is acquired. Patanjali says: "When the power of seeing and the power by which one sees have the appearance *(jiva)* of being a single-self, (this is) the feeling of personality".[218] Haughton-Woods comments: "The self is the power of seeing; the thinking-substance is the power by which one sees. The hindrance called the feeling-of-personality is a change by which these two appear to become a single essence *(svarūpa).* When there is any kind of failure to distinguish him who has the power of the enjoyer from that which has the power of being enjoyed, which are as distinct as possible and as unconfused as possible, enjoyment[219] is ready at hand. But when each has recovered its own essence, there is Isolation."[220]

The development of "point of view" in a human being has the elements both of personality and impersonality. The teachings of yoga, for example, are not true with reference to either Hinduism or Buddhism only; they are universally applicable, although specifically worked out by ascetics in India. Eliot emphasizes the element that unites the two centres of personality and this virtually becomes the basis for great poetry: "If you compare several representative passages of the greatest poetry you see how great is the variety of types of combinations, and also how completely any semi-ethical criterion of 'sublimity' misses the mark. For it is not the 'greatness', the intensity, of the emotions, the components, but the intensity of the artistic process, the pressure, so to speak, under which the fusion takes place, that counts."[221]

The fusion is the result of endless striving to correlate the physical centre with the spiritual. The process is not as simple as "by destroying personality, impersonality is achieved".[222] Eliot said: "There are two forms of impersonality: that which is natural to the mere skillful craftsman, and that which is more and more achieved by the maturing artist. The first is that of what I have called the 'anthology piece' of a lyric by Lovelace or Suckling, or of Campion, a finer poet than either. The second impersonality is that of the poet who, out of intense and personal experience, is able to express a general truth; retaining all the particularity of his experience, to make of it a general symbol."[223]

Eliot obviously gives value to the latter. In Patanjali there are four types of approach to concentration: (i) the worldly approach, (ii) the spiritual approach, (iii) the combinations of methods and intensities; and the devotion to the highest Self.[224] The goal is to achieve the highest form of concentration which alone universalizes or impersonalizes the emotion. Eliot's approach is a combination of methods and intensities which ferment in the creative cauldron of the artist and bring about a transformation. The logic is one of the still centre and the moving sphere where nothing is stable. It is a kind of *mandala* that the artist starts with. He may enter inside the *mandala* from any of the four doors and develop desired points of view on way to the centre. It is highly suggestible to study Eliot's concepts of personality and impersonality from four different angles as these concepts emerge in his essays.

Whereas Fei-Pai Lu distinguishes between two types of personality and impersonality in Eliot's essays, Rajnath discovers three types of personality and impersonality. In fact, the categorisation is extendable up to four which alone can give us Eliot's basic logic of a still centre amid a moving world. Fei-Pai Lu's dialectical approach in relation to the personality of the poet is outlined thus: "The dialectic seeks its way into Eliot's formulation about the poet through the intermediaries of such familiar doctrines as actualization (of potentialities), organisation (of interests) and maturation (through resolution of opposing elements). And both the problems of internal cohesion and external concord can be reduced to problems describable in terms of unity in diversity, identity in difference, and continuity in change".[225] Fei-Pai Lu does show the influence of Hegel in his categorisation of Eliot's personality. There are critics like Roger Sharrock who read Eliot's personal life into his theory of impersonality. "Since at least the outline of the story of Eliot's unhappy first marriage has been made public, it is impossible not to associate passages like that on the escape from emotion and personality with suppressed personal experience. Indeed the whole theory of poetic impersonality is, one suspects, fertilized by the strains of personal unhappiness".[226]

In contradiction to Lu who holds dialectic as essential to Eliot's poetry, William Righter says: "The movement of Eliot's mind, as I have said, is more that of the careful sifting of alternatives than a dialectical path to an ultimate fusion. And throughout his work words like 'coherence', 'unity', or 'order' may be used in a variety of contexts without their implying a precisely employed method. Perhaps we might view in sympathetic terms a related notion of such precision when Dr. Lure marks that 'The whole of Eliot's criticism is a calculus of the conditions of unification, without being able to find any procedures in a calculus which could be methodically employed, or any sense in the word beyond the figurative, or that of a principle underlying the unity. What seems to be fulfilled is an emotional necessity."[227]

It is more possible to agree with William Righter than with Dr. Lu. In fact, dialectical oppositions are formed out of the necessity of a process that is trying to get to a vision of the centre. Such oppositions are not part of the conscious Eliot method. The logic of sifting alternatives is in fact a variation upon the differential nature of "point of view" theory of Bradley with which Eliot agrees. The centre, in terms of my own *Mandala* theory, is in a variety of relationships to the objects in the sphere which form the centre's circumference as well as their own. The relationship is comparable to the gravitational force which varies in volume and intensity depending upon the distance of the object from the centre. If there is any passage in Eliot's essays singularly characteristic of his idea of personality, it is his obituary tribute to Charles Whibley. Whibley had a unity of personality, said Eliot: "In attaining such unity, and indeed in attaining a living style, whether in prose or in verse, the practice of conversation is invaluable. Indeed, I believe that to write well it is necessary to converse a great deal. I say 'converse' instead of 'talk', because I believe that there are two types of good writers: those who talk a great deal to others, and those, perhaps less fortunate, who talk a great deal to themselves. It is two thousand and two hundred years since, that the theory was propounded that thought is conversation with oneself; all literary creation certainly springs from the habit of talking to oneself or from the habit of talking to others. Most people are unable to do either, and that is why they lead such active lives. But anyone who would write must let himself go, in one way or the other, for there are only four ways of thinking; to talk to others, or to one other, or to talk to oneself, or to talk to God."

This four-tier structure, I have already said, has strong similarities with *Bhagavadgīta* (3.42), where it is mentioned that higher than the senses is the mind, higher than the mind is the soul; what is higher than the soul is *Ātman*. Blake also derived from the *Gīta* his central typology of characters when he said in *The Marriage of Heaven and Hell* that the Head is Sublime, the Heart is Pathos, the Genitals are Beauty, and the Hands and Feet are Proportion. In fact it is Blake's prophecies which carry Eliot's idea of personality and impersonality at its best. Krishna also tells Arjuna that he is only a medium whose beginnings or ends are not known. So in Eliot, human personality is a medium which transforms the material it receives upon the chart of its consciousness. As the medium so the transformation. Before we examine *The Waste Land*, the poem that qualifies this category in my literary theory, we could have a look at how Eliot practises his personality-impersonality criterion in his essays.

R.P. Blackmur says that "Eliot's own doctrine of poetry,

as he has united it in his personality, seems to me to turn up in what he says about the triad of feeling, emotion, and sensibility".[228] It will be seen that sensation, feeling and emotion are successive stages of shifting contours of consciousness in the circular journey of my *mandala*. Sensation, feeling and emotion constitute, together, the aesthetic sensibility. Eliot said in his book on culture: "Aesthetic sensibility must be extended into spiritual perception, and spiritual perception must be extended into aesthetic sensibility and disciplined taste before we are qualified to pass judgment upon decadence or diabolism or nihilism in art. To judge a work of art by artistic or by religious standards, to judge a religion by religious or artistic standards should come in the end to the same thing: though it is an end at which no individual can arrive."[229]

It will be seen that Eliot is trying to arrive at an Absolute personality—that comprehensiveness of perception and apprehension which is possible to the gods only. Here again Eliot comes close to Buddhism which believes that the Absolute is not formulable; it can be experienced only in parts. Eliot's concept of personality, therefore, grounded as it is in Bradley's theory of finite centres, whose one possible source could also be Buddhism, gives us gradations of consciousness which are peculiar to particular moments. Eliot's essays are such moments, and the personality that encounters an author, or a literary scene, or a social reality, is a particular personality that has its shifting gradations of perception and perspective which are peculiar to that particular moment of analysis and comprehension. Such approach gives us a personality in an impersonal overall wholeness which always self-transcends itself. Commenting upon Campion Eliot said: "I should say that within his limits there was no more accomplished craftsman in the whole of English poetry than Campion", but "we do not feel, after reading Campion, that we know the man Campion, as we do feel after reading Herrick".[230] That is why Eliot emphasized that there could be no impersonality without a personality. Another example of who has a personality and who does not is given below:

"Some poets, like Shakespeare or Dante or Villon, and some novelists like Mr. Conrad, have, in contrast to ideas or concept, points of views, or 'worlds'—what are incorrectly called 'philosophies'. . . . Mr. Conrad has no ideas but he has a point of view, a 'world', it can hardly be defined, but it pervades his work and is unmistakable."[231]

A personality for Eliot implies an idiom of thinking, linguistic orientation, and action. Points of view can be generated by minds who are capable of having them. A "World-view" can only come from a person who is capable of *thinking* about the world in relation to his particular psychosomatic organism. It is only for this reason that Massinger is inferior to Marlowe, Jonson and Shakespeare: "Mar-lowe's and Jonson's comedies were a view of life; they were, as great literature is, the transformation of a personality into a personal work of art, their lifetime's work, long or short. Massinger is not simply a smaller personality: his personality hardly exists. He did not, out of his own personality, build a world of art, as Shakesspeare and Marlowe and Jonson built."[232] A great poet always exists, integrated, at the level of *vajrakāya,* in my theory which is in the north, the symbol of the association of sensibility. The physical centre of personality and the spiritual run parallel to each other; in fact, the first is the manifestation of the latter. It is not necessary that a great poet starts with a division in his soul or mind, and gradually moves toward integration (like Eliot). Eliot writes that "The whole of Shakespeare's work is *one* poem, and it is the poetry of it in this sense, not the poetry of isolated lines and passages or the poetry of the single figures which he created, that matters most . . . . A man may, hypothetically, compose a number of fine passages or even whole poems which would each give satisfaction, and yet not be a great poet, unless we felt them to be united by one significant, consistent and developing personality."[233]

Eliot further said of Shakespeare that "No other dramatist of the time approaches anywhere near to this perfection of pattern, of pattern superficial and profound; but the measure in which dramatists and poets approximate to this unity in a lifetime's work is one of the measures of major poetry and drama".[234] The mind of the artist is an agent of transformation as in Patanjali and as not in Locke who held it to be a *tabula rasa,* an inert storage-house of impressions from outside with a mechanical reaction to them. When the two selves work in unison to each other whatever the physical self gathers by way of outer impressions, is refined, rejected and selected by the mind which always equates itself with the identity-process. Such a mind was that of Henry James, both personal and impersonal at the same time: "James's critical genius comes out most tellingly in his mastery over, his baffling escape from, Ideas; a mastery and an escape which are perhaps the last test of a superior intelligence. He had a mind so fine that no idea could violate it."[235]

Eliot's key words here are mastery and escape, something which N. Frye would put this way that for the man of vision the world and the outer environment is not an object; it is a subject. In fact, the technique of practising the yoga in Patanjali is to take an idea, internalise it by intense concentration, identify the self with it, and again by detached meditation, transcend it to attain *Kaivalya,* loneness, which equals Buddhist emptiness and *Upanishadic* "beyond the beyond". *Sūtra* 18 of Book I in *Yoga System of Patanjali* says: "The other (concentration which is not conscious of objects) consists of subliminal impressions only (after objects have merged), and follows upon that practice which effects the cessation (of fluctuations)". The artist as yogi sees the chain of impressions playing configurated games in a very detached manner. The world of apparent reality, the material of the artist, which is made of the constituents of Nature is no more a world within which the artist could be confined. The mind is open to two orders of reality: one is the reality of apparent forms manifest outside; the other is the reality of Godhood, Substance or Essence within what Eliot would call the spiritual reality.

When the artist identifies himself with the spiritual reality, the world outside is no more an inert and dead substance in a mechanical relationship, it is recreated and transcended simultaneously. Krishna declares in the *Gīta:* "For (all) this is my creative power, composed of the constituents, divine, hard to transcend. Who so shall put his trust in Me alone, shall pass beyond this (my) uncanny power" (7.14). It is for this reason that Eliot felt no orthodoxy in proclaiming himself a Christian critic, for he wanted a very creative kind of relationship between the individual and the Church. The Church should help man transcend the immediateness of his experience, what Eliot said of the task of criticism, "To bring the poet back to life—the great, the perennial, task of criticism. . . ."[236]

At places Eliot comes very close to employing the yoga terminology in which the yogi as a detached person enters into the moulds of certain ideas and comes out at will. Consider the following: "A poet like Donne, or like Baudelaire or Laforgue, may almost be considered the inventor of an attitude, a system of feeling or of morals. Donne is difficult to analyse: what appears at one time a curious personal point of view may at another time appear rather the precise concentration of a kind of feeling diffused in the air about him. Donne and his shroud, the shroud and his motive for wearing it, are inseparable, but they are not the same thing."[237] Krishna says: "The body is called the 'field' and he who knows it is the 'knower of the field', or so it has been said by those who know it" *(Gīta* 13.1). The following from the *Maitri Upanishad* 2.5 will explicate the verse from the *Gīta* as well as illuminate us on Eliot's concept of the mind which in him is performing certain yogic functions of assuming forms and dissolving them at will. The man who suffers and the mind which creates are in fact two modes of an integrated artist's personality. The *Upanishad* says: "Here (in the body) this subtle, impalpable, invisible one known as 'Person' begins to move, or rather a fraction of himself does so . . . Assuredly, this part of him is pure consciousness, reflecting the Person himself; (it is) the 'knower of the field' whose subtle body is made up of conception, will, and self-consciousness,

Prajapati under the name of 'common to all men'. By consciousness is this body set up so that it really appears to be conscious (itself): he it is who impels it (into action)."[238]

The Person in *Samkhya* philosophy is a variation upon the essence principle who cohabits material forms which are supposed to be females. In yoga, there is also the concept of *Kāyā-Kalpa,* the change from one body into another by the yogi. Of Yeats's early work Eliot said that it shows an intensity of experience which, in the later work, comes only by introspection. But Yeats does show a personality in development. "You cannot divide the work of a great poet so sharply as that. Where there is the continuity of such a positive personality and such a single purpose, the later work cannot be understood, or properly enjoyed, without a study and appreciation of the earlier; . . ."[239] The ideas of personality and impersonality in Eliot are finally related to religion and God though it at times seems all so very anxious on the part of Eliot that he had to have recourse to orthodox concepts like religious fear and the inviolable necessity of the Church irrespective of the development or degeneration of the individuals or societies. Certain of Eliot's own statements do not show that these are the utterances of a personality that has imbibed a multi-traditional culture and is bifocal in consciousness. Consider the following statement, for example: "We need to know how to see the world as the Christian Fathers saw it,[240] and the purpose of reascending to origins is that we should be able to return, with greater spiritual knowledge, to our own situation. We need to recover the sense of religious fear so that it may be overcome by religious hope."[241]

Blake was a penchant critic of the concept of religious fear which can only be generated by a God who terrorises and terrifies. God is love; He never writes "Thou Shalt Not" –

> I went to the Garden of Love
> And saw what I had never seen
> 'Thou shalt not' writ on the door
> Where I used to play on the Green.

It will be interesting to compare Eliot and Blake's views on Christian Fathers and Christianity. Whereas Blake criticised the whole Christian history as being the history of power-hungry prophets who made Church a political instead of a religious institution, Eliot does not say anything of the sort. In fact; most of his utterances on religion are submissive in nature. One just wonders what happened to that creative personality and all that individual talent! Is the creative personality afraid of its own wide ambience of consciousness which it attained after reading texts of many religions-especially Hindu and Buddhist? Why did Eliot have to say that he might have to suffer from a loss of identity if he continued his studies in Hinduism and Buddhism? I feel this is where the personality of Eliot fails to become impersonal, and fails also, in a way, though in a way only, in practising its own formulations.

God is impersonal by way of the fact that He is inside everybody, though, for Christians, He is somewhere above. And Eliot's dialectic of God and Nature brings him very close to *Bhagavadgīta* indeed. "I mean only that a wrong attitude towards nature implies, somewhere, a wrong attitude towards God, and the consequence is an inevitable doom .... The struggle to recover the sense of relation to nature and to God, the recognition that even the most primitive feelings should be part of our heritage, seems to me to be the explanation and justification of the life of D .H. Lawrence, . . . "[242] Consider the following verses from the *Gīta* in the light of Eliot's statement above: "Eightfold divided is my nature,—thus: earth, water, fire and air, space, mind, and also soul,—and the ego. This is the lower: but other than this I have a higher Nature; this too must you know. (And this is Nature) developed into life by which this world is kept in being. To all beings these (two Natures) are (as) a womb; be very sure of this. Of this whole universe the origin and the dissolution too am I (7.4-6)".

This passage relates to and explicates Eliot's entire world-view. There is a world of Nature and a world of God. When the two work in unison, integration and harmony ensue.

When the two are at enmity with each other, disintegration results. *The Waste Land* is a poem of this disintegration which we shall consider now. Eliot strongly refuted the popular view that "*The Waste Land* expresses 'The disillusionment of a generation', which is nonsense. I may have expressed for them their own illusion of being disillusioned, but that did not form part of my intention".[243]

It is significant that in the 1959 *Paris Review* Interview when asked about the intention behind writing *The Waste Land,* Eliot said: "I wonder what an 'intention' means! One wants to get something .off one's chest. One doesn't know quite what it is that one wants to get off the chest until one's got it off. But I couldn't apply the word 'intention' positively to any of my poems. Or to any poem."[244] The earlier statement seems to give the impression that Eliot had *some* intention at least in mind while writing *The Waste Land;* the latter negates even that possibility. As I suggested earlier too, in Eliot as in Buddhism, there is an absolute negative reference which *empties* the meaning of words into nothingness. This nothingness Eliot, right from his Harvard days, had been trying to achieve. *The Waste Land* is a poem of the separation of the physical self from the spiritual. In the *Gīta* Krishna is said to have set in motion two wheels: one the wheel of the spirit or the higher self and the other the wheel of the body or the lower self. The cogs of the wheel of the body were properly adjusted by God in the beginning to the cogs of the wheel of the self. However, bad times are signalled by the movement in different directions that the two wheels take. One becomes the wheel of righteousness and justice; the other the wheel of ignorance, oppression and self-imprisonment.

The ideas of Eliot's poem under consideration are precisely these. Krishna further says: "In the world there are these two persons—perishable the one, Imperishable the other. . ." (15.16). One person is the person whose centre of personality is the ego who draws to itself the mind, the intellect, and the senses and who can make only an empirical use of them. This is, in other words, an empirical projection of the self.

When the same constituents of Nature, the mind, the intellect, and the senses, are not centred in the ego but in the self which incarnates itself and is declared by Krishna to be a portion of Him, then the projection of the self changes from the material to the spiritual. This idea is put in *Svetasvatara Upanishad* (5.1) as follows:

> "In *the* imperishable, infinite city of Brahman
> Two things there are—
> Wisdom and unwisdom, but wisdom is immortal:
> Who over wisdom and unwisdom rules, He is Another."

Professor R.C. Zaehner concludes that "the relationship between the two 'persons', the two 'Unmanifests', and the two 'Natures' of Krishna in the *Gīta* would seem to be as follows:

Higher Person = liberated selves = Higher Unmanifest
= higher Nature.

Lower Person = selves in bondage
Primal matter = lower Unmanifest
= lower Nature". [245]

The ideal of *The Waste Land* is expressed by the following verse from the *Gīta:* "Whoever thus knows Me, unconfused, as the Person (All) Sublime, knows all and (knowing all) communes with Me with all his being, all his love" (15.19). The words "unconfused", "Sublime" and "love" are specifically to be noted in the context of Eliot's poem. The poem begins with a vision of Nature that is fallen. This fallen state is described by the Hyacinth girl, Madame Sosostris, and Belladonna. These ladies are three aspects of Nature compositely signifying the imprisonment of the Male Principle. Krishna says: "Subduing my own material Nature ever again I emanate this whole host of beings, powerless (themselves), from Nature comes the power" *(Gīta,* 9.8).

Krishna also says that the relationship between Him and

Nature is not fortuitous; it is Willed by Him for that is how the world comes into being. The Unreal City in Eliot contrasts with St. Augustine's *civitas dei* as well as with the *Svētāsvatara Upanishad's* following verse (5.1):

> "In the imperishable, infinite city of Brahman
> Two things there are--
> Wisdom and unwisdom, hidden, established there:
> Perishable is unwisdom, but wisdom is immortal:
> Who over wisdom and unwisdom rules, He is Another."

This city, by analogy, is the human body itself, and this body as *Kshētra,* field, is the body of history, past and present, and yet to come. The Poem's beginning in April and the use of the wheel symbol signal singularly the dislocation of man's personality. In terms of my own theory, such dislocations take place at the cardinal point of the south where the sun is at its extreme heat, though yet not able to burn and purge the ugly situation as well as the ugly man. This is the stage which advances from the lyric stage to the longer lyric, whereas the former stage was all passionate intensity and energetic expression of spontaneous ideas; such ideas at this stage are thwarted by the will that is not reluctant to live. Frustration leads to the bifurcation of the self, and a disintegrated self cannot achieve impersonality, only attempt (pretend) to do so. And this is precisely the irony of the poem. Whereas the former stage was dominated by the sense, this stage is dominate.d by the feeling. "Pity divides the soul", Blake said, and for this reason, the self unconsciously feels that this world is not what it appears to be, whereas in the earlier stage the self felt that the world is as it is feeling it. These stages are part of Eliot's four ways of perceiving the world-logic and Nagarjuna's four great sentences.

The first stage in terms of Nagarjuna was "This is" and the second "This is not". The stage under consideration, in terms of the Buddha-body, is known as the stage of *Sambhōgkāya,* the *Kaya* or the body which copulates with experience-variety that the world is, and draws inferences and effects degrees of assimilations and negations. But the intellect is not fully discriminative; in terms of the *gunās* of the *Bhagavadgīta,* whereas the first stage was dominated by the hierarchy of *tamas-rajas-sattva gunās,* so also, in the second stage, the hierarchv is *rajas-tamas-sattva,* though sometimes the *rajas* dominates and most of the time the *tamas.* The *sattva* is merely glimpsed at and remains an ideal. Matthiessen endorses such hierarchies of experience: "The poem thus embodies simultaneously several different planes of experience, for it suggests the likenesses between various waste lands".[246] Elizabeth Drew says on Eliot's sources that "His mind had already absorbed the whole literary and cultural tradition of Europe, as well as a great deal of Asiatic religion and philosophy. The point of comparison is simply what of all this 'comes together' in the poem,.. .""[247] Craig Raine alone, among a host of other Eliot critics, held that *The Waste Land* is purely a Buddhist poem: "History is repetition, a cyclic process. And this is the new thing to be said about *The Waste Land.* It is a poem about *ennui* because it is a Buddhist poem about re-incarnation. My intention is not to add another scholarly layer to a poem already obfuscated by scholarship. I wish, rather, to illuminate Eliot's master-piece by asserting the primacy of a few, basic Buddhist ideas which unify it in a simple way.""[248]

Craig Raine also draws our attention to Mr. Valerie Eliot's edition of *The Waste Land Manuscript* which shows how vast and deep a use Eliot made of Hindu and Buddhist ideas, images and symbols.

That the Fire Sermon in Eliot and Buddhism is the same is commonly agreed upon by scholars. Buddha says:

> "All things, O priests, are on Fire. And what, O priests, are all these things which are on Fire?
> The eye, O priests, is on fire; forms are on fire; eye-consciousness is on fire; impressions received by the eye are on fire; and whatever sensation, pleasant, unpleasant, or indifferent, originates in dependence on impressions received by the eye, that also is on fire.

And with what are these on fire?
With the fire of passion, say I, with the fire of hatred, with the fire of infatuation; with birth, old age, death, sorrow, lamentation, misery, grief, and despair are they on fire."'[249]

The original epigraph to *The Waste Land* came from Conrad's *The Heart of Darkness:*

"Did he live his life again in every detail of desire, temptation, and surrender during that supreme moment of complet knowledge? He cried in a whisper at some image, at some visions—he cried out twice, a cry that was no more than a breath—'The horror! the horror!'"

Craig Raine comments: "It explains, unambiguously, that the 'horror' is living one's life over again, being trapped in continual suffering *(dukkḥa).* Or, in other words, being bound upon the wheel."[250] Raine also draws our attention to certain other images and symbols whose source is basically Hindu and Buddhist. For example, the wheel, the re-incarnation, the desire, the suffering, etc. And all this since Eliot himself acknowledged his Hindu-Buddhist readings and a guarded remark by him which Bernard Bergonzi quotes without citing the source: "My own poetry shows the influence of Indian thought and mysticism."

If Eliot is taken to be the first subject of all that he wrote, then the movement and progression of his thought is very clear and it is one from bondage to liberation. He is a *tathāgatā* marching on the Buddhist way. E.K. Hay discovers in Sibyl and Tiresias the pointer to the negative way: "The Sibyl and Tiresias (who reminds one also of Tennyson's Tithonus and Eliot's own Gerontion) together offer a resounding negation: the examined life is not worth living."[251] The stage of *The Waste Land* in my theory is a variation on the stage which was full of passionate desire but where passion was not a fire. *The Waste Land* is a stage where passion attains maturity and burns instead of satisfying. The feeling performs a divisive role in personality which is largely unconscious. Tiresias, who stands midway between this division, is able to have a vision of horror of fire as well as of the remedy that lies beyond it. This stage is a precursor to the stage of the dialectical poem that we shall encounter next.

In the stage under consideration, the feeling of the world being an endless "chain" of suffering and misery is heightened—"The movement of desire", as noted by E.K. Hay, "toward silence, negation, and emptiness".[252] The stage of the unconscious negation is *The Waste Land* and that of emptiness *The Four Quartets.* Eliot himself thought of ending *The Waste Land* with a quotation from any non-Western sacred text. E.K. Hay says: "Once Eliot decided upon a different Part V (based on the *Upanishads),* he would have seen that "'The Fire Sermon' could be made Part III, continuing the vision of degraded sexuality".[253] So the third and fifth parts come under the direct influence of Indian thought. Commenting on the method in *The Waste Land,* D.E.S. Maxwell says: "Composed, as will be shown, in the figure of Coriolanus, the Fisher King, and the lost father, is the notion of a focus towards which the instability and flux of material affairs should converge. From such convergence they will be endowed with a meaning which they must lack if there is no stable centre."[251]

This again gives us the *mandala* with a centre and circumference. Maxwell also draws our attention to the ordering of different sections of *The Waste Land.* Whereas, "A Game of Chess" develops the symbols of lust and lost father, "Death By Water" relieves one from suffering, water being a refreshing symbol of purification. For this method we could look on Eliot's essay on Donne's sermons: "The method—the analogy and the repetition—is the same as that once used by a greater master of the sermon than either Donne or Andrews or Latimer: it is the method of the Fire Sermon preached by the Buddha".[255] This statement of Eliot should leave us in no doubt about his basic method which he practised throughout, that of analogy and repetition which, Eliot says, is so characteristic of Buddha's sermons. The implication of this method is very close to Nagarjuna's method (a point earlier made) of juxtaposing statement and counter-statement, and by a dialectical relationship, exhausting their formulable meaning possibilities, thus leading to emptiness. Eliot's subordination of self to a higher reality, which is always higher than the achieved and the achievable, points, in the ultimate analysis, only to this emptiness, or to the God of the *Gīta* who endlessly transcends His latest verbal formulations and remains beyond the beyond. Fishing and wheel which are in the wrong hands, distort the vision of the ultimate. Maxwell says that "The ceremony of fishing is connected with fertility ritual. In the Mahayana scriptures Buddha is referred to as the Fisherman who draws fish from the ocean, and is so represented in figures and pictures."[256] Eliot's implication is that the fishing and the wheel are in the wrong hands; hence the continuity of the cycle of pain and suffering and birth and death.

The water is also chained and not free, and "The 'freeing of the waters', the pristine object of the fertility ritual in the *Rig-Veda* to which Jessic L. Weston traces the symbolism of the Grail legend, must wait".[257] In an interesting parallel Grover Smith suggests that the bi-sexuality of Tiresias may owe its origin to a Buddhist legend in H.C. Warren's *Buddhism in Translation*.[258] I quote the legend in full: "The story is that a certain woman had married into a family of rank, but had quarreled with her husband, and, decked and ornamented, until she looked like a goddess, had issued forth from Anuradhapura, early in the morning, and was returning home to her family. On her way she met the elder, as he was on his way from Mt. Cetiya to go on his begging-rounds in Anuradhapura. And no sooner had she seen him, than the perversity of her nature caused her to laugh loudly. The elder looked up enquiringly, and observing her teeth, reality the impurity of the body, and attained to saintship. . . ." Then came her husband, following in her footsteps, and seeing the elder, he said:

Was it a woman, or a man,

That passed this way? I cannot tell.
But This I know, a set of bones
Is travelling on upon this road."[259]

It is this basic suspicion as to the identity of the individual that is the hallmark of this particular stage in the journey of Eliot's protagonist to the centre. The being is divided though hallucinations of unity still persist, though doubt no less divides and leads into the next stage of our theory which is that of the mindfully conscious of its dialectical oppositions, basically the empirical and the spiritual. The terms of Eliot which correspond to this stage are the Dissociation of Sensibility and the Objective Correlative. Eliot said that "Donne and Cowley employ a device which is sometimes considered characteristically 'metaphysical'; the elaboration (contrasted with the condensation) of a figure of speech to the furthest stage to which ingenuity can carry it".[260]

Eliot also emphasized the simultaneous co-existence and development of sensation-feeling-emotion-thought hierarchy in a unified sensibility. Eliot is not all that happy with Johnson's statement which he made upon poets like Donne, Cleveland, and Cowley, that in their poetry "the most heterogeneous ideas are yoked by violence together".[261] Eliot's trouble is that Johnson finds them yoked by violence and not united out of inner development. Eliot's divergence from Johnson comes in the following statement: "If so shrewd and sensitive (though so limited) a critic as Johnson failed to define metaphysical poetry by its faults, it is worthwhile to inquire whether we may not have more success by adopting the opposite method: by assuming that the poets of the seventeenth century (up to the Revolution) were the direct and normal development of the precedent age; and, without prejudicing their case by the adjective, 'metaphysical', consider whether their virtue was not something permanently valuable, which subsequently diasppeared,. . . Johnson has hit, perhaps by accident, on one of their peculiarities, when he observed that 'their' attempts were always analytic; he would not agree that, after the dissociation, they put the material together again in a new unity."[262] Eliot's criterion of un-dissociated sensibility is from a poetry in which imaginative equivalents of emotion and feeling are found to carry the intellectual weight of the ideas. Romantic poetry is rejected for being merely ideational, shorn of images, split and diseased, lacking centrality. Likewise, Tennyson and Browning, poets who can also think, but who "do not feel their thought as immediately as the odour of a rose",[263] meaning thereby that they do not unite thought and feeling in an instant of image. As opposed to this "A thought to Donne was an experience; it modified his sensibilily".[264] A creative and unified sensibility is recognised by the fact that howsoever disparate and chaotic the nature of experience available, it is always forming new wholes out of them.

Eliot perceived disunity and dissociation in sensibility not only of poets but of age somewhere near the Revolution in the seventeenth century. The grounds for such a perception have been debated and are debatable but Eliot's concept of the dissociation rests, primarily, on the disintegration of personality that we chiefly come across in the *Bhagavadgīta* and in *Yoga-Sūtras* of Patanjali. In the latter we read: "The Seer, who is nothing but (the power of) seeing, although undefiled *(Cuddha),* looks upon the presented-idea".[265] Haughton-Woods comments:" 'Who is nothing but (the power of) seeing means who is nothing but the power of seeing untouched by any qualification . This self becomes conscious-by-reflection *(pratisamvedin)* of the thinking-substance. He is not homogeneous with the thinking-substance nor utterly heterogeneous".[266] Here, the Self-in-Itself is untouched by impressions from outside. When, however, it reflects its relationship to the thinking-substance, it becomes conscious. This relationship escapes labelling either of homogeneity or of heterogeneity. The Self only seems to involve itself in thinking; in fact, it only looks at the mutations of matter while the object is still in the process of forming itself. At this stage the thinking-substance is under the influence of intelligence *(Caitanya).*

This stage in Eliot corresponds to the stage of thinking

or thought when the question of unification, either by violence or by unified sensibility, simply does not arise. The implication of *Patanjali's sūtra* is that the thinking substance only combines sub-conscious impressions, connects objects to organs; in other words, it acts by combining causes. The thinking-substance may well be what R.P. Blackmur says, "The mask of personality: The public shape which stands between the world and the denizens of our jungle".[267] And then we read in Patanjali: "The reason for the apperception of what the power of the property and of what the power of the proprietor are is correlation".[268] Haughton-Woods says: "The Self as proprietor becomes correlated for the purpose of sight with the object-for-sight as property. That apperception of the object-for-sight which results from this correlation is experience".[269] In Eliot's terminology, the relationship between the self and that which it sees, was not dissociated before the seventeenth century. The dissociation occurred somewhere in the middle of that century between the feeling-substance and the linguistic mask. "In the seventeenth century a dissociation of sensibility set in, from which we have never recovered; and this dissociation, as is natural, was aggravated by the influence of the two most powerful poets of the century, Milton and Dryden. Each of these men performed certain poetic functions so magnificently well that the magnitude of the effect concealed the absence of others. The language went on and in some respects improved; . . . The feeling, the sensibility, expressed in the *Country Churchyard* (to say nothing of Tennyson and Browning) is cruder than that in the *Coy Mistress*".[270]

It must be recalled that Frank Kermode had rejected Eliot's idea of the sensibility being dissociated in *The Romantic Image.* Kermode thought that Eliot propounded the dissociation theory to advance the case for the kind of verse that he was writing. How is it, Kermode asks, that such dissociation occurred for Eliot, Yeats and Hulme at different times? In fact Eliot's reading of the tradition of British poetry is highly subjective and this is quite as it should be. However, it would appear to Eliot that prior to the middle of the seventeenth century, the centre and the sense of equilibrium which the British poetry had, was lost. What we consider centres—whether purely theocentric or theocentric-literary or purely literary, are individual estimates and points of view in the first place; and since they being such they cannot avoid continual shift in their relation to literary environment and in relation to the perspectivism of perception which can never quite be escaped. Things which seem to be centred and to be having an equilibrium lose their centres when perceptions change. What was knowledge at one time is ignorance at the other. In Patanjali we read: "The reason for this (correlation) is undifferentiated-consciousness *(avidya)*".[271] Human reason and consciousness embraced all that came in its purview before the seventeenth century. In Donne's poetry, for example, the poetic image unites the sense, the sound, the feeling and the emotion—the hallmark of a unified sensibility. Such poetry has its own centre in the vital correlation, the chain-of-being so to say, which the images and the symbols perceive among themselves. In the latter poetry, the harmony is broken by a dialectic that questions the viability of the existence of a particular image and symbol, as for example, in the poetry of T.S. Eliot himself.

Haughton-Woods says that "A special correlation of each single Self with each single thinking-substance is the reason for the diversity between (individuals)".[272] This will explain the diversity of centres in poems and world-views of different poets. Although Eliot did not believe in Genetic Fallacy which implies that the poem is the experience of the poet, his general statement (for what else will it be called?) on the dissociation of sensibility is nothing but a statement which has vital links with Patanjali's *sūtra* above—the sense of perceiving correlation may be undifferentiated consciousness. The following comment by Hugh Kenner also makes us feel that Eliot fully realized that general centres are individuated in and by individual consciousness. Hence all the more reason as to why he gave that general comment upon the dissociation of sensibility: "Eliot himself at one time devoted considerable attention to the implications of hypotheses of this kind, which involve, in their various forms, an attempt to *become* the poet, on the supposition that Art works by a transfusion of personality. And just here is Eliot's point of dissent from them. For as no one will argue (he uses this figure in writing on Bradley) that the 'real' geranium is the geranium's experience of itself, just so it is meaningless to argue that the 'real' poem is the poet's experience of it. Hence, in ascertaining sources we are learning something about the process of composition, perhaps something about the poet, but not about the poem."[273]

This is what Patanjali's *sūtra* implies that all verbal formulations, as long as they are, will allow for the identity of the Self with the thinking-substance only in part and never whole. Making a distinction between philosophical and metaphysical poetry Eliot said that "in philosophical poetry the poet *believes* in some theory about life and the universe and makes poetry of it. Metaphysical poetry, on the other hand, does not imply belief; it has come to mean the poetry in which the poet *makes use* of metaphysical ideas and theories".[274] Although Eliot is having in mind the poetry of Donne and Herbert and Crashaw, it is very difficult indeed to separate technique, howsoever objective, from some sort of subjective belief at some stage or the other. I feel Eliot's distinction between the poetry of belief and the poetry which makes *use* of belief is not going to take us very far, howsoever clear his point might be. Eliot, however, would want, the poet to be in an organic relationship with the images, symbols and the syntax that he uses. There is more than one meaning of emotion, thought and feeling in Eliot. For example, the two kinds of feeling are these: "In Chapman especially there is a direct sensuous apprehension of thought, or a recreation of thought into *feeling,* which is exactly what we find in Donne."[275]

Here thought implies a sensuous apprehension of the object of perception. The sense and thought combined take us into feeling. Of the other kind of feeling Eliot says that the metaphysical poets "were, at best, engaged in the task of trying to find the verbal equivalent for states of mind and feeling".[276] Here feeling is searching for its verbal equivalents in objects outside which would imply a sensuous apprehension of them of course. Thought, feeling, emotion, are aspects of the *guna* and they do lead to the Self; they are not the Self or the Absolute to which Eliot's poetry and criticism are aspiring. In Patanjali we read that "After the aids to yoga have been followed up, when the impurity has dwindled, there is an enlightenment of perception reaching up to the discriminative discernment".[277] It is the discriminative discernment that separates the wheat from the chaff. How the object enters into consciousness, its cause and its evolution and transformation are described thus by Haughton-Woods: "Cause is ninefold, rise (into consciousness) and permanence and manifestation and modification and presentation and attainment and disjunction and transformation and sustentation. Of these (nine), 1. The cause of rise (into consciousness), (is for instance) the Central-organ (as the cause) of a mental-process *(Vijnāna)*; 2. The cause of permanence: (for instance) the fact that Self has purposes (is the cause of the permanence) of the body; 3. The cause of manifestation (is for instance) the shining (of the Self upon a fluctuation as the cause of the manifestation) of colour, just as the perception of colour (which is in the fluctuation, is the cause which manifests the shining of the Self); 4. The cause of modification (is for instance) another object-of-sense (which modifies) food to be cooked; 5. The cause of presentation (for instance) the thought of smoke (is the cause of the presentation) of the thought of fire; 6. The cause of attaining: (for instance) the following up of the aids to yoga (is the cause of attaining) discriminative discernment; 7. The cause of disjunction (is for instance) the same (following up as the cause which disjoins the Self) from impurity; 8. The cause of transformation is for instance the goldsmith (as the cause which transforms the gold. . . .) 9. The cause of sustentation (is for instance) the body (as the cause which sustains) the sense-organs, and these (organs as the cause sustaining) this (body), (and again) the great elements (as the sustaining cause) of bodies, and these (elements) reciprocally of all (element), since human and animal and supernormal bodies depend upon each other."[278]

It will be clear from Professor Woods' comment as to how forms come into existence, how they are modified, transformed and sustained. The idea that is emphasized is the interdependence of bodies—one upon the other. The moment of creation is a moment of intense concentration which realizes the aforesaid details as a simultaneous order of existence. In a letter to Harriet Monroe, Eliot said: "The test of a writer is his ability for. . . concentration AND for his power to stay concentrated till he gets to the end of his poem; whether it is two lines or two hundred". Just as in Patanjali and in Buddhism, the dependently-originated nature of things is emphasized, so Eliot said that: "The work of poetry is often said to be performed by the use of images, by a cumulative succession of images each fusing with the next; or by the rapid and unexpected combination of images apparently unrelated, which have their relationship enforced upon them by the mind of the author. This appears to be true."[279] Compare with Eliot's statement the following two *sūtras* in Patanjali: "created mind-stuffs may result from the sense-of-personality and from this alone. While there is a variety of actions, the mind-stuff which impels the many is one" (4-5, Book II). Here too, the actions (Eliot's images) are many but the uniting agency—the mind—is one.

The twofold purposes of the Self in Patanjali are that it causes the central-organ to begin the mental process from an indeterminable stage and to bring it into consciousness out of the feeling-of-personality. The images in Eliot, which are apparently unrelated because of the vacuity of consciousness, are related by a consciousness which is a consciousness of more than one personality both in Eliot and in Patanjali. In Eliot, as already said, the mind of the poet is a filament of platinum where combinations of emotions and feelings are forming new wholes.

R.P. Blackmur, quite aware of the influence of Professor Woods' translation of Patanjali's yoga upon Eliot, says that what the comparison of the poet's mind with a filament of platinum implies is in essence: "That the poet only uses language well by getting himself out of the way; that language uses him; that language is real, . . . It has always seemed to me that Eliot must have heard, read the same words I heard in Professor Woods' course in Indian Philosophy, for the notes were very old when I heard them used: 'The reality in words, gentlemen, is both, superior to and anterior to any use to which you can put them'. These words were accompanied by a strenuous forward rubbing of the hands on the desk, as if somehow the reality of words was being rubbed both into the grain of the wood and the grain of our minds. Eliot's filament of platinum may well have an ancestor in words spoken in Emerson Hall."[280] Blackmur's quotation from Woods might refer to more than one *sūtra* in Patanjali. For example, consider the verses: "And there cannot be a cognition of both (thinking substance and thing) at the same time. If (one mind-stuff) were the object-for-sight for another, there would be an infinite regress from one thinking-substance to another thinking-substance as well as confusion of memory".[281]

What Patanjali is implying is this that in order that difference in effects is produced, the functional activity has got to be differential in nature, taking into consideration the anterior and the posterior aspects within which difference can occur. The superiority and the anteriority in the quotation from Woods could be further explained by this verse from Patanjali: "The mutation into another birth is the result of the filling-in of the evolving-cause."[282] Woods' comment on this *sūtra* is this: "... The same body and organs must enter into the mutation of another birth. But this mutation does not follow from material-causes in general. For the same quantity of material-causes cannot belong to him when he attains to a supernal or to a not-supernal state-of-existence which is either more or less (than the present state)".[283] Such superior and anterior logic also develops vital relationships with words in their distinct stages of magnificence. One way of such a development is indicated by Eliot's views on auditory imagination: "The feeling for syllable and rhythm, penetrating far below the conscious levels of thought and feeling, invigorating every word; sinking to the most primitive and forgotten, returning to the origin and bringing something back, seeking the beginning and the end. It works through meanings certainly, or not without meanings in the ordinary sense, and fuses the old and obliterated and the trite, the current, and the new and surprising, the most ancient and the most civilized mentality". It is for this reason that Woods says: "The word itself, because of certain similarities and dissimilarities, is generally assumed to have the form of this or that (sound) and (so) appears in what is not its real form. For the faces as reflected in a Jewel or a sword-blade or a mirror are not parts of the real face. . . . It is brought before us or made an object by an operation *(vyāpāra)* of the presented-idea of the final (sound of the) syllable, by the operation, that is, of the subliminal impression (of the final syllable) together with the subliminal impressions generated by the experience of (sounds of) the previous syllables" (p. 242 in Woods, *Yoga System of Patanjali)*.

Eliot's views on Renaissance offer another version of the dissociation of sensibility. Eliot held, along with Babbitt and Hulme, that there was a complete breakdown between the Renaissance and the Middle Ages, for whereas the latter represented a religious approach to life, were governed by a certain theocracy, the former completely secularised the values of life and religion. There are, however, minor differences among the views of Eliot, Babbitt and Hulme on the Renaissance. For Babbitt, Bacon and Rousseau represent, respectively, the utilitarian and the emotional aspects of the Renaissance. For Hulme, the period from St. Augustine to the Renaissance constitutes the Middle Ages and the period from the Renaissance to Hulme's own time is what the Renaissance is constituted of. Hulme is as clear as this in his book *Speculations:* "It is necessary to realize that there is an absolute, and not relative, difference between humanism . . . . and the religious spirit". Hulme's attitude works by an either-or praxis and he approves Middle Ages and rejects Renaissance—even any reformulation of it such as humanism!

"All attempts to 'explain' religion on a humanist basis, whether it be Christian or an alien religion like Buddhism, must always be futile" *(Speculations*, p. 49).

Babbitt's Humanism was largely derived from Buddhism and he said that "a man may safely go into himself if what he finds there is not, like Rousseau, his own emotion, but like the Buddha, the law of righteousness."[284] Eliot's disagreement with Babbitt's humanism is well-known and he would not approve of a humanism which is devoid of religion—especially Christianity. This takes us to the formation of the dialectic at more than one level: the dialectic between Eliot and Babbitt, and the consequent dialectic between the Middle Ages and the Renaissance. Whereas Babbitt insists (in Eliot's reading of him) upon the human reason, Eliot insists upon the supernatural, the reality larger than all of us. "It is very difficult to define humanism in Mr. Babbitt's terms, for he is very apt to line it up in battle order *with* religion *against* humanitarianism and naturalism; and what I am trying to do is to *contrast* it with religion."[285]

Eliot wanted a consciousness that does not work by exclusion and separation but a consciousness that is all-inclusive—in the sense that it assimilates and transforms a variety of perceptions from a variety of fields—something which Radhakrishnan would call the "integral consciousness". Eliot summed up his "Clarke Lectures" (1926) with the following important statement on how the sensibility is dissociated: "What I have tried to do is to maintain literary values in the centre of the picture, to consider different periods of poetry by poetic values, and merely to indicate the extra-literary causes of the differences in literary value. In doing so, I have indicated a theory of what I call the 'disintegration of the intellect'. So far as I am concerned, this disintegration means merely a progressive deterioration of poetry, in one respect or another, since the XIIIth century".[286] Eliot visualized human personality very much in the sense in which Blake visualized the concept of Albion with Los, Urizen, Luvah and Tharmas forming portions of his soul, intellect, mind and senses. A mutual warfare among these zoas, as Blake calls them, results in the disintegration of Albion's being. Eliot's concept of personality, which has a direct bearing upon the dissociation theory, is very close to the concept or personality as expounded in the *Gīta* and in Patanjali. Consider, for example, this comment from Woods: "The organs of intelligence *(buddhi)* are particularized (forms) of the (personality-substance) *(ahamkara)* which is characterized as having the feeling of personality, and which has *sattva* as its dominant (aspect). But the organs of action (are particularised forms of the personality-substance) which has *rajas* as its dominant (aspect). Whereas the central-organ *(manas),* the essence of which is of both kinds, must be supposed to be the (particularised form of the personality-substance). . . the five fine elements have the thinking-substance as their cause, because they are unpar-ticularised (forms), like the feeling-of-personality".[287]

Woods' above comment is on *sūtra* 19 of Book II in Patanjali's yoga: "The particularized and the unparticularized (forms) and the resoluble only (into primary matter) and irresoluble-primary-matter—are the divisions of the aspects *(guna)*". It is these aspects which make up the personality and which, in *Bhagavadgīta,* emerge as the basic constituents of being's personality (3, 42). It is the thinking-substance in itself unconscious and unparticularised, that enervates and energises the central organ into activity. Eliot's claim that it is only the impersonality that could be expressed in Art—a theme that he develops in "Tradition and the Individual Talent" and "The Three Voices of Poetry", seems to be somewhat bypassed, as Matthiessen also notes, by Eliot's statement in 1953. The speech of Eliot is notable for comparison with Patanjali's *sūtra* above which explains how the central organ manifests itself at different pitches, levels and forms, while particularizing them. "It seems to me that what happens, when an author creates a vital character, is a sort of give-and-take. The author may put into that character, besides its attributes, some traits of his own, some strength or weakness, some tendency to violence or to indecision, some eccentricity even, that he has found in himself. . . . I believe that the author imparts something of himself to his characters, but I also believe that he is influenced by the characters he creates."[288]

This is a welcome change in Eliot's attitude and this enforces the idea, found earlier only in passing, that there is no impersonality without a strong personality, for the characters and events cannot be re-formulated or newly–imagined or transformed by a weak personality. Eliot's attacks on the Renaissance occur at several places. On Shakespeare's tragedies he says: "There is, in some of the great tragedies of Shakespeare, a new attitude. It is not the attitude of Seneca. It is not the attitude of Seneca, but is derived from Seneca; . . . it culminates, if there is ever any culmination, in the attitude of Nietzsche."[289] In Machiavelli also, Eliot finds a Nietzschean attitude: "There is a form of self-satisfaction and self-deception, which merely propogates the Jew of Malta-Nietzsche myth of Machiavelli".[290] Nietzsche's wide readings in Buddhism and Hinduism and his open use of certain ideas found in them in his creative writing generally earned him the title of a heretic, for Nietzsche freely opposed these religions to Christianity. It was because of such changes in thought that created a fissure in the sensibility of the European mind. When the dissociation occurred because of the rift among the thought-feeling-emotion trio, the problem before art arose—one—that of objective correlative – a term that has invited a variety of reactions.

It is the dialectic which makes us aware of the dual nature of our existence, and when the spirit and the matter are not only separate but in opposition to each other, different velocities of spirit and matter try to find fulfilment in different volumes of fullness-emptiness dialectic. The search for new centres of respective peripheries leads us not to the integrated whole which has a common centre, but to the divided many which perpetuate centres. The climax of the dialectical opposition, at this stage of the development of the poem in my theory, also leads into a thinking of the way out of this impasse which is likely to develop in an endless regress. The dialectical oppositions just point to a way beyond, without achieving the synthesis. This stage corresponds to Nagarjuna's third great proposition—"both this-is-and-this-is-not". The dialectic enlarges the frames of reference, often inter-contextualizes them, thus exposing the strength and weakness of both the thesis and the antithesis.

This stage is also the Buddhist *Dharmakāya,* the Body of Law, which tries to find a way beyond momentary mutations or the flux which is endless. "This body Dharma has no boundary, no quarters, but is embodied in all bodies".[291] This is where Eliot's personality becomes impersonal, and the mind shows its dual function of focussing not only upon the heart and the senses below but by uniting itself with the syncretising intellect and the faculty beyond which is *Atman* or the Self. When the synthesis of various faculties does not take place into an organic unity, the dissociated sensibility tries to achieve the sense of the fullness by creating individual, particularised centres. These centres need a body for self-expression—a body of ideas, metaphors and symbols. Eliot finds Shakespeare's *Hamlet,* an "artistic failure"; "The only way of expressing emotion in the form of art is by finding an 'objective correlative'; in other words, a set of objects, a situation, a chain of events which shall be the formula of that *particular* emotion; such that when the external facts, which must terminate in sensory experience, are given, the emotion is immediately evoked."[292] The logic of reincarnation, both in the *Bhagavadgīta* and in Patanjali's *Yoga-Sūtras,* is based upon the *samskārās* or impressions of the individual. Such *samskārās* form the individual traits and characteristics in the long run and largely determine the nature and quality of the next birth of a human being. Though God is the father of all created things, ignorance leads human beings and others away from God; they multiply individual ego-centres without finding permanent shelter in the vicinity of God. Krishna says: "In whatever womb whatever form arises-and-grows-together, of (all) those (forms) Great Brahman is the Womb, I the father, giver of the seed" *(Gīta,* 14.4). Krishna further tells Arjuna: "As a man casts off his worn-out clothes and takes on other new ones, so does the embodied (self) cast off its worn-out bodies and enters other new ones" *(Gīta,* 2.22).

Professor R.C. Zaehner elucidates: "The embodied self takes with it all the 'fruits' of the actions it has performed in this and previous lives and with it go its psychic and intellectual faculties. It is only the old body that is left behind: all the rest-intellect, will, and mind—accompany the embodied self in its endless journey through time".[293] Krishna also says: "There is he united with the soul as it had matured in his former body; and once again he strives to win perfection's prize" *(Gita,* 6.43). Eliot's insights may have also come from an article published by May Sinclair on "Jones's Karma" in *The Criterion* of October 1923. A portion of the article read: "When you talk of free-will and bondage you talk of the pairs of opposites. You are free and you are bound also. . . so long as you affirm the reality of the pairs of opposites you are subject to illusions". As per Howarth, nine years after, in 1932, Eliot said: "This kind of determination is essential to Buddhism as well as Christianity; but whether determinism is the right word for it, I leave unsettled". The pairs of opposites that Eliot refers to are *pairs* by the fact of a certain relationship between them. The relationship, though part of a larger dissociation, involves dialectical oppositions only in order to discover mutual equivalences or objective correlatives. The epistemological implication of Eliot's objective correlative theory is that it is only by correlating things one with the other that the circumference is united in relation to the centre. Just as spherical bodies revolve round a centre, so ideas, images and concepts gyrate but with a sense of mutual harmony based on the relation of the equality of volume, intensity and pitch of one object with another.

Determinism in Karma implies that a man seeks to perform those Karmas that his inherent habit would allow him to perform. The deterministic process of relating Karmas to thoughts in mind would go on until the point of climax in individual personality that will over-throw determinism not necessarily by detaching itself from Karmas performed according to determined thoughts, but by assimilating them into itself in its search for the Absolute. The epistemological implication of Eliot's objective correlative theory is the process of assimilation and annulment that it involves. All this only because an image or symbol in Eliot is always trying to be itself, trying to capture itself in relation to itself.

The above details are given to highlight the fact that the individual continues to create particular centres of repulsion and attraction in relation to the centre *(bindu)* until the time it can directly apprehend the centre (the particular *samskārās* allowing) ·which shall virtually furnish the process of objectively correlating things. As per the details above the success or the failure of relating personal feelings and emotions to situations or objects in the world of outer experience depends upon the perfection and maturity, not only of the particular ideas concerned, but upon the perfection of the yogic technique. This technique involves, on the part of the artist as yogi, a correlation of his own emotions and feelings with the emotions and feelings of the same wavelength in objects or situations outside.

This is a task precisely carried out by God Himself in the *Gīta* while continuing the round of endless births and deaths. Just as Krishna says that a yogi seeking integration has "his mind controlled, his thoughts on Me, integrated, (yet) intent on Me" *(Gīta,* 6.14), so does an artist take up his personal feelings and emotions in order to integrate them on the basis of the similarities in the wavelength of the *samskārās.* The process continues until the personal feelings and emotions are also the feelings and emotions of God which is not an instance of the objective-correlative but of the merger of the subject with the object. For Eliot, a lyric with subjective feelings expressed in the first person is an absurd way of dealing with emotion in art. The only way is to find an objective framework to fit in emotions and feelings, and the failure to do so will result in the failure of art. Eliot's case is a case of subjective and intentional fallacy, for before charging that the play *Hamlet* is an "artistic failure", Eliot has more than assured himself that his own emotions are those of Shakespeare's and that what Shakespeare wanted out of the character of Hamlet, he has failed to achieve.

Eliot's case of intentionalist fallacy has been rightly attacked by Eliseo Vivas. "The assumption, therefore, that we can criticise *Hamlet* by comparing the emotion expressed in the play with Shakespeare's emotions, or that through the play we can discover the emotions that went into it, is a confusing illusion".[294] Birje-Patil argues that Eliot "is not referring to the poet's own emotion during the act of creation. Eliseo Vivas thinks he does".[295] Birje- Patil may well represent another case of intentionalist fallacy, for in creation, emotions, howsoever dramatic, do undergo transformation only in personality. Mattheissen already reminds us that Eliot confessed in 1953 that "the author imparts something of himself to his characters" though he, in turn, is also influenced by them.[296] Allen Austin has also argued that the "identity of the emotion of the poet with that of the character is irrelevant".[297] Such thinking will have its parallel in the death of the author celebrated by Roland Barthes. But Patil's circumlocutionary way of arguing his case against Vivas falls back upon itself when he says: "Isn't Eliot in fact merely drawing our attention to Shakespeare's inability to assimilate his personal experience to his literary work? Shakespeare, Eliot explains, was unable to achieve the necessary impersonality during the act of creation."[298] And earlier Patil had claimed that Eliot is not talking of personal but dramatic emotions, as if dramatic emotions are aroused not in personality but outside it.

R.P. Blackmur, instead of arguing his case in an either-or fashion, rightly says that objective correlative is not a doctrine but "an observation put into the form of a notion . . . It is a metaphorical account of how feelings and emotions get into the words with the least interference by the 'mere' personality".[299] This obviously means that the personality is involved in a very special way in the act of transforming, received (if not one's own) emotions into words and images. What Blackmur feels about objective correlative he puts as follows: "Eliot was making a metaphor about Shakespeare's failure, as he saw it, to give the right words and actions in the right relation or sequence to express the emotions and feelings that were already there in Prince Hamlet, in his mind and the impulses of his behaviour.[300] It was not, as I see it, a metaphor about the poet's own relation to *his* feelings and emotions and to *his* language. The inconsistency with his other notions about tradition and order and behaviour and belief would make the acceptance of the objective correlative as a doctrine for poetry impossible even in a mind with such deeply divided allegiances as Eliot's. If I am right, most of the arguments about this notion as doctrine or principle take place only in the critics' own minds and concern Eliot only has a mistaken development of what he wrote in his book review of Robertson on *Hamlet.* The whole situation lacks clarity."[301]

All that it comes to is a "confusing illusion" as Eliseo Vivas said earlier. Eliot claimed: "Hamlet (the man) is dominated by an emotion which is inexpressible, because it is in *excess* of the facts as they appear. And the supposed identity of Hamlet with his author is genuine to this point: that Hamlet's bafflement at the absence of objective equivalent to his feelings is a prolongation of the bafflement of his creator in the face of his artistic problem. Hamlet is up against the difficulty that his disgust is occasioned by his mother, but that his mother is not an adequate equivalent for it; his disgust envelops and exceeds her. It is thus a feeling which he cannot understand; he cannot objectify it, and it therefore remains to poison life and obstruct action."[302] There is a point to which Eliot accepts Shakespeare's identity of himself with Hamlet. This also cuts across Birje-Patil's argument that Eliot is not talking of author's own emotion in art. Secondly, Eliot fails to persuade himself that it is only the "prolongation of the bafflement" that Shakespeare intended. Shakespeare was not trying to find an objective equivalent to either Hamlet or his mother's feelings and emotions. Shakespeare's intention, if there could be one on the basis of the reading of *Hamlet,* seems only to prolong action and obstruct thinking, leaving it to a state of indecision and confusion. This is what the theme of the play is. Eliot's objective correlative, applied indiscriminately, is, and often proves out to be, a forced error. It is astonishing that Eliot argued against Richards when the latter criticised *The Waste Land* as lacking all belief.

Eliot had said that the chaos and confusion as depicted in *The Waste Land* is also a kind of belief. Why couldn't Eliot say the same thing about Shakespeare's *Hamlet?* Why did he take his doctrine of objective correlative as good for every type of work of art? Why Eliot always looked for the objectification of emotion when the authorial intention may have been to keep it subjective? Could not we take Eliot's own personal tragedy as the cause of his personal disgust which envelops and exceeds him? Is it not what made him give undue importance to objectivity in Art? . . . in order to forget suffering that is life? This conflict in Eliot's personality is well elucidated by Victor Brombert. Eliot is also very close to Buddhism here which recognises human life and suffering as identical and asks the individual to sacrifice his individuality to the group *(samgha)* which is an objectification of personal suffering, feeling and emotion. Brombert holds that Eliot suffered from an impersonal aestheticism and personal moralism: "The fear of any aesthetic-ethical standard in criticism led Eliot to assert that from the point of view of ART only the aesthetic values were to be taken into consideration. Very soon, however, he had to concede that pure literature was only a chimera and that much entered into a work of art which could not be accounted for in purely aesthetic terms. Next, although insisting that the poet was not really a thinker, Eliot agreed that intellectual beliefs expressed in a poem could not be neglected. In his essay on Dante, Eliot maintained that the reader, in order to appreciate the poetry, was not called upon to share but merely to understand the beliefs expressed. Then followed a series of concessions: First, that it was not possible in practice to separate appreciation from belief; secondly, that there existed poets who were simultaneously thinkers; thirdly, that the beliefs expressed stood in a definite relation to the greatness of the poetry; and finally, that the reader, in order fully to judge and appreciate the poetry, could not leave out of account the beliefs and personality of the Author himself."[303]

The above is a statement on Eliot's shifting positions and the positions have been shifting because of certain dilemmas inherent in them which are precisely Eliot's dilemmas. This dialectic of scepticism and faith as Fei-Pai Lu calls it, is basic to Eliot both in his criticism and in his poetry. At the cardinal point in the west in the circle of my literary theory the sun is already on the decline after being at the climax in the south. Since the west is dominated by the mind as the east and the south were dominated by sensation and feeling, so the chief characteristic of the mind is the emotion which gives birth to the conscious dialectic and finally divides the already unconsciously-fissured self into a conscious, and even deliberate, bi-polarity both in action and in vision. But the mind occupies a place in human personality, which when attuned to the ego, the centre of physical personality, produces reptiles of division and multiplies divisive tendencies; however, there is another personality in Eliot that is spiritual. When the mind works in communion with soul, it becomes the agent of transformation too. The dialectical stage in the west is the stage in my theory where the mind does realize that the dialectical oppositions are exhausting themselves into an emptiness, that yet, rearticulates itself into a bi-polar vision of the self. The consciousness, nevertheless, of a possible synthesis beyond the dialectic, howsoever unconscious, is already visible at this stage. As Grover Smith says about "Gerontion" (the poem I considered in the first stage), that "Gerontion is not at the center, cannot attain the center, and does not believe",[305] so the journey towards the centre was continued through *The Waste Land* to the *Ash Wednesday* which we shall consider now.

The four categories of my theory, as already said, are not exclusive and apart from each other, each stage includes the qualities and characteristics of every other stage. It is always by the analogy of a macrocosm into a microcosm that each stage proceeds until the final effacement of the two into the unity of the centre. Northrop Frye says that: "The experiences in *Ash Wednesday* take place on four levels: the level of spiritual vision or high dream in III and IV; the level of nostalgic vision in VI; the level of ordinary experience, of disillusionment and distraction, in I and V, and the level of ascesis or self-denial in II. The first level is a world of identity, where the individual is identified with his community, a member of one body, without losing his individuality. . . The second level is a world where experiences of peculiar intensity are linked by memory and impose a pattern of greater significance and sadness on ordinary life . . . The third level is ordinary experience, where the ego tries to achieve identity through 'memory and desire' and the fourth level is the concentrating of consciousness designed to break up the illusions of the ego."[306]

Basically, *Ash Wednesday* is a poem of the conflict between the physical and the spiritual selves of man. The four-tier classification of personality made in my theory, *i.e.,* sense, mind, intellect and self *(Atman),* corresponds to the four levels of the poem outlined by Frye above. At the first level, in the First Section of *Ash Wednesday,* the four-tier hierarchy of personality is divided where each faculty pulls out of the other, and the very idea of the sense of unity is missing. Disillusionment over the self and the created objects overpowers feelings of unity and cohesiveness. Such drama is carried on in Section V also. This disillusionment and the extreme sense of negation leads us to self-denial in Section II. In terms of my theory, when passionate reveries fail to satisfy the full being of man, dissatisfaction with the self grows; this dejection gradually multiplies itself, and in its next development, it bifurcates itself into two parallel, though distinct, lines of action—one trying to tear across the remnants of being to the furthest distance of the disfigurement of identity, and the other trying to effect or put into practice, some method for the remedy of such a situation. This remedy in *Ash Wednesday's* second section is self-denial, very much a concept in Buddhism and in Yoga. But the attempts to re-unite the self do not succeed in the same measure as the efforts of a disintegrationist instinct do. This is made clear by the emergence of the dialectical opposition between the spiritual and the physical self at the third stage of my theory. Sections III and IV of *Ash Wednesday* constitute another aspect of the third stage of my theory, where out of the dialectical exposure and exhaustion of bi-polar terms, the desire to unite the bi-polarity grows. This desire is more in the nature of what Frye calls a "high dream" than a reality. Section VI of *Ash Wednesday* will correspond to the fourth stage of my literary theory where unity is achieved only to the extent it is achievable among the warring impulses in man.

The laboured unity at this stage, however, points beyond itself to the centre which syncretises and upholds in itself everything as a ground for possibilities. The complete surrender and identification at this stage in Eliot's poem is indicated by lines like:

> Our peace in His will
> And even among these rocks
> Sister, mother
> And spirit of the river, spirit of the sea,
> Suffer me not to be separated.

Krishna in the *Gīta* has declared that the world is not come into existence fortuitously; it is *willed* by Him. If He leaves His female consort alone, which is Nature and which includes all created things, it will turn wayward and destroy everything. It is only when the Nature's will is in consonance and harmony with the will of God that a unitive vision is achieved. Hence Eliot's prayer: "Our peace is His Will". The narrator in *Ash Wednesday* is trying to kill the ego; in a fit of bewilderment he separates farthest filaments of his being into a total vision of nihilism. But in Eliot's poem as in the *Gīta,* Nature and its concomitants are not considered exclusive hindrances in the realization of the self. What is emphasized in both is a proper moulding of Nature in consonance with the will of God in man. In fact, the structure of *Ash Wednesday* could be said to be based on the following verses in the *Gīta:*

"Raise self by self, let not the self droop down; for self's friend is self indeed, so too is self self's enemy. Self is the friend to the self of him whose self is by the self subdued; but for the man bereft of self self will act as an enemy indeed" (6. 5-5). The symbolism of the three leopards plays a significant role in redemption. Frye says that "The leopards, however terrifying, are really agents of redemption, an ambiguity which meets us often in the plays".[307]

I suggest that the three leopards are a version of the three *gunas* of the *Bhagavadgīta* which constitute material nature. This material nature binds if the individual self is not attuned to God within. It also becomes an agent of redemption if harmonised not as per the demands of material nature but the spiritual whose source is in God Himself. Krishna says: "For (all) this (Nature) is my creative power *(māyā)*, composed of the constituents, divine, hard to transcend. Whoso shall put his trust in Me alone, shall pass beyond this (my) uncanny power *(māyā)*" (7.14). The suggestion that the leopards symbolize the *gunas* of the *Gīta* is strengthened by Eliot's association of them with legs, heart and the skull which roughly correspond to the *tamas* (darkness), the *rajas* (passion), and the *sattva* (goodness). All three are fallen "having fed to satiety/On my legs my heart my liver and that which had been contained/In the hollow round of my skull". The lady in *Ash Wednesday* is very much the Nature of *Bhaguvadgīta* imagined in the form of woman with three constituents, Krishna's female consort, with the help of whom He creates the world. Look how Eliot creates the sense of dismemberment by using above concepts from the *Gīta:*

> And I who am here dissembled
> Proffer my deeds to oblivion, and my love
> To the posterity of the desert and the fruit of the Gourd.
> It is this which recovers
> My guts the strings of my eyes and the indigestible portions
> Which the leopards reject. The lady is withdrawn
> In a white gown, to contemplation, in a white gown.

It is this lady who is described in the poem by dialectical terms: "Lady of silences/Calm and distressed/Torn and most whole/Rose of memory/Rose of forgetfulness. . . " Eliot's idea by depicting the lady through such terms is to emphasize that in herself the lady is exhausted, lifeless and desert. It is only when she establishes some sort of harmony with her male counterpart that the dialectical images give birth to a unity hidden earlier. Krishna says: ". . . By my creative energy *(māyā)* I consort with Nature – which is mine – and come to be (in time)" *(Gīta,* 4.6).

The logic of *Ash Wednesday* moves round the following verses: "It is material Nature's (three constituents) that do all works whatever (works are done); (but) he whose self is by the ego fooled thinks, 'It is I who do'. But he who knows how constituents and works are parcelled out in categories, seeing things as they are, thinks thus: 'constituents on constituents act', (and thus thinking) remains unattached'." *(Gīta,* 3.27-28). It is precisely this sense of unattachment that points the way beyond the dialectic. Eliot has recourse to Buddhist as well as *Upanishadic* negation as part of yogic technique to achieve a vision of integration and liberation. The sense of pseudo-personality that accumulates at the level of the ego is to be sublimated in order that it is absorbed into the spiritual centre of the personality and transformation takes place. Eliot's division of the poem into six parts may owe something to the following in Haughton Woods' translation of Patanjali's *Yoga Sutras:* "The unparticularised (forms) are six, namely, the fine element of sound and the fine element of touch and the fine element of colour and the fine element of taste and the fine element of smell. . . And the sixth is that of which we can only say that it is the feeling-of-personality. These are the six unparticularised forms of the Great thinking-substance of whose being we can only say that it exists."[308] Each section in Eliot's poem, in some way or the other, tries to particularize the unparticularized in order to present a unitive sense of personality that always negatives the attempt at unity. Woods also draws our attention to the outer six-sheathed body in the *Mahābhārata.*[309] This six-sheathed body has a three-tier structure based on the three *gunas* of the *Gīta.* Eliot also calls them three stairs which give us three distinct kinds of vision of the Absolute or of the centre. In terms of my literary theory, the three stairs symbolize the Buddhist *Nirmānkāya, Sambhōgkāya* and *Dharmakāya,* the three circles which one has to cross in order to reach the centre. Matthiessen says that". . . Eliot's images are at the same time both exact and suggestive in their portrayal of these three spiritual stages".[310]

Matthiessen goes on to compare the three stairs with Dante's "hill of Purgatory". Eliot might as well have developed the stair imagery from the related imagery of the three circles of fire, moon and sun, in Patanjali: "In the middle of this (lotus) is the circle of the sun (and) the letter A (and) the locus of the waking-state. Above it is the circle of the moon (and) the letter U (and) the locus of sleep. Above this is the circle of fire (and) the letter M (and) the locus of deep-sleep. Above which is the highest, whose essence is the air (and) the prolonged nasal *(brahma-nāda)* (and) the locus of the fourth *(Turiya)* state (and) a half-measure. (All this) the knowers of Brahma relate."[311] Here the three circles are also related to the Hindu mystic syllable OM *(AUM)* whose three distinct sounds capture the movement of flux and stillness in their entirety. In Eliot also, the suggestion is a marginal decrease in evil from one stair to another until the good is attained— the stillness of the sound "M" which closes the movement of the vocal chords. In Eliot's poem the place of the lotus which is symbolically used to describe the complex of body-plexuses is taken by the rose whose meaning implications remain the same as that of lotus. Eliot, however, emphasizes the struggle which always turns into a dialectic: "Eliot does not rest satisfied with the vision of 'Ash Wednesday' IV, but returns to the struggle in the world that lies about him".[312]

Grover Smith thus summarises the four parts of the poem: "After the four central parts of *Ash Wednesday,* exhibiting respectively the rejection of carnal love, the involuntary persistence of desire, the lost vision of light, and the inability of human weakness to reach the Word, the poem concludes with a renewed prayer to the Virgin for humanity and for an end to the painful separation from grace."[313] My interpretation is that the lady is Nature of the *Gīta* and she can approximate Christian Mary only when malleated into the will of God. Northrop Frye says that the narrator in *Ash Wednesday* is a middle aged person, "beginning to realize that life is a parabola, He is not content however with the chagrin of ordinary experience: he wants to kill the ego, . . . He descends from despair founded on disillusionment to despair founded on reality, the despair of finding anything in the past worth clinging to. . . It is only when the narrator's very bones have stopped clinging together that he can become aware of any other reality. . ."[314] The narrator's position and mental state imply that he has lost faith in Word, in himself and in the communicability of language. This total negation which is used in Buddhism, often consciously, leads to total affirmation. In Eliot's poem too, the narrator is made aware of his spiritual-self only when his physical-self is dead. The poem of com-plete affirmation, or rather integration, is *The Four Quartets,* the poem which corresponds to the fourth stage of my literary theory which I shall consider now. The circle comes full at the cardinal point north where a complete negation is also achieved: "Neither-this nor this-is-not". The achievement of this absolute negative reference, on the one hand, kills the personality centred in the ego by negativising all that it claimed true, and, on the other, regenerates it by linking it to the spiritual personality within. It is in this sense that the *Gīta's* two wheels, originally set in motion by God, in consonance to each other (the movement of the one being changed in the other direction by the ego-centred man), are again set in motion as per the original principle with the spirit providing the centre and the ego manifesting it instead of accumulating outer experiences on to itself, thus obfuscating the vision of the spirit. The spiritual state achieved at this level is called *Mahāsukha* or the *Vajrakāya,* often called the Diamond Body of Buddha. The mental state at this level fully achieves the logic of a still centre amid a moving world, fixity within flux, and centre within circumference.

The male and the female triangles meet; Nature is no longer the wayward lady devoid of the control of the will of God as we meet in *Ash Wednesday.* God exercises full control of His will and Nature has no separate will as such; it only becomes God's creative power out of which He spins human bodies into integrated structures. The thousand-petalled lotus comes in full bloom; the six body-plexuses are transcended into this flowering, and *samādhi* (concentration) is attained by the individual consciousness, which, in silence alone, gives a vision and experience of the absolute. The achievement of this Whole, howsoever relatively, with all our concepts and categorical way of thinking, is the achievement of Eliot's poetry as well as theory of poetry. Consider these verses from the *Gīta:* "Stand fast in Yoga, surrendering attachment; in success and failure be the same and then get busy with your works. Yoga means 'sameness-and-indifference'. For lower far is (the path of) active work (for its own sake) than the spiritual exercise of the soul *(buddhi-yoga).* Seek refuge in the soul... Whoso performs spiritual exercise with the soul *(buddhi-Yukta)* discards here (and now) both good and evil works. . . For those wise men who are integrated by the soul *(buddhi-Yukta),* who have renounced the fruit that is born of works, these will be freed from the bondage of (re-) birth and fare to that region that knows no ill. When your soul passes beyond delusion's turbid quicksands, then will you learn disgust for what has been heard (ere now) and for what may yet be heard. When your soul, by scripture once bewildered, stands motionless and still, immovable in ecstasy, then will you attain to sameness-and-indifference". *(yoga) (Gīta,* 2.48-53).

Grover Smith says: "Eliot's treatment of time and place concedes certain limits to human experience. The ideal of 'turning', even if once actual or partly actual, has vanished from actuality in the present; and only the present of things 'as they are' has validity. If this fact causes pain, nevertheles it means that the sins of the past are not actual either. By the same token the present torment need not determine the future. Boundaries of time and place justify not only grief but rejoicing. At this point the attitude toward the 'nothing' of actuality, on its highest level the *nāda* of the Spanish mystics, is sustained by the doctrines of St. John of the Cross. If renunciation of 'the blessed face' and 'voice' is a resigned act of detachment from a human being, then it may create, from the negative point of view, the occasion for rejoicing in service to God. On the other hand, if it is a despairing rejection of a spiritual vision, whether embodied in a human being or not, it may signal a rejoicing which is illusory."[315] Grover Smith emphasizes two kinds of detachments: detachment which renounces not only the fruits of all action but the desire itself, and the detachment which yet nourishes within itself the savouring of the fruits of action. The former kind of detachment establishes an absolute negative point, in relation to which all referentiality acquires mere negative meanings—a sort of emptying process at work in language, thought and action, that eschews all meaning-illusions in order to grasp the Whole—an affirmative act which is simultaneous with the singular act of total negation.

The past and the present can become the yardstick of the future only to determinable being—being whose mind is not attuned to the soul within. Krishna also obliterates dis inctions of the past, present and future, and promises Arjuna regeneration in the present: "Give up all things of law, turn to Me, your only refuge, (for) I will deliver you from all evils; have no care" *(Gīta,* 18.66). Self-surrender, surrender of works and of fruits of works are as much emphasized in the *Gīta* and the *Upanishads* as in Eliot. The "'nothing' of actuality" in Grover Smith's quotation reminds of Buddhism as well as the *Upanishadic neti neti* which simultaneously negates as well as affirms. The Spanish *nāda* in fact is a Sanskrit word which literally means sound, but this sound is a very rare sound audible only to those yogis in whom the thousand-petalled lotus has already bloomed. The centre is virtually the *bīja,* the seed, out of which all visible and imaginable forms are carved on the earthly canvas. ". . . God is prior to all that moves toward Him, the failure of a particular and only hypothetical potentiality to achieve its own actual form does not nullify its meaning. The true meaning is perpetual at the still point."[316]

It is a point of multifoliate propensity whose farm is its own pleasure and whose pleasure its own consummation (in the centre). It is thus *svayambhu,* self-created as well as self-absorbed. It is the movement as well as the still point. Eliot believes in the wheel of *samsāra,* of becoming as found in Buddhism, and after a relative degree of integration, abandons all verbal constructs in favour of the experience of the absolute or the whole. Craig Raine, who has pointed out in Buddhism the source of certain images and concepts in Eliot, says: "The Wheel is *Samsāra,* the Wheel of Becoming or Rebirth, as the Lama expresses it in *Kim:* 'I go to free myself from the Wheel of things by a broad and open road'. In both of the major Buddhist schools of thought, the Theravada and the Mahayana, the Wheel plays a vital part in the idea of rebirth and the journey towards Nirvana."[317] This symbolism explains what Eliot was now ready to achieve—a complete poem of integration, a *mandala,* that is, the *Four Quartets.* Harold F. Brooks says that all the first movements in the *Quartets* are movements of proposition; the second movements are movements of negation antithetical to the first. The third movements are movements of acceptance, reconciliation, and transformation. The fourth movements are lyrics of communion between the human and the divine whereas the fifth movements achieve integration in three phases.[318] Brooks, in fact, has described, in a way, the structure of my own theory. First of all, the division of the poem into four sections corresponds to my four-tier classification of human personality, the sense, the mind, the soul, and the *Atman* *(Gīta,* 3.42). The correspondences may be many more. Secondly, the proposition in the first movement and its negation in the second is how Nagarjuna's propositional dialectic also works: "This is" is negatived by "This is not", and "Both this-is and this-is-not" is negatived by "Neither-this nor this-is-not". The fifth movement in Nagarjuna is a movement in silence, which, on the one hand, recognises the impotency of all verbal formulations—an exhaustion of terms—and, on the other, descends into the silent Absolute, which in Eliot (following the *Gīta)* is called integration.

The first stage of my theory produced a protagonist who believed his first hand experiences for what they were—a passionate fulfilment in lyric of a passionate desire in emotions quite rudimentary and simple. The dialectic at this stage is at the farthest limit of consciousness—in fact unconscious—and very rarely does it manifest itself at this level in outlines distorting the identity-process. At this stage, sensation, feeling and emotion are united—a sensuous apprehension of thought as Eliot would call it. The desire to *know* the felt-experiences divides the feeling while the unconscious dialectic of the first stage gradually acquires conscious chords of growing disharmony. The shape of the dialectic already acquires the texture of disillusionment and the maturation of the dialectic leads us into the third stage which sees the climax of dialectical thinking into two relatively absolute terms of yes and no. The achievement of absolute negativity and absolute positivity *(Ash Wednesday)* is only a prelude to the process of assimilation, ab-sorption and integration that is achieved in the fourth stage which is the *Quartets.* Lama Anagarika Govinda says: "The *pratītyasamutpāda,* however, is not confined to a sequence in time, but can also be interpreted as a simultaneous cooperation of all its links, in so far as each of them represents the sum total of all the others, seen under a particular aspect".[319] That is how Eliot's *Four Quartets,* categories of my theory, and in fact Eliot's poetic theory and whole poetry are to be read. The four distinct stages form four distinct *mandalas* as per the nature of the inherent potentiality of the seed. There should, however, be no doubt, especially after E.K. Hay's book, *T.S. Eliot's Negative Way,* that Eliot used the Buddhist method of extreme negation which relapses into silence. Citing Scarfe's approach as a wrong one which contrasts the precision and exactness of Eliot's imagery with the vagueness of imagery in Louis MacNeice.[320] B. Rajan says that "Such a procedure seems to me to impose quite the wrong demands upon the poetry. In fact the imagery is inexact—deliberately so, because what Mr. Eliot has to say cannot be said pictorially. The effect depends on disparate 'hints and guesses' reaching to the paradox of music that is not heard and rising from thence to the truth of Incarnation."[321]

It must again be recalled that Buddha always remained silent whenever Ananda queried him on God. Buddha followed the empirical method only to expose its limitations and by doing so he showed the way to what the limitations pointed to. In an unpublished lecture on "English Letter Writers" which Eliot delivered at New Haven in the winter of 1933, he was stimulated by Lawrence's plea for the language of poetry to be without any deflection or that poetry should use the "stark, bare, rocky directness of statement".[322]

Eliot said: "This speaks to me of that at which I have long aimed. . . to write poetry which should be essentially poetry, with nothing poetic about it, poetry standing naked in its bare bones, or poetry so transparent that we should not see the poetry, but that which we are meant to see through the poetry, poetry so transparent that in reading it we are intent on what the poem *points to,* and not on the poetry, this seems to me the thing to try for. To get *beyond poetry,* as Beethoven, in his later works, strove to get *beyond music.*"[323] B. Rajan gives us further interesting comparisons. Eliot said in 1938: "The poetry is something to be looked through not at" *(The Townsman,* July 1938, p. 10). In *A Choice of Kipling's Verse* in his Introduction (pp. 14-15), Eliot said in 1941: "The great poet's craft may sometimes fail him: but at his greatest moments he is doing what Kipling is doing on a lower plane—writing transparently so that our attention is directed to the object and not to the medium". Eliot insisted upon the incremental repetition of terms, a poetry of incantation which his theory of auditory imagination emphasized. To this we shall return in a short while.

Helen Gardner says upon Eliot's method in the *Quartets* that "Mr. Eliot is here writing in the tradition of those mystics who followed the negative way. It is a tradition that goes back beyond Christianity to the Neo-Platonists, who turned what had been a method of knowing—the dialectical method of arriving at experience of the One".[324] In fact, prior to Christianity and Neo-Plantonism, the dialectical tradition goes back to the Buddhists in India. Buddha used this method of propositional argument by positing and negating all *isms*—materialism, substantialism, essentialism, theism, agnosticism, etc, etc., for his endeavour was to keep the flux going, the movement, which is very vital to him. It is only by accepting the movement that the seeker can look beyond the movement into the still centre as one of my own poem says:

How curious the world becomes
When a man reacheth the centre
And sees the wheel moving from thence
Where divinity danceth in exhuberant splendour.[325]

Buddha recognized the distinct and discrete nature of each self and many selves that the time process *throws* (in the Heideggerean sense) as the manifestation of momentariness. The relationship between cause and effect is not always that of mutual dependence though more often than not it is. The psychophysical individual is said to be dependent upon consciousness *(Vinnāncapaccaya namarūpam, Digha Nikaya,* II 56) as the consciousness is said to be dependent upon the psychophysical individual *(namrūpapaccaya vinnānam, loc.cit.).* Buddhaghosa rightly says that thc Pali word *samuppāda* is *Pratītya-Samutpāda,* dependent-origination, means a plurality of conditions that give birth to a result. Buddha argues against the theory of integral selves in the *Potthapada Sutta.* I quote K.N. Jayatilleke: "It is argued that from the experimental point of view when self (1) is real (sacco), selves (2) and (3) are not real and when self (2) is real, selves (1) and (3) are not real, etc. . . .[326] Since these 'selves' were attained at different times, it does not make sense, it is said, to say that anyone of them is real in an absolute sense but only that each is real at the time of attaining it while the others were not real *at that time*",[327] This is what the logic of the four in Eliot means. Each stage of my own theory is only relatively real in terms of its own capacity to manifestation in terms of form and meaning. Objects in the world are the way they are. Metaphors exist; they are very rarely created. They indeed are perceived. That is why Buddhists do not consider cause to be a subjective thing; they emphasize its objectivity and universal movement without bothering for its origin. Eliot's plan in the *Quartets* was to make the existence of language possible at two simultaneously"existent levels: the level of language pertaining to common speech and the level of language pertaining to music. "Whether poetry is accentual or syllabic, rhymed or rhymeless, formal' or free, it cannot afford to lose its contact with the changing language of common intercourse".[328] However, Eliot is more than conscious (at each stage of his correlating the common language with the music inherent in words) of sight of *the beyond* the words point to—a *beyond* which is beyond the circumference or apparent meaning-dimensions of words. ". . . While poetry attempts to convey something beyond what can be conveyed in prose rhythms, it remains, all the same, one person talking to another. . ."[329]

Part of the sense of what poetry as incantation means to Eliot was given to him when he listened to Yeats reciting his on poems. "To hear him (Yeats) read his own works was to be made to recognise how much the Irish way of speech is needed to bring out the beauties of Irish poetry: to hear Yeats reading William Blake was an experience of a different kind, more astonishing than satisfying".[330] Eliot is emphasizing the concept of word as *mantra* and reminds one of Aurobindo's concept of future poetry as *mantra.* A word is, precisely, the vibration of certain sounds; these sounds may be ennobling as well as disparagingan effect which solely depends upon its context—the context which made the formation of those particular sounds (and not the other) possible. In words, as Heidegger said, the realities of the earth meet the mysteries of heaven. For Eliot a musical word is the intersection of time and eternity. Words are allusive by nature and they always mean something more than, and apart from, themselves. The musical poem is defined by Eliot as "a poem which has a musical pattern of sound and a musical pattern of the secondary meanings of the words which compose it, and these two patterns are indissoluble and one".[331]

Grover Smith considers four layers of sound as necessary for an understanding of the *Quartets:* "Thus the music of the *Quartets,* as developed by 'instruments', extends from the colloquial to the oratorical, and from the homiletical to the analytical. In it may be heard the voices of personal reflection and discursive philosophy, the terms of market place and inkhorn".[332] Lama Anagarika Govinda thus expounds the four planes of the existence of the frequencies and vibrations of sound: "On the first plane we have to consider the pure sound value of a mantra and its 'psychological associations', on the second plane its verbal meaning (as far as this can be established) and its mental and traditional associations; on the third plane its creative or evocative value (which depends on the particular experience of initiation in the supreme moment of the transference of power); and finally its growing and expanding spiritual value in the practice and experience of progressive *sādhana.* In such a *sādhana* the mantra takes on different dimensions and evokes different mental images and visualizations, depending on whether the mantra is applied to the universal realm of the *Dharmakāya,* or to that of the *Sambhōgakaya,* the realm of creative vision and spiritual enjoyment, or to that of the *Nirmānakāya,* the realm of action and transformation of both body and mind. In the case of *bīja* or seed-syllables, we have furthermore to consider in which connection or combination they are used, because—as in a chemical formula—it is the combination that determines their specific meaning."[333]

The above quotation makes it clear how the three circles in my *mandala* theory receive different vibration-intensities of the sound on the basis of the nature of the seed which emanates that sound and the context that contextualizes it. The seed-syllable sound may be contextualized either by the individuals who themselves are distinct contexts on the basis of their nature and inclinations, or the sound may gradually change its colour and tenor and intensity and frequency of vibration as it passes from the lowest *(Mūlādhāra-Cakra)* to the highest plexus *(Sahastrār-Ċakra)* in the human body. In fact, the seed-syllable sounds widen and open the gates of human perception until the *nāda,* the sound that is the vital *Prāna* or consciousness, is audible.

By harmonising distinct planes of existence and different mental levels, what Eliot is trying to achieve in the *Quartets* is unity that is the chief work of unparticularised consciousness. Woods says that "That which is prior to the unparticularised (forms) is that of which we can only say that it is resoluble (primary-matter), the Great-Substance *(mahat-tattva)*".[334] This is what the centre of the *mandala* intends to show. There is a point beyond the unity of the *Quartets* in Eliot's poem that, as we say, passes understanding. It is to this that Woods' statement above refers. But this process of the total absorption of relative sounds into the seed-syllable is a highly gradual process. It is for this reason that in Eliot's point it is the fifth movement, directly emanating from the centre, that gives the movement of integration. But even the integration at this level is shown to have three phases in Eliot's poem. Brooks says: "First in these movements of integration, the truth attained is applied to the poet and to us, so that he in his vocation, and we in ours, are seen to have a place in the experience depicted. . . Next comes recapitulation: earlier themes, particularly from the preceding Quartet when there is one, are recalled and integrated into new wholes, since at the stage now attained they can be seen differently".[335]

The third phase of integration is that of complete resolution of the latent formal-constructs which are resolved earlier too but only relatively. Northrop Frye notes that "the *Four Quartets* form a single cycle that begins and ends at the same point".[336] This is true of Buddha's life too, for Buddha was born on the full moon day; He gained *nirvāna* on this day; he broke his fast at Bodhgaya and achieved enlightenment on this day itself. The wheel has come full-circle. Earlier commentary on the wheel occurs in varying capacities in Eliot's poetry and even criticism. Upon the following lines in *The Waste Land* –

London, the swarming life you kill and breed
Huddled between the concrete and the sky;
Responsive to the momentary need,
Vibrates unconscious to its formal destiny.

Ezra Pound has commented: "London, your people is bound upon the wheel".[337]

The image again occurs in the manuscript: "The inhabitants of Hampstead are bound forever on the wheel."[338] The wheel in Buddhism as in yoga could be taken to perform the twin roles—it imprisons as well as liberates. "The machine-wheel is the symbol of *Samsara*, of ever recurring birth and death, of the inescapable law of existence".[339]

The same wheel is transformed into *nirvāna* by the *siddhas* or enlightened persons.[340] Eliot was constantly trying to be one and John Peter has already noted that Eliot, in the *Criterion*, "In commentary after commentary" was "emphasizing the virtues of detachment, of independent thinking, of 'solitary, rather than group thought', of 'that balance of mind which a few highly-civilized individuals, such as Arjuna, the hero of the *Bhagavadgīta*, can maintain in action"'.[341] There is not much left for me to comment upon Eliot's use of the *Bhagavadgīta* in general and in *Dry Salvages* in particular. The influence of Indian religion and philosophy upon Eliot was so overpowering that he thought its study essential for anyone trying to go deep into metaphysics or mysticism. When Donald Adamson told Eliot that he had been brought up along the devotees of theosophy, pat came Eliot's reply: "It has saved you years of research into Indian religion".[342] Donald Adamson also tells us that "he (Eliot) had become aware that the *Bhagavad-Gīta* was a classic of the mystical life which for many years he preferred to St. Paul's *Epistles*; and throughout the years he returned as often to Arjuna as to Dante".[343] Eliot rejected Western epistemology and the point is well made by Edward Lobb in *T.S. Eliot and the Romantic Critical Tradition*. Even Dante whom Eliot acknowledged to have been "the most persistent and deepest influence upon my own verse",[344] could not exactly help Eliot discover his own "way".[345] Even if the idea of Heraclitean flux comes closest to Buddhism in the Western tradition, there is hardly much emphasis on the still point or the centre in Heraclitus as compared to the Indian tradition which includes Buddhism. Eliot had already told K. Hazareesing that he "wondered if, in writing 'Ash Wednesday', he had not been unconsciously influenced by some aspect of Indian philosophy".[346]

Eliot read Buddhaghosa during 1912-1913 with Charles Lanman. Eliot's main source for rejecting Western epistemology was chiefly Indian and he often drew inspiration from his Indian readings to elaborate certain points in Christianity. Eliot's symbolism of three and four, so basic to the structure of many of his poems, is not really Christian. For example, the three stairs in *Ash Wednesday* which E.K. Hay compares with the *Visuddhimaggā, Way of Purification,* of Buddhaghosa. She further says: "We shall see again in *Four Quartets* that Eliot drew effectively from early Buddhist texts in support of Christian experience. In 'Ash Wednesday' the difficulty of understanding why Eliot was only three steps, rather than the ten of the Christian mystics, can be solved if we remember Nagarjuna's and Buddhaghosa's teaching about the saint (called the *arhāt)* who has achieved the complete detachment that leads to perfect release, or *Nirvāna.* The four stages leading to *arhātship* require a passage up three steps: first, the step of devotion and intellectual discipline. . .; second, the step of returning once to repeat the cycle of earthly life; and third, the step on which he frees himself from 'the lower bonds' of belief in a permanent self, of doubt, and reliance on mere morality and rituals, while also freeing himself from sensual passions. This third step gives the Buddhist *arhat* access to the highest possibility of man, which is freedom from death, for he is now free from even the desire for existence."[347] The three steps as gradual ways of the purification of the body also meet us in the *Bhagavadgīta* in the form of three *gunās* or dominant qualities— Goodness *(Sattva),* Passion *(Rajas)* and Darkness *(Tamas).* Their different combinations form the tenor and texture of different personalities. Their dialectical (as in Nagarjuna), contextual (as in Dinnaga) and gradual elimination would render one fit to attain to the highest stage.

Eliot makes use of all the three methods to annul categories and attain to the centre that contains all these, yet is beyond them. Consider the following lines from the *Quartets:*

> At the still point of the turning world.
> Neither flesh nor fleshless;
> Neither from nor towards; at the still point, there the dance is,
> But neither arrest nor movement. And do not call it fixity,
> Where past and future are gathered. Neither movement from nor towards,
> Neither ascent nor decline. Except for the point, the still point,
> There would be no dance, and there is only the dance.

Harold E. McCarthy, who quotes more lines than the lines quoted, says that "The thought which is here being expressed by Eliot is incredibly complex, but no more complex than many such statements one can find in Buddhist writings. The mode of expressing the thought, *i.e.,* in terms of negation and paradox, is not distinctively Buddhist, but it is at least characteristic of Buddhism. The image of the turning wheel which underlies the entire passage is a basic image in Buddhism. . ."[348]

As for the "turning wheel" image, when Buddha first of all preached the tenets of his religion to the five monks, that event is known as the event of *Dhann-Cakra-Parivartana,* the changing of the wheel of righteousness and law. Buddha was setting the spokes of the wheel of carnal desire in accordance with the wheel that will virtually lead to *Nirvana.* The same use of wheel Krishna also makes in the *Gīta* as already pointed out. But, in the equivocation of terms which alone permits transcendence, Eliot is more close to the *Gīta* than to Buddhism. The *Gīta* defines yoga as "sameness-and-indifference" (2.48). In the *Gīta* (11.37) Arjuna describes

Krishna as "The Imperishable, what IS and what is not and what surpasses both". Krishna Himself says that the whole world is an emanation from His own being; all beings reside in Him and He in them, but He transcends them all. Why Eliot's "Still Point" needs circumlocutionary terms of equivocation is because that is all the language can do. The *Gīta's* following verse comes close to Eliot's "still point": "By soul held fast in steadfastness he must make the mind (too) subsist in the self; then little by little will he come to rest; he must think of nothing at all" (6.25). Eliot had written to Paul Elmer More in 1936 that "(your) spiritual biography... is oddly, even grotesquely, more like my own . . . than that of any human being I have known."[349] More was a very serious student of Indian philosophy and religion, especially, *Bhagavadgita* and the *Upanishads*.

Eliot was concerned with the "Application of our religion to the criticism of any literature."[350] He further said: "I repeat that when I am considering Religion and Literature, I speak of these things only to make clear that I am not concerned primarily with Religious Literature. I am concerned with what should be the relation between Religion and all Literature."[351] To this end Eliot used the term "religious literature" in three senses. In the first sense we could take the Authorised translation of the Bible in the same way as we take the writings of Gibbon or Clarendon. Eliot's chief criteria for distinguishing literature from non-literature is of course language, for writers not specifically writing literature "had a gift of language which makes them delightful to read to all those who can enjoy language well written even if they are unconcerned with the objects which the writers had in view".[352] The second kind of use that Eliot visualizes for religion in relation to literature is that of devotional or religious poetry. Such poetry is available in most of the traditions whether Hindu, Christian or Sufi. Eliot admits that such poetry could be minor or major depending upon the author's areas of awareness. Dante, Cornielle or Racine are major religious poets because their range of awareness and the ability to contextualize religious ideas, symbols and concepts in relation to poetic frameworks is unquestionable. The inability to do this is what makes Eliot class Vaughan, Southwell or George Herbert, or even Hopkins, as minor poets.

Expounding why a majority of religious poets remain minor, Eliot says: "The religious poet is not a poet who is treating the whole subject matter of poetry in a religious spirit, but a poet who is dealing with a confined part of this subject matter: who is leaving out what men consider their major passions, and thereby confessing his ignorance of them."[353] About the third sense of the use of religion that literature can make, Eliot says that "I am concerned with' what should be the relation between Religion and all literature."[354] Eliot was sure that if deeply dug into inductively and deductively, religion, in fact all religions, could come to certain identical principles of methods of evolution, transformation and realization seen in the context of language. This is what *my mandala* theory precisely aims to do. *Mandala,* though a tool of meditation in Hinduism and Buddhism, is basically a technique of self-attainment, the attainment of the "still point" of Eliot. The terminology, metaphor and symbols used, do not belong to a particular tradition but are apprehensible by the literary and philosophic minds of all traditions, for *mandala* is basically a being-centred technique which annuls language through language in order to reach the centre. Eliot, however, seems to me to be somewhat *un*doing all his noble attempts by proclaiming: "What I want is a literature which should be unconsciously, rather than deliberately and defiantly, Christian."[355] Is it a fall from the Sublime to the Grotesque? Eliot might be defended by saying that he had realized it very well that the universal could only be reached through the local and the particular. Therefore, just as a literary critic, belonging to the Western literary-critical-philosophical tradition, would search for universal literary principles only within the context of Christianity whether conscious or unconscious, so a critic belonging to some other tradition must look for those principles within the context of a religion which is his and to which he professes. E.K.

Hay feels that the Buddhist "way" leads the individual, *by* choice, to respond to the centre.[356] The way is both a path as well as a motivating force in "Burnt Norton" III, she says.

The fifth movement of "East Coker" begins: "So here I am, in the middle way". The middle way, as Eloise Knapp Hay rightly says, is not Eliot's age but his situation: "We are surely intended here to think of (among other things) 'the middle way' of early Buddhism: the forest sage Nagarjuna's 'Fundamentals of the Middle Way' where the phrase refers to a middle path between existence and non-existence. . . . For Nagarjuna the Middle Way is way of liberation achieved by freeing oneself from all 'patterns', including all fixed formulas concerning non-being or being. But while insisting that man can know no eternal reality independent of changing existences, Buddhist followers of the Middle way focus on *the relation* between changing forms and the emptiness *(sunyata)* in which forms exist."[357] Nagarjuna says: "We state that whatever is dependent arising, that is emptiness. That is dependent upon convention. That itself is the middle path. A thing that is not dependently arisen is not evident. For that reason, a thing that is non-empty is indeed not evident".[358] This will indicate Eliot's singular achievement in the *Quartets.* Eliot's poetry and his theory of poetry aspire to achieve this emptiness and this is evidenced by Eliot's thesis on Bradley too.

Eliot's basic method is that of a "disinterested intelligence" as discovered by Roger Sharrock[359] and which Eliot himself says at so many places. This disinterested intelligence works towards contextual elimination of terms *by* using them equivocally and paradoxically, so that the essential emptiness of things is exposed. Roger Sharrock outlines Eliot's negation as operative on three levels, all connected: "The most familiar of these is represented *by* the alienation of the writer from the prevailing assumptions of *bourgeois* society. However, at a deeper level this denial of social and moral conventions is matched by a metaphysical denial of the 'reality' of the extended, objective world. . . Life is a series, an infinite regress, of finite centres of consciousness; 'thinking of the key, each confirms a prison': the limited point-of-view of the individual consciousness and the complexity of the series inhibit true knowledge and permit only guesses about any God or Absolute in whom all the finite centres or monads are reconciled."[360] This Absolute for Eliot is Emptiness, for the God of the *Gita* is always de constructing Himself, and so is Patanjali de constructing God in his *Yoga-Sūtras.* Whereas Krishna aligns Himself with Buddhist emptiness by telling Arjuna that whatever he has preached is "mere words", Patanjali says that God is not the highest thing to be attained; *Kaivalya* (loneness) is. It is here, in this basic emptiness that the philosophies of Eliot, *Gīta* and Patanjali meet. They also largely determine Eliot's tradition howsoever dogmatic and orthodox certain of Eliot's statements on Christianity might appear to be. This fact is very strongly testified by Eliot abandoning the use either of the American tradition of religious poetry as noted by E.K. Hay or not returning to the American Quartet in the last movement of "The Dry Salvages" as noted by Northrop Frye. Eliot further turned, more often, to the Hindu and the Buddhist *via negativa* than to the Christian methods of negation in order to arrive at the truth, the whole, or the Absolute, howsoever relatively.

Eliot had said that Blake followed a philosophy of his own and Northrop Frye finds that "whatever influences there may be from Bradley or Patanjali or St. John of the Cross or Heraclitus, we darkly suspect Eliot too of indulging in a philosophy of his own".[361] This may be very broadly true because of the fact that the poet's mind is a catalytic agent amalgamating distinct experiences and transforming them into new wholes. But if Eliot comes close to any living religion, it is Indian, both Buddhism and Hindu. Eliot's concern with emptiness, its realization in the nerves and arteries and the tender filaments of the being of his poetry, is evident from the beginning to the end of his poetic career. This he achieves by following the Buddhist middle path which involves a negative perception leading to the overall emptiness out of which objects emerge and into which they subsist and disappear. This negativism is paralleld in the *Upanishads* and even in the *Gīta* by the expression *neti neti* – "not this", "not this" which ultimately leads to the realization of emptiness or *Kaivalya,* loneness. Eliot also makes use of the lotus symbol as found in the yoga to denote the full-flowering and culmination of the climaxes of negativity. When, by persistent negation, the energy passes from the lowest to the second highest plexus, figuratively depicted in yoga symbolism as the tube of the lotus, the lotus blooms in the head the place of the highest plexus, generally called the blooming of the thousand-petalled lotus. In Section III of the "Little Gidding" there are three flowers who

> Flourish in the same hedgerow:
> Attachment to self and to things and to persons, detachment
> From self and from things and from persons; and, growing between them, indifference
> Which resembles the others as death resembles life.

When the negation is complete, the flower blooms and this is where Eliot realizes another aspect of Buddhist emptiness – complete integration by negation. E.K. Hay rightly says that "Eliot's lotus is of course the Buddha's, not Tennyson's lotus of indifference and forgetfulness".[362] Buddha also used the onion symbol to denote the inherent emptiness of all objects for the onion is all husk with nothingness at the centre. That this nothingness is also everything is what the lotus means.

Notes and References

1. Fei-Pai Lu, *T.S. Eliot: The Dialectical Structure of His Theory of Poetry* (Chicago: University of Chicago Press, 1966), p. 39.
2. *The Art of T.S. Eliot* (London: Faber, 1969), p. 173n. First publication 1949.
3. *Ibid.*
4. *Ibid.*, p. 2.
5. The point is also made in Damayanti Ghosh, *Indian Thought*

in T.S. Eliot (Calcutta: Sanskrit Pustak Mandir, n.d.), p. 2.

6. F.O. Matthiessen, *The Achievement of T.S. Eliot* (N.York: Oxford University Press, 1959), p. 51.
7. *Ibid.*, p. vii.
8. *Ibid.*
9. Philip Wheelwright, "Eliot's Philosophical Themes" in B. Rajan (ed.), *T.S. Eliot: A Study of His Writings by Several Hands* (London: Dennis Dobson Ltd., 1971), pp. 103ff., first pub. 1947.
10. The article appeared in *Philosophy: East and West,* II (1952-53) brought out by Hawai University Press.
11. William Blissett, "The Argument of T.S. Eliot's *Four Quartets*", *University of Toronto Quanerly,* xv, no. 2 (Jan. 1946).
12. Hyatt Howe Waggoner, *The Heel of Elohim* (Norman: University of Oklahoma Press, 1950).
13. B. Rajan, (ed.), *T.S. Eliot: A Study of His Writings By Several Hands,* p. 87.
14. T.S. Eliot, "The Humanism of Irving Babbitt", in Frank Kermode (ed.), and Intro., *Selected Prose of T.S. Eliot* (London: Faber, 1980), p. 284, F. Pub. 1975.
15. See *Criterion* XIII (October, 1933), commentary. . .
16. Hugh Kenner, *T.S. Eliot: The Invisible Poet* (London: Methuen, 1965), p. 34.
17. Herbert Howarth, *Notes on Some Figures Behind T.S. Eliot* (New York, 1964), pp. 199-200.
18. *After Strange Gods* (New York: Harcourt, Brace & Co., 1934), p. 43.
19. *Philosophy: East and West,* II (1952-53), Hawai University Press, p. 35.
20. T.S. Eliot, *After Strange Gods,* pp. 43-4.
21. Irving Babbitt, *The Dhammapada* (New York & London: Oxford University Press, 1936), p. 101; Quoted in McCarthy, "T.S. Eliot and Buddhism", *Philosophy: East and West,* II (1952-53), p. 35, f.n. 14.
22. D. Ghosh, *Indian Thought In T.S. Eliot,* p. 25, f.n. 11.
23. *Ibid.*
24. M.S. Ramaiah Compiled, *Indian Responses to T.S. Eliot* (Calcutta·

Writers Workshop, 1988).

25. R.S. Sharma, "Indian Response to T.S. Eliot: Potentialities and Directions", p. 9. Dr. Sharma is Prof. of English, Banaras Hindu University, Varanasi.
26. London: Harvard University Press, 1982.
27. *Ibid.*, p. vi.
28. J. Birje-Patil, *Beneath the Asie-Tree* (Delhi: Macmillan, 1977).
29. Elizabeth Drew, *T.S. Eliot: The Design of His Poetry* (New Delhi: Doaba House, 1970), Indian reprint, p. 114.
30. Northrop Frye, *T.S. Eliot: An Introduction* (Chicago: University of Chicago Press, 1981), p. 49, F. Pub. 1963.
31. *Ibid.*, p. 50.
32. *Ibid.*, p. 77.
33. Stephen Spender, *T.S. Eliot* (New York: The Viking Press, 1976), p. 20.
34. "Remembering Eliot", in Allen Tate (ed.), *T.S. Eliot: The Man and His Work* (1966), pp. 55-6.
35. Henry Clarke Warren, *Buddhism in Translation* (Cambridge, Mass.: Harvard University Press, 1953), pp. 202-08. F. Pub. 1896.
36. *Ibid.*, p. 205.
37. *Ibid.*
38. *Ibid.*, p. 206.
39. Stephen Spender, *T.S. Eliot,* p. 25.
40. Elizabeth Drew, *T.S. Eliot: The Design of His Poetry,* p. 114.
41. H.C. Warren. *Buddhism in Translation,* pp. 355-56.
42. *Ibid.*, p. 363.
43. *Ibid.*
44. *Ibid.*, pp. 363-64.
45. D.J. Kalupahana, *Nagarjuna: The Philosophy of the Middle Way* (New York: State University of New York Press, 1986), see pp. 370-76 and translation of verses 1 & 2 of Nagarjuna's *Mumadhyamak-Karika, Ibid.*
46. H.C. Warren, *Buddhism* in *Translation,* p. 365.

47. *Bhagavadgita,* Chapter 6, verses 5-6, Zaehner, p. 409. All references to *Bhagavadgita,* henceforth, will be from R.C. Zaehner, *The Bhagavad-Gita* (London: Oxford University Press, 1975), first published 1969.
48. "Dante" in *Selected Essays* (London, 1948), p. 113.
49. *Notes Towards the Definition of Culture* (London, 1948), p. 113.
50. "Introduction" to G. Wilson Knight's *The Wheel of Fire* (London, 1930), p. 14. 51. T.S. Eliot *The Sacred Wood* (Delhi: B.I. Publications, 1976), p. 160. Indian reprint.
52. "Blake" in *The Sacred Wood,* pp. 157-58.
53. *Ibid.,* p. 158.
54. See R.C. Zaehner, *Bhagavad-Gita,* p. 178.
55. Eloise Knapp Hay, *T.S. Eliot's Negative Way* (Cambridge, Mass.: Harvard University Press, 1982), p. 69.
56. Henry Clarke Warren translates four Buddhist *Jhanas* as "The Four Intent Contemplations". See the Chapter under the same title in his *Buddhism in Translation.*
57. Fei-Pai Lli. *T.S. Eliot: The Dialectical Structure of His Theory of Poetry,* p. 117.
58. Elizabeth Drew, *T.S. Eliot,* p. 114.
59. *Buddhism in Translation,* p. 495; Warren's translation is from The Fourteenth chapter of the *Visuddhi Magga.*
60. *Ibid.,* p. 492.
61. *Ibid.*
62. *Ibid.,* p. 495.
63. James Haughton-Woods, *The Yoga-System of Patanjali* (Delhi: Moti Lal Banarasidass, 1983), Book II, verse 5, p. 110, first published 1914; first Indian reprint 1966.
64. *Ibid.,* II, 13, p. 123.
65. *Ibid.,* James Haughton Woods' commentary on verse 13 of Book II, p. 124.
66. Verse 19, Book II, pp. 148-53, See Woods' commentary too.
67. *Ibid.,* p. 149; Cf., Eliot's "Whole of feeling" with Patanjali's "feeling of personality".
68. Hugh Kenner (ed.), *T.S. Eliot: A Collection of Critical Essays*

(Englewood Cliffs, N.J.: Prentce-Hall, 1965), p. 7.

69. *Ibid.*, p. 10; Eliot's statement quoted from *The Use of Poetry and the Use of Criticism* (1933).

70. *Vikalpayonayah sabda Vikalpah sabdayonyah* – Dinnaga quoted in Stcherbatsky, *Buddhist Logic,* II, p. 405n.

71. For Eliot's development in philosophy and method during 1913-14, see Grover Smith (ed.), *Josiah Royce's Seminar* 1913-14, *as Recorded in the Notebooks of Harry T. Costello* (New Brunswick, 1963).

72. Eliot gave an account of this paper in his "Introduction" to Charlotte Eliot's *Savonarola* (1926).

73. Richard Woliheim, "Eliot and F.H. Bradley: An Account" in Graham Martin (ed.), *Eliot in Perspective: A Symposium* (London: Macmillan, 1970), p. 171.

74. T.S. Eliot, *Knowledge and Experience In the Philosophy of F.H. Bradley* (London: Faber & Faber, 1964), p. 126.

75. Richard Wollheim, "Eliot and F.H. Bradley: An Account" in Graham Martin (ed.), *op.cit.*, p. 172.

76. *Ibid.*, pp. 176-77.

77. *Knowledge and Experience In the Philosophy of F.H. Bradley,* p. 76.

78. Richard Wollheim, "Eliot and F.H. Bradley: An Account" in Graham Martin (ed.), *op.cit.*, p. 178.

79. *Ibid.*, pp. 178-79.

80. T.S. Eliot, *Knowledge and Experience*. . ., p. 35.

81. *Ibid.*, p. 36.

82. *Ibid.*, p. 37.

83. *Ibid.*, p. 40.

84. *Ibid.*

85. *Ibid.*, p. 43.

86. *Ibid.*, p. 83.

87. "Eliot and F.H. Bradley: An Account" in Graham Martin (ed.), *op.cit.*, p. 179. 88. *Ibid.*, p. 182.

89. *Ibid.*, p. 183.

90. Frederick J. Streng, *Emptiness: A Study in Religious Meaning*

(New York: Abgindon Press, 1967), p. 168.

91. David J., Kalupahana, *Nagarjuna: The Philosophy of the Middle Way* (State University of New York Press, 1986), p. 19.
92. *Majjhima-Nikaya,* 3. 230.
93. *Mulmadhyamak-Karika,* 18.8, in David J. Kalupahana's translation, *op.cit.,* p. 269.
94. *Ibid.*
95. Streng, *Emptiness, op.cit.,* p. 68.
96. *Ibid.,* p. 69.
97. Translation followed here is that of Frederick J. Streng.
98. Cited in Margolis, *T.S. Eliot's Intellectual Development,* n. 142, quoted in E.K. Hay., *T.S. Eliot's Negative Way,* p. 32.
99. Streng, *Emptiness,* p. 155.
100. E.K Hay, *T.S. Eliot's Negative Way,* p. 16.
101. *Ibid.,* p. 69.
102. Quoted in D.J. Kalupahana, *Nagarjuna: The Philosophy of the Middle Way,* p. 271.
103. This should be taken to mean that language at the literal level is rejected.
104. Commonality implies literality's dialectical counterpart—the metaphor.
105. This reality is to be taken to be the reality of the Buddhist middle path.
106. Streng, *Emptiness,* p. 155.
107. Quoted in David J. Kalupahana, *Nagarjuna: The Philosophy of the Middle Way,* pp. 10-11. The veracity of the sermon is confirmed by Ananda, Buddha's closest disciple, and accepted by major schools of Buddhism.
108. E.K. Hay, *T.S. Eliot's Negative Way,* pp. 71-2.
109. Quoted in H. Howarth, *Some Figures Behind T.S. Eliot,* p. 95.
110. Stephen Spender, *T.S. Eliot* (New York: Viking Press, 1975), p. 20.
111. E.K Hay, *T.S. Eliot's Negative Way,* p. 75.
112. "Reflections on the Unity of European Culture", *Adam* 14, No. 158 (May 1946): 1-3, also cited in Howarth, *Notes on Some Figures Behind T.S. Eliot,* p. 95.

113. "Eliot & F.H. Bradley: An Account", in Graham Martin (ed.), op.cit., p. 184.
114. "Tradition and the Individual Talent", in T.S. Eliot, *The Sacred Wood,* Indian reprint (New Delhi: B.I. Publications, 1976), p. 49.
115. D.E.X. Maxwell, *The Poetry of T.S. Eliot* (London: Routledge, 1961), p. 20.
116. *The Achievement of T.S. Eliot: An Essay on the Nature of Poetry* (New York: Oxford University Press, 1959), p. 4.
117. N. Frye, *T.S. Eliot: An Introduction* (Chicago: University of Chicago Press, 1981), p. 11.
118. *Ibid.*
119. M.C. Bradbrook, "Eliot's Critical Method", in B. Rajan (ed.), *T.S. Eliot: A Study of His Writings by Several Hands,* p. 124, f.n.
120. *Ibid.*
121. Quoted in Samuel Hynes, "The Trials of a Christian Critic" in David Newton-de Molina (ed.), *The Literary Criticism of T.S. Eliot* (London: The Athlone Press, 1977), p. 67. Samuel Hynes feels that by reorganisation Richards means acceptance of a scientific view of the world. I feel it is rather on the other side; reorganisation means the reorganising of the mind and the sensibility in relation to the challenges thrown by the landscape of contemporary reality.
122. *Ibid.,* pp. 67-8.
123. T.S. Eliot, *The Sacred Wood,* p. x.
124. "Andrew Marvell", *Selccted Essays,* p. 304.
125. Frank Kermode (ed.), *Selected Prose of T.S. Eliot* (London: Faber, 1980), "Reflections on Vers Libre", p. 32, First Published 1975.
126. "The Function of Criticism", in Frank Kermode (eds.), *Ibid.,* p. 73.
127. *Visuddhi Magga,* Chapter VIII, translated in H.C. Warren, *Buddhism in Translation,* p. 150.
128. "The Use of Poetry and the Use of Criticism", in Frank Kermode (ed.), *op.cit.,* p. 87.
129. *T.S. Eliot's Negative Way,* p. 3.

130. "The Aims of Education: The Issue of Religion", *To Criticise the Critic,* p. 119.

131. T.S. Eliot: *The Dialectical Structure of His Theory of Poetry,* p. 81.

132. "Tradition and the Individual Talent", in *The Sacred Wood,* p. 50.

133. T.S. Eliot: *The Design of His Poetry,* p. 115.

134. See pp. 80-84 in his book, *T.S. Eliot: The Dialectical Structure of His Theory of Poetry.*

135. "Tradition and the Individual Talent", *The Sacred Wood,* p. 52.

136. Rajnath, *T.S. Eliot's Theory of Poetry* (New Delhi: Arnold-Heinemann, 1980), pp. 47 ff.

137. "The Three Provincialities (1922) *With a Postscript* (1950)", *Essays in Criticism,* 1 (January 1951), p. 41.

138. Rajnath, *op.cit.,* p. 48.

139. "Eliot and the Criterion", in David Newton-De Molina (ed.), *The Literary Criticism of T.S. Eliot,* p. 25.

140. "The Use of Poetry and the Use of Criticism", in Frank Kermode (ed.), *Selected Prose of T.S. Eliot,* pp. 82-5.

141. *Some Figures Behind T.S. Eliot,* p. 206.

142. D.E.S. Maxwell. *The Poetry of T.S. Eliot,* p. 47.

143. James Haughton Woods (ed.), and translated, *TIre Yoga-System of Patanjali* (New Delhi: Motilal Banarsidass, 1983), Book IV, 24; first published in 1914 in Harvard Oriental Series, volume seventeen.

144. "Religion and Literature", in Frank Kermode (ed.), *op.cit.,* p. 100.

145. "The Humanism of Irving Babbitt", in Frank Kermode (ed.), *Selected Prose of T.S. Eliot,* pp. 278-79.

146. *Ibid.,* p. 278.

147. James Haughton Woods (ed.) & trans, *The Yoga-System of Patanjali,* Book I, aphorisms 11, 12 & 13.

148. Woods' footnote says: "The object as such is not directly perceived, but only its form *(akara)* as reproduced in the thinking substance *(buddhi-sattva)* which in its turn reflects the image cast' upon it by the Self." *Ibid.,* p. 31.

149. *Ibid.*

150. "Tradition and the Individual Talent", in *The Sacred Wood,* p. 52.

151. *Ibid.,* p. 52.

152. Woods, *Yoga-System of Patanjali,* p. 31.

153. *Ibid.,* pp. 31-2.

154. *Ibid.,* pp. 32-3.

155. "Tradition & the Individual Talent", *The Sacred Wood,* p. 55.

156. "The Humanism of Irving Babbitt", in Frank Kermode (ed.), *Selected Prose of T.S. Eliot,* p. 284.

157. *Ibid.,* pp. 283-84.

158. Book-I, aphorism 5 in Haughton Woods, *op.cit.,* p. 17.

159. *Ibid.*

160. *Ibid.*

161. *Ibid.,* Book IV, aphorism 6, p. 304.

162. N. Frye, *T.S. Eliot,* p. 17.

163. *Ibid.,* p. 50. The same circular criteria Eliot applied in his criticism: "Certainly we may say that in Swinburne's verse the circuit of impression and expression is, complete;. . ." "The Perfect critic" in *The Sacred Wood,* p. 7. And further: ". . . the relations, proportions, values of each work of art toward the whole are read-justed;. . .",*Ibid.,* p. 50.

164. Attention was drawn previously to Edward Lobb's book, *T.S. Eliot and the Romantic Critical Tradition* where he took Eliot's Clark Lectures of 1926 as base for his conclusion that Eliot rejected Western epistemology of "psychologism".

165. *Ibid.,* p. 49.

166. See my *The Chariot of Fire: A Study of William Blake In the Light of Hindu Thought* (Salzburg: Salzburg University Press, 1981).

167. *The Thirteen Principal Upanishads* (London: Oxford University Press, 1931).

168. E.K. Hay, *T.S. Eliot's Negative Way.* p. 69.

169. *Time,* March 6, 1950, p. 23.

170. *T.S. Eliot's Negative Way,* p. 70.

171. Irving Babbitt, *The Dhammapada* (New York: New Directions

Paperbook, 1965), p. 78. E.K. Hay says that "Eliot refers admiringly to this posthumous work of Babbitt in his essay in *Revelation*, ed. John Baillie and Hugh Martin (London, Faber, 1937), pp. 15-6. Eliot's immense regard for Babbitt as a *religious thinker* survived his conclusion that neohumanism was a 'decayed form of religiosity"'. p. 197. in *T.S. Eliot's Negative Way*.

172. N. Frye, *T.S. Eliot*, p. 58.

173. F.O. Matthiessen, *The Achievement of T.S. Eliot* (New York: Oxford University Press, 1959), p. 19.

174. "Eliot's Philosophical Themes", in B. Rajan (ed.), *T.S.Eliot: A Study of His Writings by Several Hands*, pp. 97-8.

175. The Translation followed is that of Prof. R.C. Zaehner.

176. From the *Anguttara-nikaya* iii, 134, in *Buddhism* in *Translation*, p. xx.

177. "T.S. Eliot and Buddhism", p. 41, in *Philosophy: East and West*, *op.cit.*

178. Grover Smith, *T.S. Eliot Poetry and Plays: A Study in Sources and Meaning* (Chicago: University of Chicago Press, 1971), p. 15.

179. *Ibid.*, p. 61.

180. S.B. Dasgupta, *An Introduction to Tantric Buddhism* (Calcutta: Calcutta University Press, 1974), p. 178.

181. *T.S. Eliot's Poetry and Plays*, p. 109.

182. *Ibid.*, p. 108.

183. "Tradition and the Individual Talent", in *The Sacred Wood*, p. 53.

184. (Delhi: Primal Publications. 1986).

185. *Ibid.*, p. 20.

186. Translated from the *Milindapanna* (40) in Henry Clarke Warren, *Buddhism in Translation*, pp. 148-50.

187. "Tradition and the Individual Talent", *op.cit.*, p. 54.

188. Translated from the *Samyutta-Nikaya* (XII.621) in Henry Clarke Warren, *Buddhism in Translation*. p. 151.

189. *Knowledge and Experience in the Philosophy of F.H. Bradley*, pp. 116-17.

190. *T.S. Eliot's Negative Way,* p. 16.
191. Translated from the *Milindapanna* (251) in H.C. Warren, *Buddhism in Translation,* pp. 132-33.
192. Translated from the *Visuddhi-Magga* (Chapter XVIII), *Ibid.,* pp. 134-35.
193. "Eliot's Classical Standing", *Lectures in America* (London: Chatto & Windus, 1969), p. 33.
194. *The Language as Criticism* (London: Methuen, 1966), p. 94.
195. "Critical Note", *The Collected Poems of Harold Munro* (London, 1933), p. xv.
196. In *Selected Essays,* p. 93.
197. Stephen Spender, *T.S. Eliot,* p. 22.
198. *Ibid.,* p. 164.
199. T.S. Eliot: *The Dialectical Structure of His Theory of Poetry,* p. 73.
200. *Beneath the Axle-Tree,* p. 12.
201. Book I, *Sutra* 13, in Haughton Woods (ed.), & trans., *The Yoga-System of Patanjali,* p. 34.
202. Book I, *Sutra* 16, *Ibid.,* p. 37.
203. Book I, *Sutra* 17, p. 40. *Ibid.*
204. Book I, *Sutra* 18, pp. 41-2, *Ibid.*
205. Quoted by Eliot in *To Criticise the Critic* (London, 1965), p. 175.
206. "Shakespeare and the Stoicism of Seneca", in *Selected Essays* (London, 1970), p. 135.
207. Book I, *Sutra* 20, p. 45., *Ibid.*
208. Cf. Pound's "inspirational emotion" in the quotation from Eliot above.
209. Cf. Pound's idea of the remoteness of inspirational emotion.
210. *The Yoga System of Patanjali,* p. 46.
211. J. Birje-Patil, *Beneath the Axile- Tree,* p. 12.
212. "What is a Classic" in Frank Kermode (ed.), *Selected Prose of T.S. Eliot,* p. 126.
213. Book II, *Sutra* 3, in Haughton-Woods, *op. cit.,* p. 106.

214. *The Yoga System of Patanjali,* pp. 111-12.
215. See Rajnath, *T.S. Eliot's Theory of Poetry,* p. 80.
216. The John Hayward Bequest, King's College, Cambridge, p. 3, quoted in Rajnath, *op.cit.,* p. 80.
217. "Humanist, Artist and Scientist", *The Athenaeum* (October, 1919), p. 1015.
218. Book II, *Sutra* 6, *Yoga System of Patanjali,* p. 115.
219. Eliot's "Point of View".
220. *Yoga System of Patanjali,* p. 115.
221. "Tradition and the Individual Talent", *The Sacred Wood,* p. 55.
222. See J. Birje-Patil, *Beneath the Axle-Tree,* p. 10.
223. "W.B. Yeats", in on *Poetry and Poets* (London: Faber, 1969), p. 255.
224. See *Sutras* 19-23, Book I, in Woods, *Yoga System of Patanjali.*
225. *T.S. Eliot: The Dialectical Structure of His Theory of Poetry,* pp. 71-2.
226. "Eliot's Tone" in David Newton-De Molina (ed.), *The Literary Criticism of T.S. Eliot,* p. 173. See also Richard Ellmann, *Golden Codgers* (1974) for biographical background of *The Waste Land.*
227. "The 'Philosophical Critic", in De Molina (ed.), *Ibid.,* p. 137.
228. "In the Hope of Straightening Things Out" in Hugh Kenner (ed.), *T.S. Eliot: A Collection of Critical Essays* (N.J.: Prentice Hall, 1965), p. 145.
229. Quoted in Blackmur, *Ibid.,* p. 147.
230. "What is Minor Poetry?" *On Poetry and Poets,* pp. 46-7.
231. "Kipling Redivivus", *The Athenaeum,* May 9, 1919, p. 298.
232. "Philip Massinger", *The Sacred Wood,* p. 139.
233. *Selected Essays,* p. 179.
234. *Ibid.*
235. "Henry James", in Frank Kermode (ed.), *Selected Prose of T.S. Eliot,* p. 151.
236. "Andrew Marvell", *Ibid.,* p. 161.
237. *Ibid.*
238. Quoted in *Bhagavad-Gita,* translated and ed. by R.C. Zaehner. (London: Oxford University Press, 1975), p. 334.

239. "Yeats", in Frank Kermode (ed.), *op.cit.,* p. 256.

240. Whither Tradition and the individual talent!

241. "The Idea of a Christian Society", in Frank Kermode (ed.), *op.cit.,* p. 291.

242. *Ibid.,* pp. 290-91.

243. "Thoughts After Lambeth" (1931) in C.B. Cox and Arnold P. Hinchliffe (eds.), *T.S. Eliot: The Waste Land* (London: Macmillan, 1968), p. 26.

244. *Ibid.*

245. *The Bhagavad-Gita,* p. 367.

246. "The Achievement of T.S. Eliot" in C.B. Cox and A.P. Hinchliffe (eds.), *T.S. Eliot: The Waste Land,* p. 111.

247. *T.S. Eliot: The Design of His Poetry,* p. 52.

248. " 'The Waste Land' as a Buddhist Poem", *Times Literary Supplement,* May 4, 1973, p. 503.

249. "The Fire Sermon" in H.C. Warren, *Buddhism in Translation,* p. 352.

250. "'The Waste Land' as a Buddhist Poem", *op.cit.,* p. 503.

251. *T.S. Eliot's Negative Way,* p. 52.

252. *Ibid.,* p. 54.

253. *Ibid.,* p. 60.

254. *The Poetry of T.S. Eliot,* p. 97.

255. *Athenaeum;* November 28, 1919, p. 1252.

256. *The Poetry of T.S. Eliot,* p. 108.

257. Grover Smith, *T.S. Eliot's Poetry and Plays: A Study in Sources and Meaning,* p. 95.

258. See p. 94, *Ibid.*

259. *Buddhism in Translation,* pp. 297-98.

260. "The Metaphysical Poets", in Frank Kermode (ed.), *Selected Prose of T.S. Eliot,* p. 60.

261. *Ibid.*

262. *Ibid.,* p. 63.

263. *Ibid.,* p. 64.

264. *Ibid.*

265. James Haughton Woods, *The Yoga System of Patanjali,* Book II, *Sutra,* 20, p. 154.
266. *Ibid.*
267. "In the Hope of Straightening Things Out", in Hugh Kenner (ed.), *T.S. Eliot: A Collection of Critical Essays,* p. 143.
268. Book II, *Sutra* 23, Woods, *op.cit.,* p. 160.
269. *Ibid.,* pp. 160-61.
270. "The Metaphysical Poets" in Frank Kermode (ed.), *Selected Prose of T.S. Eliot,* pp. 64-5.
271. Book II, *Sutra* 24, p. 166 in Woods, *op.cit.*
272. *Ibid.,* p. 167.
273. Hugh Kenner, "Introduction" in *T.S. Eliot: A Collection of Critical Essays,* ed. by him, p. 9.
274. 1930 broadcast talk on Donne, "Rhyme and Reason: The Poetry of John Donne".
275. "The Metaphysical Poets", *Selected Essays,* p. 286.
276. *Ibid.,* p. 289.
277. Book II, *Sutra* 28, Haughton Woods, *Yoga System of Patanjali,* p. 172.
278. *Ibid.,* pp. 173-74.
279. "Prose and Verse", p. 7; quoted in Rajnath, *T.S. Eliot's Theory of Poetry,* p. 123.
280. "In the Hope of Straightening Things Out", in Hugh Kenner (ed.), *T.S. Eliot: A Collection of Critical Essays,* p. 144.
281. *Sutras* 20-21, Book IV, in Woods, *op.cit.,* pp. 330-31.
282. Book IV, *Sutra* 2, p. 300, *Ibid.*
283. *Ibid.,* pp. 300-01.
284. *Rousseau and Romanticism,* p. 28.
285. "The Humanism of Irving Babbitt", in Frank Kermode (ed.), *op.cit.,* p. 279.
286. "Clarke Lectures", p. 183; Quoted in Rajnath, *T.S. Eliot's Theory of Poetry,* p. 142.
287. *The Yoga System of Patanjali,* p. 151.
288. Quoted in F.O. Matthiessen, *The Achievement of T.S. Eliot,* p. 211.

289. "Shakespeare and the Stoicism of Seneca", *Selected Essays,* p. 129.
290. "Nicolo Machiavelli", *For Lancelot Andrews,* pp. 50-1.
291. S.B. Dasgupta, *An Introduction to Tantric Buddhism,* p. 178.
292. "Hamlet and His Problems", *The Sacred Wood,* p. 100.
293. R.C. Zaehner, *The Bhagavad-Gita,* p. 133.
294. *Creation and Discovery* (Chicago, 1955), pp. 288-89.
295. *Beneath the Axle-Tree,* p. 18.
296. See Quotation No. 288.
297. "T.S. Eliot's Objective Correlative", *University of Kansas City Review,* Winter, 1959, p. 136; quoted in Birje-Patil, *op.cit.,* p. 18.
298. *Beneath the Axle-Tree,* p. 18.
299. "In the Hope of Straightening Things Out", *op.cit.,* p. 145.
300. Again a very difficult and complex point to argue, for how does one completely separate Hamlet's problems with author's and 'on what grounds?
301. "In the Hope of Straightening Things Out", *op.cit.,* p. 145.
302. "Hamlet and His Problems", *The Sacred Wood,* p. 101.
303. Victor Brombert, *The Criticism of T.S. Eliot: Problem of an 'Impersonal Theory of Poetry'* (N. Haven, 1949), p. 33.
304. See pp. 102-03 'in his *T.S. Eliot: The Dialectical Structure of His Theory of Poetry.*
305. *T.S. Eliot's Poetry and Plays,* p. 63.
306. *T.S. Eliot: An Introduction,* pp. 76-7.
307. N. Frye, *T.S. Eliot,* p. 75.
308. *Yoga System of Patanjali,* p. 149.
309. XII, 305, 5f = 11332-3; *Ibid.,* see f.n. 2 on p. 44.
310. *The Achievement of T.S. Eliot,* p. 66.
311. Woods, *Yoga System of Patanjali,* p. 75.
312. D.E.X. Maxwell, *The Poetry of T.S. Eliot,* pp. 145-46.
313. *T.S. Eliot's Poetry and Plays,* p. 136.
314. *T.S. Eliot,* p. 75.
315. Grover Smith, *T.S. Eliot's Poetry and Plays,* p. 142.
316. *Ibid.,* p. 267.

317. Craig Raine, " 'The Waste Land' as a Buddhist Poem", *Times Literary Supplement,* May 4, 1973, p. 503.
318. "*Four Quartets:* the Structure in Relation to the Themes", in Graham Martin (ed.), *Eliot* in *Perspective: A Symposium* (Macmillan, 1970), pp. 137ff.
319. *Creative Meditation and Multi Dimensional Consciousness* (London: George Allen & Unwin, 1977), p. 10.
320. See his *Auden and After* (London, 1942), pp. 62-7.
321. "The Unity of the Quartets", in B. Rajan (ed.), *T.S. Eliot: A Study of His Writings by Several Hands,* p. 89.
322. See Matthiessen, *The Achievement of T.S. Eliot,* p. 89.
323. Quoted in Matthiessen, *Ibid.,* p. 90.
324. "Four Quartets: A Commentary" in B. Rajan (ed.), *op.cit.,* p. 65.
325. Poem No. XXVIII, *Tapascharanam* (New Delhi: Samkaleen Prakashan, 1981), p. 46.
326. Self (I), (2) and (3) are respectively, the self formed of the essence of food, the mental self, and the cognitive self.
327. *Early Buddhist Theory of Knowledge* (Delhi: Motilal Banarsidas, 1980), p. 318. First pub. 1963 by George Allen & Unwin, London. See also *Diggha Nikoya,* I.199 and I.201.
328. "The Music of Poetry" in Frank Kermode (ed.), *Selected Prose of T.S. Eliot,* p. 110.
329. *Ibid.,* p. 111.
330. *Ibid.,* p. 112.
331. *Ibid.,* p. 113.
332. *T.S. Eliot's Poetry and Plays,* p. 252.
333. *Creative Meditation and Multi-Dimensional Consciousness,* p. 78.
334. Haughton Woods, *Yoga System of Patanjali,* p. 149.
335. "*Foul' Quartets:* the Structure in Relation to the Themes", in Graham Martin (ed.), *Eliot* in *Perspective,* p. 139.
336. *T.S. Eliot: An Introduction,* p. 79.
337. See Craig Raine, " 'The Waste Land' as a Buddhist Poem", in *TLS,* May 4, 1973, p. 503.
338. *Ibid.*
339. Lama Anagarika Govinda, *op.cit.,* p. 185.

340. *Ibid.*, p. 187.
341. "Eliot and the 'Criterion' ", in Graham Martin (ed.), *Eliot in Perspective*, p. 255.
342. Donald Adamson (ed.), *T.S. Eliot: A Memoir* (New York: Dodd, Mead & Company, 1971), p. 22.
343. *Ibid.*
344. "What Dante Means to Me", *To Criticise the Critic*, p. 123.
345. "Dante's 'Way' Was not Exactly Eliot's" E.K. Hay, *T.S. Eliot's Negative Way*, p. 163.
346. *The Times* (London), January 12, 1965, p. 11.
347. *T.S. Eliot's Negative Way*, pp. 93-4.
348. "T.S. Eliot and Buddhism", in *Philosophy: East and West, op.cit.*, p. 48.
349. Quoted in E.K. Hay, *op.cit.*, p. 163.
350. "Religion and Literature" in Frank Kermode (ed.), *Selected Prose of T.S. Eliot*, p. 98.
351. *Ibid.*, p. 99.
352. *Ibid.*, p. 98.
353. *Ibid.*, p. 99.
354. *Ibid.*
355. *Ibid.*, p. 100.
356. *T.S. Eliot's Negative Way*, p. 168.
357. *Ibid.*, p. 173.
358. Chapter 24, Verses 18-19, *Mulmadhyamak-Karika* by Nagarjuna translated in David J. Kalupahana and edited by him as *Nagarjuna: The Philosophy of the Middle Way* (Albany: State University of New York Press, 1986), pp. 339-41.
359. "Eliot's 'Tone' ", in David Newton-De Molina (ed.), *The Literary Criticism of T.S. Eliot*, p. 169.
360. *Ibid.*, p. 166.
361. *T.S. Eliot: An Introduction*, p. 49.
362. *T.S. Eliot's Negative Way*, p. 187.

ESSAY II

Jacques Derrida, Buddhism, and A Buddhist Poetics

In the first part I briefly outline Indian contribution to the shaping of what Derrida calls Western logocentrism. The seminal figures of this tradition—Hegel, Kierkegaard, Schopenhauer, Nietzsche, Heidegger and Saussure—acknowledge their debt to Indian thought directly or indirectly. Derrida rightly points out that this logocentrism is part of Eastern tradition. *The Upanishadic* (and even *Vedic)* logocentrism was deconstructed by Buddha who invented the methods of dependent-origination and the propositions best expounded by Nagarjuna, a second century A.D. Buddhist monk. In the second part I argue that Derrida's central concepts bear a very close resemblance to concepts in Buddhism, and that his method of deconstructing Western logocentric tradition is, by and large, derived from Nagarjuna. The third part briefly focusses upon what I feel a possible Buddhist poetics could be. The fourth part gathers the ground covered and makes such generalisations as are warranted.

I

There are valid reasons for Nietzsche considering Plato's thought as "anti-Hellenic".[1] "That Jesus is the last prophet of Israel or even that he is a development of Judaism is only a prejudice of dogmatic theology, but is not a historical truth".[2]

Long before Clement of Alexandria in 220 B.C. who mentions Buddha by name: "Buddhist doctrines had made heavy inroads in the Western world",[3] Indian connections with the West go back at least to the sixth century B.C. After the fall of Babylon in 538, Darius had established the Persian empire which included Greece and the Indus Valley.[4] Under the Persian rule Indians knew of Greek lonians.[5] Radhakrishnan rightly holds that looians were the first to question the authenticity of Homeric religion. Such connections apart, there were certain mystery cults which greatly shaped Western logo-centrism. We know through Plato's *Phaedrus* (69c.) that Orpheus' religion consisted of a mystical theology and certain purificatory rites.[6] Eleusinianism borrowed many ideas from Orphism and often refined upon them. Herodotus (ii. 81) noticed the similarity between these mystery cults and Pythagoras. Aeschyleus, Sophocles, and Euripides were already familiar with these cults. Pythagorean universe is made of equal proportions generating *harmonia.* The fact of Pythagoras having visited India is well documented by Apuleius[7] who says that ". . . the Brahmins taught him the greater part of his philosophy; what are the rules and the principles of understanding: what the functions of the body; how many are the faculties of the soul, how many the mutations of life; . . ."[8] The doctrine of *Logos,* introduced into Christianity from Philo, H.G. Rawlinson says, "superficially resembles the personifications of *Vāch* 'Speech' as a goddess in the *Rig Veda.* But there is no *Vāch* doctrine, *Vāch* being merely an unimportant abstraction".[9] Rawlinson thoroughly misunderstands the Vedic *Vāch* concept which forms the basis of Bhartrihari's theory of *sabda-brahman,* the Word as Logos.

Gnosticism was another important sect which "was a deliberate attempt to fuse Greek (Platonic) and Hindu elements".[10] This sect flourished in the eastern provinces of the Roman empire, and represented most of the Hindu and 'Buddhist ideas, often in an untainted form. Radhakrishnan says that what Gnosticism did was "to introduce into Christianity not the pure spirit of Greek philosophy but conceptions of Eastern religions which by the first century had taken their place everywhere in the Roman empire".[11] After Pythagoras, who flourished round about the latter half of the sixth century B.C., Socrates (470-399 B.C.) obviously did not accept the ritualistic religion of Greece. "He perhaps accepted the Orphic view that the soul is immortal and that happiness means the achieving of immortality by renunciation of the world, and that all men are brothers whatever their conditions be".[12]

By the time of Plato (427-347 B.C.) conceptions of the *Logos,* emanation, and a hierarchy of existence are already well-formulated. There is a soul that is beyond change, indissoluble and eternal, which is conjoined to a body that is corruptible and mortal. Plato also believed in the Pre-existence of the soul, its birth into the cyclic world, and its consequent liberation. Plato attributes his knowledge to a "sacred story"[13] and to "men and women who were wise in the sacred lore".[14] Stutfield wrote: "The mind of Plato was heavily charged with Orphic mysticism mainly derived from Asiatic sources. India, always the home of mystical devotion, probably contributed the major share".[15]

Radhakrishnan thus delineates the roots of logocentric tradition in Plato: "We have in Plato, as in the *Upanishads,* the highest God, the idea of the Good in the *Republic,* the Demiurgus and the Soul of the World in the *Timaeus.* Towards the end of the sixth book of the *Republic* Plato describes the endeavour to ascend to the first principle of the universe which transcends all definite existence".[16] The god of the *Upanishads (Brahman),* who is transcendent and beyond all conceptions, is given a thoroughly logocentric status in the *Gīta;* but *Gīta's* God deconstructs Himself and aligns with Buddhist Nothingness.

Taking a long jump in time I come now to Derrida's immediate tradition which itself presents versions of logocentrism influenced by Indian thought. Hegel quotes verses from the *Gīta,* seventh and tenth chapters, to emphasize that in the *Gīta* the particular is "relegated in its turn to the accidental, over which the One is superimposed in the sublimity thus conjoined with it",[17] Hegel further says: "In the true type of the Sublime. . . the most excellent objects. . . are employed merely as the ornament of God, and as servants to celebrate the splendour and majesty of the One, ..."[18] It is lamentable that Hegel does not bring in the *gunās* (qualities) which themselves are tools of terrific individuating process. Hegel, no doubt, *deconstructively* read Gita for Krishna nowhere belittles Arjuna's individuality; He, instead, restores it so that Arjuna might carryon the fight aroused by *Kārmic* immediateness. In fact, the doctrine of *kārmic* inevitability subjects the individual to assume particularised forms in order to carry out a *particular* variety of action. Hegel's deconstructive argument regarding *Gīta's* doctrine is not tenable. The pioneers of German romanticism—Schelling, Schelegels, Goethe, among many others—were already familiar with Indian thought. Schopenhauer, who needs be mentioned because he influenced Nietzsche a great deal, mentions his familiarity with Hindu and Buddhist ideas in *Parerga* and *Paralipomena* at many places. Charles Muses quotes McGill on Schopenhauer who said that by 1830 Schopenhauer had access to a second-hand rendering of Buddhism.[19] In the Preface to *Die Welt als Wille und Vorstellung,* Schopenhauer had said: "I might assert that each of the individual and disconnected utterances that make up the *Upanishads* could be derived as a consequence from the thought I am to impart, although conversely my thought is by no means to be found in the *Upanishads*".[20] Schopenhauer's debt to *Upanishadic* logocentrism is complete and well-acknowledged.

In 1888 Georg Brandes had recommended Nietzsche. Kierkegaard's writings. Kierkegaard shows no deep understanding of Indian thought. He said that "The prolixity and diversity found in Indian poetry—which has led some to characterise it as romantic—is not romantic; it is vegetative prolification; on the whole, life in the East is vegetative; indeed their gods are borne by a calyx, grow out of flowers".[21] The apparent multiplicity of gods and goddesses Kierkegaard mistakes for polytheism and God's immanence he wrongly interprets as vegetative. Nietzsche shows his familarity with Buddhism rather with a sense of inversion. Schopenhauer and Buddhism are accepted and rejected, much in a deconstructive way by Nietzsche, because the former presents pessimism in the half-Christian, half-German narrowness, while the latter, as Nietzsche understood Him (Buddha), could not transcend the delusion of morality. Mistaking Buddhism for what it is, Nietzsche approaches a much clear vision of the *Bhagavadgita,* which he obviously must have read in a host of translations available.[22] "Whoever with an Asiatic and super—Asiatic eye has actually looked inside, and into the most world-renouncing of all possible modes of thought—beyond good and evil, and no longer like Buddha and Schopenhauer, under the dominion and delusion of morality, . . ."[23] Nietzsche hated a religion which produced an "autonomous herd" (the reference is to the Buddhist *Samgha,* group) and obliterated distinctions of the "master" and the "slave", for this leaves no one to demand any "right" as all-are equal. Commenting upon Buddhist notions of the sympathy for the suffering and compassion for all, Nietzsche said: ". . . in their involuntary beglooming and heart-softening, under the spell of which Europe seems to be threatened with a new Buddhism. . . the consolation of the present, the great discharge from all the obligations of the past; altogether one in their belief in the community as the *deliverer,* in the herd, and therefore in 'themselves'."[24] Buddhism spread like a contagion in Europe and scholars soon realised how serious a consideration it merited. In *The Genealogy of Morals,* Nietzsche shows an understanding of Indian religion in an historical perspective. Tracing the origin of the "ascetic idea" and the way it acquired the status of a religion, Nietzsche says that the ascetic ideal is "the awe-inspiring catastrophe of a two thousand-year training in truth, which finally forbids itself the *lie of the belief* in *God* (The same course of development in India — quite independently, and consequently of some demonstrative value — the same ideal driving to the same conclusion the decisive point reached five hundred years before the European era, or more precisely at the time of

Buddha — it started in the Sankhya philosophy, and then this was popularised through Buddha, and made into a religion". Nietzsche's own method of appropriation (of meaning) and its forgetfulness (Buddhist "emptiness"?) already contains seeds of deconstructive strategy.

Heidegger, who, Derrida says, comes closest to his method, struck the key note of Dcrrida's thesis when he said that Western metaphysics is gradually led away from Being in the course of its development from Plato. Heidegger owes his key concepts to Buddhism and he acknowledges it. "The word 'way' probably is an ancient word that speaks to the reflective mind of man. The key word in Laotse's poetic thinking is Tao, which 'properly speaking' means way".[26] As reported by William Barret, Heidegger once confessed: "A German friend of Heidegger told me that one day when he visited Heidegger he found him reading one of Suzuki's books. 'If I understand this man correctly', Heidegger remarked, 'this is what I have been trying to say in all my writings'."[27] The vital notion of the Void or Nothingness Heidegger derived from Buddhism as did his disciples Karl Jaspers, Paul Tillich, Martin Buber, among many others. In the following dialogue Heidegger is the inquirer while the Japanese answers his queries: *"Inquirer."* That emptiness then is the same as nothingness, that essential being which we attempt to add in our thinking, as the other, to all that is present or absent. *Japanese:* Surely. For this reason we in Japan understood at once your lecture 'What is Metaphysics'? When it became available to us in 1930 through a translation which a Japanese student then attending your lectures had ventured. . . . We marvel to this day how the Europeans could lapse into interpreting as nihilistic the nothingness of which you speak in that lecture. To us, emptiness is the loftiest name for what you mean to say with the word 'Being'."[28] Heidegger's Being as empty and full simultaneously serves as a model to Derrida's meaning, strategy where he puts keywords under erasure.

II

In the only valuable study on Derrida in the light of Buddhism,

Robert Magliola refers to Derrida's charge that the East has a stronger logocentric tradition than the West, and says: "The suspicion in question leads one to expect from Nagarjuna's Madhyamika the name 'voidism' (non-presence) or at least 'Taoism' (interdependence of presence and non-presence) that supposedly represent the whole of Oriental philosophy, . . Derrida's own characterisation of Eastern thought charges that the East offers no more than variations of logocentrism".[29] I, however, draw Magliola's attention to the following remark Derrida made in *Positions* where he shows a better understanding of the East by pointing out to the tradition when logocentrism was subverted. Replying to Ronse's question on the irreducibility of writing in Derrida, Derrida says that this irreducibility is "measured less well in France, it appears, than abroad, and significantly, less well in the West than in certain Eastern countries".[30] The pointer is towards Nagarjuna, the second century A.D. Buddhist thinker, who subverted *Upanishadic* logocentrism. At places, however, as Robert Magliola says, Derrida seems "egregiously misinformed"[31] as for example in regarding the Buddhist void another variation on the notion of the centre.

Derrida makes a direct reference to Buddhism in *Of Grammatology;* the subject is the exploitation of man by man in "writing". The idea first occurs in Levi Strauss' *Tristes Tropiques* in the description of the Nambikwara tribe. Derrida says: "Our question is therefore no longer only 'how to reconcile Rousseau and Marx but also: 'Is it sufficient to speak of superstructure and to denounce in an hypothesis an exploitation of man in order to confer a Marxian pertinence upon this hypothesis? A question that has meaning only through implying an original rigor in Marxist criticism and distinguish it from all other criticism of suffering, of violence, of exploitation, etc.; for example, from Buddhist criticism. Our question clearly has no meaning at the point where one can say 'between Marxist criticism. . . and Buddhist criticism. . . there is neither opposition nor contradiction'."[32] All suffering in Buddhism is realised as differential. Difference arises from ignorance which manifests itself in the form of twelve *nidānās.*

The name of the doctrine is *Pratītya Samutpāda,* Dependent-Origination, which constitutes the momentary world of becoming. *Pratitya Samutpāda Hrdaya*[33] (Tanjure Mdo XVII) contains seven *āryās* by Nagarjuna. Prof. T.R.V. Murti says that *Bodhicaryavatārapanjika* (p. 351) quotes a couplet and a half from Nagarjuna's text to the effect that "in the phenomenal sphere, *Pratītya-samutpāda,* or the twelve-link causal chain with its three sub-divisions, continues without intermission in this and other lives conditioned as it is by *klesa* and *karma*".[34]

These twelve principles may be said to constitute Derrida's "general text". Derrida designates the effect of the structure of general text upon the subject as an inescapable "chain": "And it would be ridiculous to overlook the necessity of this chain. . . Without it, in effect, there would be neither 'subject', nor the 'symbolic', etc. . ."[35] Derrida says that his differential list has no taxonomical closure. "Differences" spread out in a chain over the practical and theoretical entirety of a text,..."[36] Nothing precedes difference ("a" implying difference's infinite generative power) for notions of subject and object are its effects rather than causes.[37] There are six spheres of sense which make all contact possible. These are material form, sound, smell, taste, touch and concepts. Combined with these spheres of sense are five aggregates, which, together, produce, *becoming.* The "causal" into which the individual (Derrida's sign under erasure or play) finds himself enmeshed right from the time of its birth, involves endless change, transformation, and taking of one position after another. Likewise, there are four forms of propositions, the four *mahāvākyās,* as propounded by Nagarjuna, though Sanjaya before him is said to have originated them. The four propositions are: "No existents whatsoever are evident anywhere that are arisen from themselves, from another, from both, or from a non-cause. There are only four conditions, namely, primary condition, objectively supporting condition, immediately contiguous condition, and dominant condition. A fifth condition does not exist".[38]

Nagarjuna's four propositions are also summarised as:

"this", "not this", "both-this and not-this", and "neither-this nor not-this". Nagarjuna is denying first cause here as does Derrida. Nagarjuna disagrees both with *Satkārvādins,* who believe that the effect is identical with the cause, and *sarvastivādins* who posit a permanent entity. Prof. Murti says: "The Madhyamika shows by his dialectic that not only causality but every category or doctrine leads to contradiction... Criticism dissolves their plausibility, and establishes the real as Absolute, as devoid of thought-determinations *(Sūnya)".*[39] The *Sūnya,* or Nothingness, neutralises binary oppositions and results in trace —the last resort for thinking mind in Derrida. The endlessness of the play of the sign does not seek origin, for there is none. It results in *trace,* a movement that has neither beginning nor end. Heideggerian model is overthrown, as per Derrida's understanding of Heidegger, for Heidegger tried to *restore* everything to "Being". Using Heidegger's terms to deconstruct Heidegger's own text, Derrida says: ". . . the trace is neither a ground, nor a foundation, nor an origin, and that in no case can it provide for a manifest or disguised ontotheology."[40]

Derrida comes very close to the Buddhist theory *of Apōha,* which establishes negativity as the essence of meaning. The propounder of this theory was Dinnaga who wrote *Pramānasamuccaya. Apōha* theory rejects *Mimāmsaka* and *Naiyāyika* theorists who believe that words have direct reference to objective realities. It must be recalled that Derrida's disagreement with Saussure and Husserl is precisely because both establish arbitrary relationship between signifieds and signifiers. As Derrida says in *Positions* that for Husserl "The relationship between meaning and sign, or between the signified and the signifier, then becomes one of *exteriority:* or better, as in Husserl, the latter becomes the exteriorization *(Ausserung)* or the expression *(Ausdruck)* of the former".[41] The whole Western metaphysics is rejected because it systematizes the transcendental illusion, a variation on logocentrism. Although Heidegger's *Being* transcends all signifier-signified relationships, and does away with its own distant lineaments (of *identity),* as Gayatri Chakravorty agrees,[42] Derrida disagrees with Heideggerian void or *sūnyata*, thinking that it still means and evokes notions of *Presence*. Dinnaga's theory of negative reference, like Derrida's, implies "contextual elimination" of one term by another in an endless process. Words evoke conceptual images which are not objectively real but subjective constructs *(vikalpās)*. Derrida also says: "I have never said that there is not a 'subject of writing' ".[43] All our meaning-notions are derived from this conceptual image *(vikalpā)* whose essence (and existence) is based on a constant negation of all its counter-correlates *(anyāpōha)*.[44] As K. Kunjunni Raja says: "The word produces the purely subjective concept, which is negative in nature, consisting as it does in the exclusion of other concepts to make it distinct. Hence, the meaning of a word has to be considered as the negation of the concept's counter-correlate, as the exclusion of everything other than the concept *(anyapoha)*".[45]

Derrida's language is characterised by what Levi strauss calls *bricolage*, a language that is fissured and fractured before it has articulated anything. It is *the* Nothing which can exist only by negation and exclusion. Language is an equivocation, a paradox (parody?) of terms, which, like Nagarjuna's propositions, is both "is" and "is not" and is neither "this" nor "this is not". Language simply cannot be viewed in terms of Saussurean *Langue* and *Parole* which point towards a determinate ontology. The Derridean concepts of the supplement, the *gram*, the irreducible space, the hymen—all are neither negative nor positive. Containing though both, they are neither, and they always transcend their own latest mental fabrications in order that they might get on to the *trace* which has no destination but the vacuity of the vacuum, the *sunyata* of the *sunya*. The position of the subject, both in Derrida and in Buddhism, as existentialism, is self-deferring and self-postponing, for all the three believe in an ever-changing dynamic continuum which keeps the subject away from itself, in spite of endless supplementation and substitution. Derrida's concept of *arche-writing (ecriture)* is none other than the Buddhist "silence", the Book as Totality which is lost forever; What remains now is the endless movement. Nagarjuna, likewise, says what if causes are self-sufficient, they cannot be expected to have relations with other entities; "and if they are not 'real' causes, then what is called 'a cause' when it is effecting a result is something different from what it is before the result is effected".[46] Streng goes on to show that by the same method of reasoning, Nagarjuna denies any real nature to the conditioning causes.

Kalupahana disagrees with T.R.V. Murti who thought that the self-causation theory belonged to Hindu schools while the early Buddhists brought in the theory of external causation.[47] Kalupahana says: "When Nagarjuna said, 'The self-nature of an existent is not evident in the causal condition, etc., . . .' he was not rejecting or denying conditions, but only self-nature *(svabhava)* that some philosophers were positing in the conditions *(pratyaya)* in order to account for the arising of the effect".[48] Nagarjuna's point is that if entities are taken to exist by themselves *(svabhavat)*, then they will have to be thought of as uncaused; if they are thought to be dependent upon each other, as *Pratītya-samutpāda* says, then they are relative to each other, not merely in point of time, but, as Prof. Murti so significantly says, "relative to each other in nature".[49] Derrida treats writing in the sense of inscription which was already there before all our conceptions about it developed. The *hollow* is the surplus, the immeasurable plenitude, which notions of form or equation cannot bind into harmony, unity or structure. Derrida goes out of metaphysics by putting the sign under erasure (debt to Heidegger is acknowledged). The expressed is always short of its own motivating expressive power which it cannot contain. Derrida's concept of the void comes much closer to that of Sunya in Buddhism. He says that "thought means nothing" for it is "the substantified void of a highly derivative ideality, the effect of a *difference* of forces,.. ."[50] And since there is no meaning (for all meaning is relative to differences; Husserl's intentionality and pure consciousness are also rejected), all thought means nothing. The following statement by Derrida will show how meticulously he has applied

Buddhist *Pratītya-samutpāda* doctrine to his method: "To be entangled in hundreds of pages of a writing simultaneously insistent and elliptical, imprinting, as you saw, even its erasures, carrying off each concept into an interminable chain of differences, surrounding or confusing itself with so many precautions, references, notes, citations, collages, supplements—this 'meaning-to-say-nothing' is not, you will agree, the most assured of exercises".[51]

Derrida further says that this "nothing" into which everything seems heading towards, is not exactly a "nothing" either[52] (Derrida escapes all designations), and no notion of *Presence* can be subsumed under it. It is for the same reason that Derrida denies that "the other" is a category.[53] Prof. K. Bhattacharya says of Nagarjuna's method that "the best way for him to refute his opponent's criticisms is to show the inner contradictions of the latter's thought and to use against him his own logic".[54] To the query as to why all things are void *(sūnya)*, or devoid of intrinsic nature *(nihsvabhāva)*, Nagarjuna says that because they are dependently-originated *(pratityasamutpanna)*. Much like Derrida, Nagarjuna says that he has not negated anything for there is nothing to be negated: "I do not negate anything, nor is there anything to be negated *(pratisedhāyami nāham kimcit pratisedhyam asti na ca kimcit)*. You, therefore, culminate me when you say: 'You negate' *(tasmat pratisedhayasity adhilaya esa tvaya kriyate)*".[55] Nagarjuna is a mystic but his mysticism is not thought-renouncing. Nagarjuna exposes our relational way of thinking and the fallacy of objective knowledge, or pure consciousness, or being as the primordial source of all knowledge and thought. Like Nagarjuna, who neither affirms nor denies the world, Derrida's thought concerns neither Presence nor Absence; it is *sunya*, the void, which, in itself, is not a category. Since the world appears only to the ignorant who manufactures *vikalpās ad infinitum*, the unending substitutionary chain has no meaning for the enlightened. For the enlightened there is not the slightest of difference between the world *(samsāra)* and *Nirvāna:* " *'Nirvānasya ca ya kotih samsāranasya ca/na tayor antaram kimcit susuksman api vidyate'*: What is the extremity of the life-process, between them not even a subtle something is evident".[56] F.J. Streng rightly says that Buddhist emptiness "does not mean a definition of something conceived as an essence with attributes but is a term used to shift the mode of apprehending 'existence' and 'ultimate reality'".[57]

Phonocentrism, logocentrism and ethnocentrism are related terms in Derrida. Ferdinand de Saussure, a professor of Indo-Aryan languages, is commended by Derrida for his differentialism but criticised for his privileging speech over writing. Derrida quotes from Saussure's *Course* and says: "Saussure, for essential, and essentially metaphysical, reasons had to privilege speech, everything that links the sign to phone".[58] Derrida is aware, however, that Saussure recognises that the faculty which constitutes language is more natural to man than the spoken language.[59] Saussure, like Heidegger, by privileging speech over writing, leads to an ontology of Presence which Derrida cannot accept. Statements in the *Course* like "Writing is foreign to the internal system (of language)" (p. 44), and "Writing veils our view of language: it does not clothe language, but travesties it" (p. 51), are the sort of statements which almost *spur* Derrida into his theory of the *gram* as the new science of writing, though the status of a "science" to *gram* is immediately denied by Derrida. "Whether in the order of spoken or written discourse, no element can function as a sign without referring to another element which itself is not simply present. This interweaving results in each 'element'—phoneme or grapheme—being constituted on the basis of the trace within it of the other elements of the chain or system. This interweaving, this textile, is the text produced only in the transformation of another text. Nothing, neither among the elements nor within the system, is anywhere ever simply present or absent. There are only, everywhere, differences and traces of traces".[60] It can clearly be seen how well Derrida's new science of writing compares with Nagarjuna and Dinnaga's methods of mutual exclusion and contextual elimination. The process of Dependent-Origination leads to infinite regress, annulment of causality, into the void or *sūnya.* "Those who posit the substantiality of the self as well as of discrete existence—these I do not consider to be experts in the meaning of the (Buddha's) message".[61] Identity and Difference exist in a certain war of attrition with each other, for if only identity is there it will end as absence for both the subject and the object as there would be no difference. If the difference is maintained between the definition and the difiniendum, the latter would have no distinguishing mark. Relation accomplishes two functions: it connects the two terms finding links that join them to some form of approximate identity; it differentiates between them because it links two distinct entities. T.R.V. Murti concludes: "These insuperable difficulties impel us to the conclusion that cause and effect, substance and attribute, whole and parts, subject and object, etc., are mutually dependent, relative; hence they are not things in themselves".[62] Denying any point of origination, Nagarjuna says: "Someone becomes manifest by something; something is manifest by someone. How would someone exist without someone?"[63] Denoting emptiness as the supreme meaning or the meaning of meanings, Nagarjuna gives logical explanation for this: "If the cause is empty of a product, how would it produce the product? A non-empty product would not be originated, (and) and non-empty product would not be destroyed. Then that is non-empty which will not originate or not disappear. How would that be produced which is empty? How would that be destroyed which is empty? It logically follows, then, that which is empty is not originated and not destroyed".[64] Jonathan Culler, commenting upon Derrida's notion of meaning, says: "Derrida suggests, on the contrary, that the inexhaustibility identified here is not that of richness, depth, complexity of an essence, but rather the inexhaustibility of a certain poverty. . . a condition of 'designification' produced, for example, in Freud's writings, where metapsychological concepts such as the Unconscious, Death instinct, Pleasure of Drive, connect with the signs from which they derive but empty them of their meaning and oppose further semantic actualization".[65]

Dissemination, another important concept in Derrida, says Gayatri Chakravorty Spivak, is a "sowing that does not produce plants, but is simply infinitely repeated. A semination that is not insemination but *dissemination,* seed spilled in vain, an emission that cannot return to its origin in the father",[66] for all fathers are variations on logocentrism. This view implies Being as a concept of origin which determines the sheer "erruptive" force of emptiness and implicates itself into false teleologies. "Play" is a crucial word both in Nietzsche and in Derrida, and I suggest that Nietzsche had discovered it in the *Gīta.* Krishna's uncanny power is known as *māyā*, which produces not only the illusions *(vikalpās),* but also endlessly transforms them. Whereas ordinary mortals are caught in its web, Krishna enjoys in its play, for *māyā* cannot bind Him. "These works (of mine) neither bind-nor-limit Me: as one indifferent I sit among these works (of mine), detached".[67] Krishna's indifference, Buddhist *sūnya*,. and Derrida's *"thought to Nothing"* meet. Just as Derrida says that "the other" is not a category, so does Nagarjuna deny the status of a proposition to his "void". Robert Magliola also says, and rightly, that the *sūnyata* is not a material or a mental category.[68] Derrida's view that the void is also a kind of centrism, is not tenable. The Buddhist middle way is virtually this void: *"yah Pratītya-samutpādah sūnyatam pracaksmahe/ sa prajnāptir upādaya pratipāt saiva madhyama:* Dependent Origination is that which we call Voidness. It is a mere designation based on something, and it is the Middle way".[69] Magliola thus compares the methods of Nagarjuna and Derrida: "It will be noticed that the 'Derridean' methodology—(1) entrapment of adversary in self-contradiction, (2) resort to another conclusion, (3) the placement of the conclusion *sous rature,* and (4) discernment of *lueur* given off by *difference,* from between the marks of erasure—all characterise the Nagarjunist trail. . . ."[70]

III

The following *mandala,* in a nutshell, will represent my theory of poetry and poetic process. (See page 177)

To the many circles, intersecting circles, the square, the circle enclosing the square, and the two triangles in opposition each to the other, there is a single centre, called in tantric terminology, the *parā bindu,* the Centre beyond centres, The three circles outside the intersecting complex (which I have designated as forming the three bodies of the Buddha) are, from the outside, the manifestations of the *Nirmā nkāya,* the *Sambhō gkā ya,* and the *Dharmakā ya.* I make them correspond to my three basic categories of poetry, viz., the lyric, the long poem (longer poem) and the epic. The three categories also correspond to the *sattva,* the *rajas,* the *tamas* qualities *(gunas)* of the *Bhagavad Gīta.* The qualities are translated as Goodness, Passion and Darkness. When the artist as yogi transcends peripheral boundaries of such categories, there is a churning or melting-pot beyond the three in which there is a consummation or transumption of categories. The body is exhumed of defilements, pilferages, wastes of energy, and, finally, attains to its androgynous nature, symbolised in the figure by the intersecting male and female triangles. This is, however, a stage where dualities still exist, and a final effort will naturally involve the consummation of this as well into

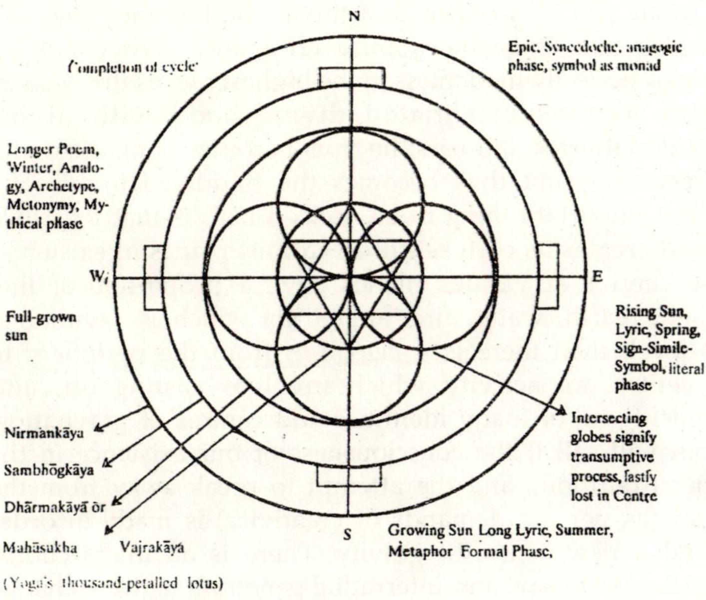

(Yoga's thousand-petalled lotus)

the inner potency of the Centre, which cannot be designated, though for communication's sake, Buddhists call it "emptiness". This *parābindu* assimilates many *bindus*, centres, in itself. Prof. S.B. Dasgupta says: "The lowest *ċakra* of the body (whether the *Nirmān-Ċakra* of the Buddhists or the *Mūladhara-Ċakra* of the Hindus) is the material plane and *Mahāsukha (parāb-indu)* remains here in its grossly physical form—it is the sex-pleasure; and in this plane *bodhicitta* is the physical *bindu* (seed); through further downward motion the *bindu* becomes transformed into the physical body. But as the *bindu* marches up from the physical plane to higher and higher planes it casts off its physical nature and approximates its original nature as the motionless and changeless; this motionless and changeless *Mahāsukha* in the highest plexus is the Absolute in which the self and the not-self merge. The *bindu* in the *Nirmān-Ċakra* is composed of earth, water, flre, air and ether; but when the *bindu* in its upward march leaves the *Nirmān-Cakra,* the element of earth merges itself in water, and in this way, with further march of the *bodhicitta,* the element of water merges itself in fire, fire in air and air in *ċitta,* and this is the highest plane, *i.e., Usnīsa-kamala,* it becomes pure effulgence. When *bindu*... becomes perfectly motionless in the highest plexus the *sādhaka* attains a transubstantiated divine body with divine (immaterial) eyes and ears; he thus becomes ominscient and all-pervading and thus becomes the Buddha Himself'.[71]

The important thing to be noticed here is that the *bindu* as seed creates its own centre at various planes of existence; these centres at various planes have a proportion of life-element (earth, water, fire, air, ether) which is peculiar to that level; then there is a *movement* from the periphery to the centre, an activity which involves casting off, and embracing in, of many identities and centres of gravitation. Bloom will call it the consciousness of our existence in the Father (tradition); and the attempt to break away from the Father (as per the demands of creativity) is made in order to find a new centre of gravity. There is an intersectional interstice, so to say, and interradial penetration, the exchange of microcosmic limbs of the body for the macrocosmic and *vice versa.* There is an interpenetration of bodies—tonal, metaphorical, metonymical, synecdochic, and metaleptical, several times and at several levels. This hybridization is the creative process itself, and is the source of all poetic forms. It is here that the time and eternity meet and create. While the creative process begins from the outermost circle, it is not necessary that every artist is able to pierce through all the *cakras.* The artist locates the centre of gravity in terms of his own level of consciousness and it depends upon his propensity to create larger or smaller forms.

Beginning with the outermost circle, which is the Buddhist *Nirmānkāya,* and which constitutes my lyric, the description quoted from Dasgupta rightly says that this stage is marked by a desire to please the senses. The motivational component of the lyric form is the subject's desire to *grasp* or *crave for* the object. This is the stage, where, of the five elements, the earth element dominates, and passions rule the mind. This means no denial of other elements, for my line of argument is that everything exists in everything else. Since the *tamas* element dominates over the protagonist of the lyric, "insatiate desire" *(Gīta:* 16.10) is the vital component of most of the lyrics written, and the tendency on the part of the subject to conceive falsely, in terms of his beloved or a situation, or his expectation that the impossible will happen, are features common enough. I have associated the subject of the lyric with the East—a symbol of growing energy, rising sun, laden with ideas whose maturity or immaturity it does not care for. But the whole *mandala* complex (one's own body) is a dynamic continuum, and each stage has got its own transformational potentialities in terms of the enactment and re-enactment of the real potency of the Centre, possibilities for a kind of ritual rehappening which will initiate the original ritual. Therefore, the lyric as *Nirmāukaya* also has the seeds of other *kāyās,* bodies, within itself. The linearity of the narrative is not yet open which delays the inevitable in time; what is open is a conceited notion of the world, misconceptions about the self and others, and the time-duration of this activity is brief, like the flicker of a moment. At the level of the *Sambhōgkāya,* the lyric desire expands its own impulse in terms of time-duration, and creates conscious bipolarity in the subject. It is the impulse along with the subject's intellect that governs this level of the longer lyric. The difference of each stage from the other is exhibited in terms of the existential stature, mode, manner, and duration of stability of the lineaments of form.

In terms of the language-incarnation or the *avatāra* of instinct in terms of figures of speech, I would place the lyric at the confluence of literal-descriptive and formal-mythical phases. The parameters of language will function much within the periphery of the sign and the symbol, though the role of the symbol as archetype and the symbol as image, cannot be ruled out. The latter will come in flashes of illumination but will not stay. In terms of *mythos* or mode, the lyric will have all the four elements—comedy, romance, tragedy and irony and satire, but the dominant mode would be romance, irony (of situation) will be subordinated, and tragedy (of total result) will be implicit. Under the long lyric category, I have the lyric which is longer than the lyric discussed in the first stage; then there is the lyric that I call the longer poem—longer than the lyrics discussed in the first and the second stages. Taken together, poems like the sonnet (first stage lyric) and the ode (second stage lyric) are the spring and the summer figments, basically poems of nascent desire, where the experience of ambient dimensionality is yet unknown. From the lyric to the poem longer than it, there is a gradual widening of the body-circles, body-movement, and body-dimensionality. Whereas in the shorter lyric, the formal-mythical phase was dominated by the literal-descriptive, and the purely subjective character of the lyric was distinguished by the gross involvement of the "I", in the larger form 'of the lyric there is not only a consciousness of the conflicting forces and tendencies, implying thereby that the process of disintegration has set in, and a boundary is being created within the confluence point of the subject and the object, but a need is also felt to overcome the bi-polarity which, in fact, is never overcome. There are lamentations, as for example, in Gray's *Elegy,* or the chorus, which tries to perform the original ritual in order to re-live primeval times, which, it knows, will never come. In the lyric of the second stage, irony comes to acquire an increasingly important role. The romance is subordinated and the tragedy is still implicit. The language functions as a trope of deceit and delusion. The intent of the images is bifurcated; they acquire, not necessarily Fryean apocalyptic and demonic labels, but surely show a tendency towards imprisoning and liberating movements.

At the lyric of the third stage (longer lyric), the dialectic is really born. The lyric of the first stage corresponds with Nagarjuna's first proposition "this is", where the subject feels in tune with himself and his environment. The lyric of the second stage which showed the first glimmerings of the conflict within the subject corresponded with Nagarjuna's second proposition: "this is not" which already includes the earlier "this is". The nature of the conflict at this stage is the faint refutation by one part" of the self to the false claims to knowledge by the other. The lyric of the third stage, which shows dialectic at its intensest and most poignant, corresponds to Nagarjuna's third proposition: "both this and this is not", where the one self is in a perpetual war of attrition with the other, each trying to cancel out the other. Substitutions or tropes are variations upon the four forms of basic propositions already examined. These four propositions can only be negated by "emptiness" which is neither a concept nor a proposition. Emptiness is Nothing. The lyric of the third stage, in terms of the Buddha body, is born at the confluence of the *Nirmānkāya* and the *Sambhōgkāya*. The *Dharmakāya,* which alone unites the triplet into a unity, is achieved at the epic stage which forms my last poetic category. In the lyric dominated by the dialectic, metonymy is no stable figure of speech as it is in continuous circulation of ambiguities, each claiming its own position as true. Since the dialectic exposes the relative merits and demerits of the contents, the need for transcending respective positions is immediately felt. In terms of literary phase, this level is formal-mythical. Myth has an unavoidable element of ritual, and ritual is often known to be the cure for many psychological diseases. The form of the poem itself is a ritual which repeats auguries that go well beyond man's sense of written history. For this reason, I join the mythical to the merely formal, so that the door to its regeneration is opened. Irony and satire, which were lurking in the background in the lyric and the longer lyric, are now not only manifest, they have achieved and were capable of achieving—the death of the unity of the protagonist's being—which is what the dialectic does. All knowledge of good and evil, in the first instance, is not needed; and, in the second, is relative to the original innocence that has 'been lost. This cruel fact is achieved by the birth of the dialectic (Adam & Eve) in the Biblical story of creation.

The epic is characterised by a magnitude of infinite possibilities where difference and identity are at work at their widest of parameters. The epic is the infinite breeding ground of characters, parading them round the iron-wheel of desire, making them part of the dependent-origination logic, and, finally, joining their interdependent nature to the axis of the centre. The element "air" dominates the epic; the direction assigned to the epic is north, which completes the sun-cycle and comes in a bi-polar relationship with the south; this is equally true of the east and the west. The strings are pulled and the centre keeps the balance of the sphere. This stage of the *Dharmākaya,* though manifesting itself in the triple world, is free from impurities and desires. It unfolds itself here, there, and everywhere (responding to the call of *karma)*. . . "This body of *Dharma* has no boundary, no quarters, but is embodied in all bodies".[72] Beyond the epic stage is the stage of the *Vajrakāya,* Buddha's Diamond Body, which is eternal, the confluence of serenity and gravity, which I designate as the total effect of the artist's striving to create the largest form and see it as part of his own body. After all the *rasās* (aesthetic pleasures) that a work of art may generate, all genuine art-works lead to *Śanta-rasa,* the *rasa* of tranquillity and sereneness, supremely exhibited by Buddha images found anywhere in the world,[73] what Charles Tomlinson said of Oc-tavio Paz that ", . . in the art of India... he (Paz) admires that combination of ecstasy and gravity which, in another form, characterises much of his own mature poetry".[74]

IV

Reasons for beginning with the importance of Indian ideas in the Greco-Roman world were to show how in the very process of receptivity the method of deconstruction has been at work. Ever since the *Vedas, Upanishads,* and Buddhism made their inroads into the Western world, Western texts have not only been de constructing their own tradition in the light of such ideas, Indian tradition itself has deconstructed its own centrist premises which is what is the precise achievement of Buddha. The chain of Indian ideas, which took a positive (or negative?) turn since Plato, continues its influencing trend in all notable thinkers, down to this day, and it is the burden of the first section to indicate precisely this. This chain obviously finds its fuller and often (its) complete manifestation in Schopenhauer, Nietzsche, and Heidegger. The intention is to show that Derrida's acquaintance with Indian thought, especially Buddhism, is not direct; it is also through the deconstruction of the notable texts of the thinkers in the Western tradition that Derrida has shown degrees of receptivity to Nagarjuna in particular and Buddhism in general. Nevertheless, few doubts should now exist as far as the similarity between Nagarjuna and Derrida's methods is concerned. This is what the second section tries to conclude. Tantric typology, concepts of the *mudrās, mandalās,* and *yantrās* in Buddhist (Hindu) tradition are the sort of concepts deeply inbred into poetic sensibility having inherently creative bases. The source of all poetic forms, or for that matter of forms other than poetic, resides in human psyche. This was exhibited by what we now call the archaic religion.[75] Moreover, it would appear that I have again created a centrist poetics by positing concepts of the circle and the centre, concepts with which some versions of

Buddhism may not agree. Heidegger had already drawn his "hermeneutic circle" and claimed that there is no escape from it, and therefore from the centre. This, by no means, implies that Heidegger's being is a centrist concept as Derrida often leads us to believe. Heidegger's Being, put under erasure, transcends itself by itself, and is beyond the beyond (much like the *Brahman* of the *Upanishads).* That Buddhism celebrates *movement* is well known;[76] it, however, does not amount to a denial of the centre. *Movement* does have a source of generation round which it moves. Even Derrida, who is often misunderstood, acknowledges the place of the centre and the subject: "First of all, I didn't say there was no centre, that we could get along without the centre. I believe that the centre is a function, not a being—a reality, but a function . . . . I don't destroy the subject; I situate. That is to say, I believe that at a certain level both of experience and of philosophical and scientific discourse one cannot get along without the notion of subject. Therefore I keep the concept of the centre, which I explained was indispensable, as well as that of the subject."[77] Buddhist emptiness is what makes the centre functional, for it does not determine a point of origination. Queried so many times on God, Buddha always maintained a silence that was its own answer. This silence is the road to the ultimate meaning in literature, which, in all verbal formulae, can only be grasped through endless supplementations. By acknowledging a functional centre and confessing to *situate* the subject in his texts, while yet keeping the possibilities open, is what brings Derrida and Buddhism very close indeed.

Notes and References

1. See his *Will to Power,* ed., Dr. Oscar Levy, Vol. I (1909), p. 346.
2. S.M. Melamed, *Spinoza and Buddhism: Visions of a Dead God* (Chicago: Chicago University Press, 1933), pp. 321-22.
3. *Ibid.,* pp. 323-24.
4. As we know through Herodotus, iv.44, that the first book on India was written by Seylax, a Greek sea-captain, whom Darius sent to explore the. course of the Indus Valley.

5. *Yona* is Prakrit equivalent of *Yavanani*, used in Asoka inscriptions to describe Hellenic princes; Panini speaks of Greek script as *Yavani-lipi*, iv. 1.49.
6. Orphism is mentioned in Plato's *Cratylus*, 402b; *Laws*, ii. 669d, viii. 829d; *Republic*, ii.364e; *1011*, P. 536b.
7. "The Florida of Apuleius", xv, Works of Apuleius, pp. 388-89.
8. Apuleius quoted in John Drew, *India and the Romantic Imagination* (Delhi: Oxford University Press, 1987), p. 118.
9. *Intercourse Between India and the Western World* (Delhi: Rai Book Service, 1977), p. 176.
10. S. Radhakrishnan, *Eastern Religions and Western Thought* (Delhi: Oxford University Press, 1975), p. 198.
11. *Ibid.*, p. 200.
12. *Ibid.*, p. 144.
13. *lon*, p. 534.
14. *Phaeedo*, 70c.
15. *Mysticism and Catholicism* (1925), p. 74; Quoted in Radhakrishnan, *op.cit.*, p. 149.
16. Radhakrishnan, *op.cit.*, p. 147.
17. Hegel, *The Philosophy of Fine Art*, trans. F.P.B. Osmaston (London: Give Bell & Sons, 1920), Vol. II, p. 90.
18. *Ibid.*, p. 93.
19. See Charles Muses, *East-West Fire: Schopenhauer's Optimism and the Lankāvatāra Sūtra* (London: John M. Watkins, 1955), p. 20.
20. Arthur Schopenhauer, *The World as Will and Representation*, trans. E.F.J. Payne, 2 Vols. (Colorado, Indiana Hills: Falcon's Wing Press, 1958), I, xxiii-xxiv.
21. See p. 53 in Gregor Malantschuk (ed.), *Kierkegaard's Thought*, trans. Howard V. Hong and Edna N. Hong (Princeton: Princeton University Press, 1971).
22. Nietzsche might have read the *Gita* in German translation made by F. Von Mayer, *Aus Dem Bhagavadgita* (incomplete translation based on Charles Wilkins' translation of the *Gita* in English), Zurich; 1801; other translations available were *Bhagavadgita Oder des Hohe Lied des Indus* (Leipzig, 1834); *Bhagavadgita oder des Lied der Gottheit* (Berlin, 1870). J.G. Herder had made a free translation

of *Hitopadesa* and *Bhagavadgita* entitled *Thoughts of Lone Brahmins;* 1792.

23. In *Beyond Good and Evil,* abstracted in Richard Gill and Ernest Sherman (cd.), *The Fabric of Existentialism: Philosophical and Literary Sources* (N. Jersey: Prentice-Hall, 1973), p. 278.
24. *Ibid.,* p. 280.
25. *Ibid.,* p. 287.
26. Martin Heidegger, *Unterwegs zur Sprache* (Pfullingen: Gunther Neske, 1959), p. 198.
27. William Barrett (ed.), *Zen Buddhism* (New York: Doubleday, 1956), p. xi.
28. Heidegger, *op.cit.,* pp. 108-09.
29. Robert Magliola, *Derrida on the Mend* (Indiana: Purdue University Press, 1984), p. 88.
30. Alan Bass, trans. & annot., *Positions: Jacques Derrida* (London: The Athlone Press, 1981), p. 11.
31. Robert Magliola, *Derrida on the Mend,* p. 88.
32. J. Derrida, *Of Grammatology,* trans. Gayatri Chakravorty Spivak (Baltimore: Johns Hopkins University Press, 1976), p. 120, first published 1974. Derrida quotes from Levi Strauss the following: "In its own way, and on its own level, each of them corresponds to a truth. Between Marxist criticism which sets man free from his first chains, and Buddhist criticism, which completes that liberation, there is neither opposition nor contradiction (The Marxist teaches that the apparent significance of Man's condition will vanish the moment he agrees to enlarge the object that he has under consideration). Marxism and Buddhism are doing the same thing, but at two different levels." *Ibid.* Mark Derrida's insistence on *levels* and *liberation* (of metaphysics). L de la V. Poussin's monumental *Bibliotheca Buddhica,* Vol. 4, St. Petersberg, 1913, was already there to consolidate Derrida's Ideas on Buddhism. It was here that a translation of Nagarjuna's *Madhyamak-Karika* appeared.
33. Tibetan text and translation, ed. by Poussin as Appendix IV to his *Theorie des douze Causes,* Gand, 1913. Pandit N. Aiyaswami has translated this into English from a Chinese version (Taisho, Vol. XXXII, 1654), in *K.V. Rangaswamy Aiyangar Com., Vol.* pp. 485-91.

34. *Bodhicary Avatara Panjika* by Prajnakarmati (Bib. Ind.), p. 389; See T.R V.Murti, *The Central Philosophy of Buddhism* (London: George Allen & Unwin, 1980), p. 90.

35. *Positions,* p. 88.

36. *Ibid.,* p. 40.

37. For twelve factors of the causal-chain, see David J. Kalupahana, *Nagarjuna: The Philosophy of the Middle Way* (New York: State University of New York Press, 1986), pp. 370-76.

38. Kalupahana, *Ibid., Mūlmadhyamak-Kārtika,* verses 1 & 2.

39. *The Central Philosophy of Buddhism,* pp. 121-22.

40. *Positions,* p. 52.

41. *Ibid.,* p. 32.

42. See her translation of *Of Grammatology,* p. xvi.

43. *Positions,* p. 88.

44. See Dinnaga: *Vikalpayonāyah sabda vikalpah sabdayonayah* as quoted in Stcherbatsky, *Buddhist Logic,* II, p. 405n.

45. K. Kunjunni Raja, *Indian Theories of Meaning* (Adyar: Adyar Library and Research Centre, 1963), p. 82.

46. F.J. Streng, *Emptiness: A Study in Religious Meaning* (New York: Nashville: Abingdom Press, 1967), p. 60.

47. Kalupahana, *op.cit.,* p. 28.

48. *Ibid.*

49. *Central Philosophy of Buddhism,* p. 122:

50. *Positions,* p. 49.

51. *Ibid.,* p. 14; *cr.* the account of Nagarjuna and Dinnaga's methods given.

52. *Ibid.,* p. 92.

53. *Ibid.,* p. 95.

54. Kamaleswar Bhattacharya, trans. *The Dialectical Method of Nagarjuna Vigrahavyartani,* ed. by E.H. Johnston and Arnold Kunst (Delhi: Motilal Banarsidass, 1986), p. 89; first pub. 1978.

55. *Ibid.,* verse LXIII *(Vigl'havyavartani),* p. 131.

56. *Mūlmadhyamak-Kārtika,* Kalupahana's translation, Chap. XXV, verse 20, p. 367. 57. Streng, *Emptiness,* p. 21.

58. *Positions,* p. 21.
59. *Ibid.*
60. *Ibid.,* p. 26.
61. *Mūlmadhyamak-Kārika,* Chap. X, verse 1, Kalupahana, p. 195.
62. Murti, *Central Philosophy of Buddhism,* p. 138.
63. Nagarjuna quoted in Streng, *Empliness,* p. 62.
64. *Mūlmadhyamak-Kārika,* Chap. XX, verses 16-8, in Streng, *Ibid.,* p. 65.
65. J. Culler, *On Deconstruction* (London: Routledge, 1987), p. 209.
66. *Of Grammatology,* p. lxv.
67. R.C. Zaehner, ed. & trans. *The Bhagavadgita* (London: Oxford University Press, 1975), Chap. 9, verse p. 277.
68. *Derrida on the Mend,* p. 99.
69. K. Bhattacharya, *The Dialectical Method of Nagarjuna,* p. 93.
70. *Derrida on the Mend,* p. 106.
71. *Sékoddésa-tika* (Gaekwad Series), pp. 7, 45, quoted in S.B. Dasgupta, *An Introduction to Tantric Buddhism* (Calcutta: Calcutta University Press, 1974), p. 178.
72. *Ibid.,* p. 11.
73. My theory would appear in greater detail in one of my forthcoming books.
74. See p. 13, in Charles Tomlinson (ed.), *Octavio Paz: Selected Poems* (Penguin, 1979).
75. Two important studies on the subject of religion and poetic form are: H. Zimmer, *Artistic Form and Yoga* in *the Sacred Images of India* (Delhi: Oxford University Press, 1984), trans. from German into English by Gerald Chapple & James B. Lawson; the other book is by Roderick S. Bucknell and Martin Stuart Fox, *The Twilight Language: Explorations* in *Buddhist Mediation and Symbolism* (London: Curzon Press, 1986), published simultaneously by St.Martin's Press, New York.
76. See especially Padmasiri de Silva, "Two Paradigmatic Strands in the Buddhist Theory of Consciousness", in Ronald S. Valle and Rolf Von Eckartsberg (ed.), *The Metaphors of Consciousness* (New York: Plenum Press, 1981).
77. The remark came as a reply to one of the questions put to

Derrida after he read his paper, "Structure, Sign, and Play in the Discourse of the Human Sciences", remark quoted in Murray Krieger, *Theory of Criticism* (Baltimore: Johns Hopkins University Press, 1976). p. 231.

Essay III

Perspective and Structure: Hindu Contexts for Blake and Whitman

I

NORTHROP FRYE has remarked that in the eighteenth century England, "New contributions were pouring in from as far afield as Persia and India, and Blake was among the first of European Idealists able to link his own tradition of thought with the *Bhagavadgīta*",[1] Blake had painted Charles Wilkins in the act of translating the *Gīta* and entitled his painting, "The Bramins: A Drawing". Placing it at No. X in his *A Descriptive Catalogue* Blake wrote: "The subject is, Mr. Wilkin(s) translating the *Gīta;* an ideal design, suggested by the first publication of that part of the Hindoo Scriptures translated by Mr. Wilkins. I understand that my Costume is incorrect, but in this I plead the authority of the ancients, who often deviated from the Habits to preserve the Manners, as in the instance of Laocoon, who, though a priest, is represented naked",[2] A.C. Swinburne is the earliest critic who not only ushered in modern Blake criticism with the publication of his essay[3] but also brought out some of the similarities between Blake and Whitman.[4] S. Foster Damon was another important critic whose book on Blakes provided many powerful insights into the poetry and thought of Blake and Whitman.

In *A Descriptive Catalogue* (1809) Blake invokes the older

literatures of the world, by which he means the literatures of the ancient Greeks, Egyptians, Persians, and Hindus, In the exhibition of his paintings, the first two paintings were of Nelson and Pitt. Of these Blake wrote: "The two pictures of Nelson and Pitt are compositions of a mythological cast, similar to those Apotheosis of Persian, Hindoo, and Egyptian Antiquity, which are still preserved on rude monuments, being copies from some stupendous originals now lost or perhaps buried till some happier age."[6] Whitman's interests were similar to those of Blake. Whitman spent many hours in the libraries of New York city and "in the 1850s he frequented the Egyptian Museum on lower Broadway, where he acquired an interest in the history of the human race and the myths and religions of ancient peoples that broadened his intellectual horizon."[7] Here Whitman also met Dr. Henry Abbot, the owner of the Egyptian Museum, and many other learned persons. In *A Backward Glance O'ver Travell'd Roads* (1888) Whitman recalled: "I used to go off, sometimes for a week at a stretch, down in the country, or to long island's seashores—there, in the presence of outdoor influences, I went over thoroughly the Old and New Testaments, and absorbed Shakespeare, *Ossian,* the best translated versions I could get of Homer, Eschylus, Sophocles, the old German Nibelungen, the ancient Hindoo poems and one or two other masterpieces, Dante's among them."[8] Both Blake and Whitman thought in terms of old Bibles, epics and classics, and both had a comparatist's attitude to ancient civilizations and literature. Blake had also written: "No man can believe that either Homer's mythology, or Ovid's were the invention of Greek Artists; perhaps the Torso is the only original work remaining; all the rest are evidently copies, though fine ones, from greater works of the Asiatic Patriarchs."[9]

Critics who tend to give undue emphasis on Blake's and Whitman's reading of the Bible have to confess that Blake and Whitman were not reading the Bible in terms of Christian orthodoxy. Milton O. Perceival thus described Blake's tradition: "The Orphic and Pythagorean tradition, Neoplatonism in the whole of its extent, the Hermetic,

Kabbalistic, Gnostic, and Alchemical writings, Erigena, Paracelsus, Boehme, and Swedenborg—here is a consistent body of tradition extending over nearly twenty-five hundred years. In the light of this tradition, not in the light of Christian Orthodoxy, Blake read his Bible, weighing and deciding for himself, formulating a 'Bible of Hell'."[10] Malcolm Cowley, whose edition of *Leaves of Grass* gave a new perspective to Whitman scholarship, said that *Leaves of Grass* should be studied in the light of the tradition as established by the *Bhagavad-Gīta*, the *Upanishads*, Christopher Smart's long crazy inspired poem *Jubilate Agno*, Blake's Prophetic books (not forgetting *The Marriage of Heaven and Hell)*, Rimbaud's *Illuminations*, *The Chants of Maldoror*, and Nietzsche's *Thus Spake Zarathustra*, as well as *The Gospel of Sri Ramkrishna* and a compendious handbook, *The Philosophies of India*, by Heinrish Zimmer (New York, 1951).[11]

The foregoing perspective is given with a view to establishing the Blakean-Whitman-Hindu tradition. It is assumed that the proximity of relationship between Blake and Whitman, and its effect upon their work, is not hitherto realized by scholars. Because of the same source material at hand, Blake had created a poetic mythology for which he has been placed outside the Christian tradition[12] and Whitman is termed no better for apotheosizing the human soul in all its naked beauty and pristine grandeur singing the song of the primeval.[13] I shall now establish a Blake-Whitman relationship, and show, with the help of the material available to them, especially the *Bhagavadgīta*, how they developed their mythic archetypes into larger poetic structures with reference to *The Four Zoas* and the *Song of Myself.*

II

In 1868 William Michael Rossetti published an edition of *Leaves of Grass* in England. In the same year had also appeared Swinburne's essay on Blake in which Swinburne had remarked: ". . . in breadth of outline and charm of colour, these poems (of Whitman) recall the work of Blake; and to neither poet can a higher tribute of honest praise be paid than this."[14] Hotten had sent a copy of Swinburne's book to Whitman and when in March 1968 Whitman read it he knew that "Swinburne had ended his book with a flattering comparison of him with Blake."[15] John Swinton, Whitman's old friend, had also acquired a copy of the poems of William Blake published from London in two volumes. Swinton read these poems of Blake along with Whitman's, and had this to say in Whitman's own words: "He, Swinton, gives me rather new information in one respect—says that the formal resemblance between several pieces of Blake, and my pieces is so marked that he, S. has with persons that partially know me, passed them off temporarily for mine, and read them aloud as such. He asked me pointedly whether I had not met with Blake's productions in my youth, and C.—said that Swinburne's idea of resemblance and C. was not so wild, after all. Quite funny isn't it?"[16] William Michael Rossetti, in 1869, had sent O'Connor a letter along with copies of critical appreciation of the poems of Whitman. These appreciations were written by Anne Gilchrist, the widow of Blake's biographer Alexander Gilchrist. Rossetti, however, did not identify the woman describing her only as "wife and mother."[17] Whitman later sent a photograph of himself to Rossetti asking him to pass it on to the lady. Whitman also wrote in the letter that he was "deeply touched by these sympathesies and convictions, coming from a woman and from England, and am sure that if the lady knew how much comfort it has been for me to get them, she would not only pardon you for transmitting them to Mr. O'Connor but approve that action. . ."[18] Whitman further promised to send early copies of new editions of *Leaves of Grass* to Rossetti and ended the letter by saying: "I want you to loan this letter to the lady, or if she wishes it, give it to her to keep".[19] Mrs. Gilchrist read the unexpurgated *Leaves* in the copy that Whitman had prepared for the printer. Mrs. Gilchrist's reading resulted in the publication of an article in the May issue of Boston Radical: "A Woman's Estimate of Walt Whitman".[20]

Among Whitman's family influences, that of Thomas Paine is important. Whitman's father had read Paine's political essays and was deeply influenced by the "inner light" concept of the Quaker Elias Hicks. "Walt Whitman idolized both of these independent-spirited men".[21] Thomas Paine had criticised the perversions of Biblical teachings in his lectures. Bishop R. Watson had attacked Paine by writing annotations to "An Apology for the Bible in a Series of Letters addressed to Thomas Paine by R. Watson, D.D., F.R.S." (London, MDCCXCVII). Blake was reading both Paine's writings and Watson's annotations. Blake concluded that "Paine has not attacked Christianity. Watson has defended Antichrist".[22] The purpose behind referring to W.M. Rossetti, Mrs. Gilchrist, Tom Paine and John Swinton, was to show the obvious relationship between Blake and Whitman. While John Swinton's acquisition of Blake's work leaves us in no doubt of Whitman having read them; Mrs. Gilchrist's settlement in Philadelphia in 1876 and Whitman's occasional visits to the lady presupposes that Blake figured prominently in the discussions between the two. Secondly, W.M. Rossetti, who was constantly in correspondence with Whitman and who had published the first London edition of Whitman's poems, was also responsible for the publication of William Blake's poems in 1911. Whitman not only read Blake thoroughly, he also selected a design from William Blake to be implanted on a small mausoleum he wanted to build for himself in 1892 at Harleigh cemetery.[23]

Whitman's debt to, and his relation with, Emerson and Thoreau, makes for another major Hindu influence. Emerson in 1838 had given a lecture at Harvard University comparing the divine in man to the Hindu *Aтman-Brahma* concept. Thoreau was Emerson's neighbour between 1837 and 1862. In July 1846 Emerson noted that Thoreau had been reading to him extracts from *A Week on the Concord and Merrimack Rivers.* This work contains eulogies of the *Gīta* and other works from Indian philosophy. The "Transcendental Club" was founded round 1840 (Whitman was its member) and in the Club's quarterly journal *The Dial,* Margaret Fuller was publishing translations from Oriental languages. In 1854, the Englishman, Thomas Cholmondeley, the nephew of the bishop

Reginald Heber, visited Concord and became friendly with Thoreau, Emerson and Whitman. On his return to England, Cholmondeley sent Thoreau a collection of Oriental classics in 44 volumes. Thoreau said that it was impossible to find any of these works in America. Therefore, when Whitman said that he had read the "ancient Hindoo poems" in preparation for *Leaves of Grass*[24] he was just stating a truism. When Thoreau had compared *Leaves of Grass* as a work "wonderfully like the Orientals", and asked Whitman if he had read any of the Oriental works, Whitman is believed to have replied in the negative. But as Gay Wilson thinks that "this may have been disingenuous or it could have been modesty before a man who obviously knew a great deal about oriental scriptures,[25] is most likely and possibly true.

III

The structure of *Leaves of Grass* has defied the efforts of many a scholar though "some recent ones profess to find a thematic structure in it".[26] Thus Carl F. Strauch reads the poem at five levels:[27] the mystical interpretation of Self with all life; Selfs identification with all life and the transfiguration of the degraded; life issuing from and coming into the Self; the description of the Superman and questions concerning life, death, immortality, etc. In his edition of 1855 of *Leaves of Grass,* Malcolm Cowely read the poem at nine levels. Harold W. Blodgett and Sculley Bradley, in their edition of *Leaves of Grass,* maintain that *Leaves of Grass,* especially the "Song of Myself', expresses the poet's wish "to improve and transform life (the poet as maker and reformer), to discern and set forth its miraculousness (the poet as celebrator), and to sing the transcendence of human love, envisioned as divine (the poet as lover).[28] My reading of "Song of Myself' has been stimulated by Whitman's poem "A Sight in Camp in the Daybreak Gray and Dim" (1865). In this poem Whitman describes three forms lying on stretchers and covered with blankets. Unfolding the blanket of the first form the poet asks:

> Who are you elderly man so gaunt and grim
> well-gray'd hair,
> and flesh all sunken about the eyes?

Next, the poet advances to the second form:

> . . . and who are you my child and darling?
> Who are you sweet boy with cheeks yet blooming?

And finally to the third:

> . . . a face nor child nor old, very calm, as of
> beautiful yellow-white ivory;
> Young man I think I know you—I think this
> face is the face of Christ himself,
> Dead and divine and brother of all,
> and here again he lies.

In *A Descriptive Catalogue* (1809) of his paintings, Blake placed at No. V the painting "The Ancient Britons". Characterising the three ancient Britons as the Strong Man, the Beautiful Man, and the Ugly Man, Blake wrote: "The Strong Man represents the human sublime. The Beautiful Man represents the human pathetic, which was in the wars of Eden divided into male and female. The Ugly Man represents the human reason. They were originally one man who was fourfold; he was self-divided, and his real humanity slain on the stems of genera-tion, and the form of the fourth was like the Son of God."[29] This fourfold man is the Primal Man of the *Purush-Sūkta* of the *Rig Veda:* "When (the gods) divided the *Purusha,* into how many parts did they cut him up? The Brahman was his mouth, the Rajanya was made his arms, the being (called) Vaisya was his thighs, and the Sudra sprang from his feet".[30]

The three men which Whitman describes in his poem, and the three men described by Blake, are variations of the same Primal Man archetype that we come across in the *Rig-Veda.* Blake's Ugly Man corresponds with Whitman's gaunt and grim elderly man whose flesh is sunken round his eyes due to the tyranny of perverted reason. Blake's Beautiful

Man corresponds with Whitman's darling child, the symbol of growing energy, whose cheeks are blooming. Blake's Strong Man corresponds with Whitman's third person neither child nor old and whose face is the face of Christ himself. These three persons in both Blake and Whitman are archetypes and they represent the natural divisions of humanity as described in the *Bhagavadgīta* (Chapters XVI, XVII, and XVIII). The typological division in the *Gīta* is described thus: "Exalted are the senses, or so they say; higher than the senses is the mind; yet higher than the mind the soul; what is beyond the soul is the *(Ātman)*".[31] Archetypes are the organs of the psyche; they are dynamic intellectual complexes and Jung calls them *dominants* of the Unconscious.[32] Then there are "universal dynamic forms" —the Primal Man being all the dynamic forms into one—which constitute Jung's Collective *Unconscious*. The three types of men that we are discussing with reference to Blake and Whitman constitute "primordial images". Their qualities and characteristics transcend time and space hypothesis. They are eternal lineaments which have implanted themselves upon the memory of the human race, which have been "stamped as it were upon our physical organism".[33] Frye says: "I mean by an archetype a symbol which connects one poem with another and thereby helps to unify and integrate our literary experience".[34] It is this vital fact that exists between poems under discussion and Whitman was not ignorant of what he was doing.[35]

Myth is central to the archetypal study of literature. Both *The Four Zoas* and *Song of Myself* have, at their background, the myth of a Primal Man, the *Purusha* of the *Rig Veda,* the Brahma of the *Laws of Manu,* the Hebrew Adam Kadmon, the *Gīta's* Krishna (Chapter XI), or even a more orientalised Christ of unorthodox Christian conception (that of Blake and Whitman for example),[36] whose body contains both the abysmal deep of the mysteries of the universe, and the manifest world of meaning and form, comedy and tragedy, order and chaos, etc. *The Primal Man* is a stage in the imaginative development of the human race where "contraries are equally true" but who, by the sheer power of his divine will and spiritual majesty, transcends opposites and mingles into the process of self-identification, and creates an integral atmosphere where atmospheric atoms cling on to his body as pearls of a bead cling on to the body of Krishna in the *Gīta.* While in *The Four Zoas,* as would apparently seem, the poet has depersonalised in his quest for a certain order of narrative (T.S. Eliot's comments notwith-standing),[37] Whitman has preferred, somewhat voluntarily, even whimsically, (for so the assumption is), to impose his egotistical sublime upon the reader.[38]

The narrative structure of the *Gīta* is advanced by a succession of verbal sequences relating to the obstinate questionings of Arjuna, the hero, and the God-incarnate, Krishna's answers. The climax comes in Chapter XI where Krishna, talking in the same characteristic "I" in which Whitman talks, shows Arjuna the world inside his body, the macrocosm in the microcosm, the infinite and indefinite in the finite and the fixed. Comedy, whose theme is the integration of society, aims at the metamorphosis of character or a change in his outlook and behaviour. Arjuna, who starts as a man devoid of intellect and vision of the true nature of things, ends with the positive affirmation that he is ready to fight. The *Gīta* ends with the enlightenment of the hero; there is an advancement from a state of ignorance and delusion *(pistis)* to a state of knowledge *(gnosis).* There is, very often,. some kind of ritual[39] before the new society crystallizes round the hero. This ritual in the life of Arjuna takes place when Krishna makes him cast his natural eye and gives him a celestial eye.[40] Arjuna, before his enlightenment, is a barren land where desires in the form of shrubs grow but decay for want of the water of life. Arjuna, therefore, is an autumn figure in terms of Frye's theory, and the fertilization of his mind takes place due to Krishna who is obviously the spring figure and the source of comic resolution.

Both *The Four Zoas* and *Song of Myself* are comedies in the first instance; both of them are concerned with a certain cosmological disorder (the action of comedy) and the re-emergence of the proper order (the comic resolution). Both the poems use the myth of Primal Man which Blake and Whitman might have derived from any of the numerous sources outlined in the first section, especially the *Gīta,* the *Laws of Manu,* and the *Rig Veda.* The three levels at which the action of comedy operates are: the rebellion of the hero against the society of senex, a society disrupted by folly, obsession and forgetfulness; hero's triumph over this society; and, finally, the attainment of the golden age or the integration of society. These three stages of comedy may well correspond with Blake's Ugly, Beautiful and Strong men and Whitman's three men already described. These three characters are also the autumn, the winter, and the spring figures, who share among themselves the fossilized beliefs of inertia and neurosis, and then are restored, according to the demands of comedy, to the "unbroken current of energy and memory".[41]

Blake, as early as the writing of *The Marriage of Heaven and Hell* (1790-1793), had divided human personality into "The head Sublime, the heart Pathos, the genitals Beauty, the hands and feet Proportion".[42] We may now look at the qualities of each of these three men. The *Gīta* exemplifies these qualities in terms of food, sacrifice, ascetic practice, alms-giving, and metaphysical doctrine, etc. The following quotation will serve our purpose: "The kind of knowledge by which one sees one mode of being changeless, undivided in all contingent beings, divided (as they are), is Goodness, (knowledge). Be sure of this. But (that kind) of knowledge which in all contingent beings discerns in separation all manner of modes of being, different and distinct—this, you must know, is knowledge born of passion. But that (kind of knowledge) which sticks to one effect as if it were all,—irrational, not bothering about that Real as the (true) object (of all knowledge, thinking of it as) finite,—this (knowledge) belongs to Darkness."[43]

IV

Out of the source material outlined above, Whitman used the typology of characters (as described in the *Gīta)* in relation to the myth of the Primal Man whose qualities he appropriated on to himself giving his own personality a cosmological meaning, while Blake segmented the Primal Man—Albion—into Tharmas (sense), Luvah (mind), Urizen (soul), and Urthona/Los *(Ātman)*. Thus the Primal Man myth in Blake and Whitman takes different textures in terms of different formulations only; the mythic mode, despite being central to both the poems, fits into different moulds, but the reality of meaning (the thematic content) does not change. We may divide *Song of Myself*, then, into three broad categories: 1. Paragraphs 1-18, the self in man in relation to the world without (sensory level); 2. Paragraphs 19-25, nature of Self and its power to transform life (mental level); 3. Paragraphs 26-52, the transformed Self (microcosm) succeeds in containing the world (macrocosm) within the myth of the Primal Man fully realized (the level of the soul).

Blake begins *The Four Zoas* with the following assertion:

> Four Mighty Ones are in every Man; a Perfect Unity
> Cannot
> Exist but from the Universal Brotherhood of Eden
> The Universal Man, to Whom be Glory
> Evermore. Amen.

Of the "four mighty ones" in Blake, three we have related to the three *gunās* of the *Gīta*. The fourth one, Urthona (Earth-Owner?), is a symbol of the *Atman*, and therefore, outside the confines of the world of nature. For this reason Urthona does not take part in Blake's poem as a character. It is only his temporal form Los[44] who guides the other three zoas and restores them to unity. In Whitman's poem "A Sight in Camp in the Gray and Dim", we have already identified these three men. The multitudinous voices thronging all over the poetry of Whitman have their source in the personality of the poet and the poet has the source of his personality in these verses from the *Rig Veda*: "*Purusha* has a thousand heads, a thousand eyes, a thousand feet. On every side enveloping the earth, he overpassed (it) by a space of ten fingers. *Purusha* himself is the whole (universe), whatever has been and whatever shall be. He is also the lord of immortality, since (or when) by food he expands. . . With three-quarters Purusha mounted upwards. A quarter of him was again produced here. . . When the gods performed the sacrifice, with *Purusha* as the oblation, the spring was its butter, the summer its fuel, and the autumn its (accompanying) offering."[45] In the *Gīta,* Arjuna, beholding Krishna's universal form, exclaims: "O God, the gods in your body I behold and all the hosts of every kind of being; . . . Arms, bellies, mouths and eyes all manifold—so do I see you wherever I may look—infinite your form! End, middle, or again beginning I cannot see in you, 0 Monarch Universal, (mani-fest) in every form!"[46]

Whitman appropriated these universal qualities on to himself. He wrote *Leaves of Grass* because he wanted "to articulate and faithfully express in literary or poetic form, and uncompromisingly, my own physical, emotional, moral, intellectual, and aesthetic personality, in the immediate, and of current America.. .."[47] Here we can clearly see the physical, emotional, moral, intellectual and aesthetic aspects of Whitman's personality (Self). Whitman did not want to celebrate great events, personages and romances, etc. He wanted to celebrate the "natural propensities in himself; and that is the way he celebrates all".[48] The *Purusha,* we have just described, Whitman envisions as male and female, "a great composite democratic individual". This *Purusha* in Hindu mythology, is also a hermaphroditic figure, and in the creation myth, when he comes out breaking the egg-shell *(Brahmānda),* a female form separates itself out from his body.[49] The three *gunās* of the *Gīta* collectively exist in the personality of each of the four zoas as well as in Whitman's three men, separately and collectively. They are levels of consciousness and point to the imaginative development of each man with varying degrees of perception. Albion's and Whitman's personalities, in respective poems, are a result of the collective efforts of the sense, mind and soul forces. They are the agents of civilization. It is these forces who give an existential meaning to an otherwise abstract concept of the Primal Man myth. Thus, Whitman's sensory faculty, believing in sexual enjoyment of, and interrelation with, phenomenal things, exclaims:

"I am satisfied. . . I see, dance, laugh, sing."

This sensual man Whitman described as "gaunt and grim, with well-gray'd hair, and flesh all sunken about the eyes?" Compare the description of this man with the following verses from the *Gīta:* "Some men there are who, without regard to Scripture's ordinance, savagely mortify (their flesh), buyoed up by hypocrisy and self regard, yielding to the violence and passion and desire, and so torment the mass of (living) beings whose home their body is, the witless fools—and (with them) I Myself within (that same) body abiding: how devilish their intentions".[50] The hypocrit element in this man of darkness is that outwardly he mortifies his flesh but the passions and desires within take a stronger turn and become violent without being creative. Blake described the Ugly Man as "one approaching to the beast in features and form, his forehead small, without frontals; his jaws large; his nose high on the ridge, and narrow; . . . The Ugly Man acts from love of carnage, and delight in the savage barbarities of war. . ."[51]

It is clear that Blake and Whitman modelled their third type of man upon the description found in the *Gīta.* Tharmas, who represents this man in Blake, is described thus:

> Struggling to utter the voice of Man, struggling to take the features of Man, struggling
> To take the limbs of Man, at length emerging from the smoke
> Of Urizen dash'd in pieces from his precipient fall,
> Tharmas reared up his hands & stood on the affrighted ocean: (*F.Z.,* Night III, 117-20).

In both Blake and Whitman, the man under consideration has disfigured himself not only in his bodily shape but also in his actions. Whitman describes the second man as "child and darling. . . sweet boy with cheeks yet blooming". Blake's Beautiful Man is not only a man of intellectual beauty, his "face and limbs that deviates or alters least, from infancy to old age, is the face and limbs of greatest Beauty and Perfection".[52] This is Blake's Luvah (mind), the symbol of growing energy, the sun-figure, who, unguided by the man or zoa above him, may bring self-ruin. He is virtually the centre of personality of both Whitman and Albion. In *The Four Zoas,* Luvah marched from the heart of Albion into his brain (where Urizen lived), and seized Urizen's horses. This resulted in the imbalance of Albion's personality and Urizen's retaliation set in the process of disintegration. In *Song of Myself,* the child, a symbol of passion and curiosity, a spring figure, fetches a patch of grass to the poet seeking for an answer. The poet replies:

> I guess it must be the flag of my disposition, out of
> hopeful green stuff woven.

It should be borne in mind that Blake's *The Four Zoas* starts with an act of fall and that the process of affirmative celebration of life starts only after characters have overcome the process of disintegration. In Whitman's *Song of Myself,* there is no fall and life is celebrated at all levels right from the beginning, with, of course, a plea for cleansing perception. The third type of man, whose face resembles the face of Christ, is the *sattvika* man of the *Gīta* and the Strong Man of Blake: "The Strong acts from conscious superiority, and marches on in fearless dependence on the divine decrees, raging with the inspirations of a prophetic mind."[53] Whitman describes the third man as neither "child nor old, very calm, as of beautiful yellow-white ivory", and concludes that this is the "face of Christ himself'. In the *Gīta,* the qualities of "Calm, self-restraint, ascetic practice, purity, long suffering and uprightness, wisdom in theory as in practice, religious faith"[54] are assigned to the *sātivika* man. In Whitman's poem this man (within Whitman himself) exclaims:

> Divine am I inside and out, and I make holy whatever
> I touch or am touched from;

In Blake's poem, the unfallen Urizen, who appropriates these qualities, is quite unaware of his real majesty. It is only when he realizes his true nature that he marches back from heart to the mind of Albion and Albion's being is integrated.

In both Blake and Whitman the unity and disintegration of the three archetypal characters is also responsible for the integration and disintegration of society which is the body of the Primal Man. From section forty-four up to the end of the poem *Song of Myself,* Whitman assumes the role of the Super-Man and gives a vision of the world in his body—the vision similar to the one Krishnā gave to Arjuna in the *Gītā.* "One essential principle of archetypal criticism is that the individual and the universal forms of an image are identical.[55] This applies to Whitman's *Song of Myself* (I contain multitudes./I concentrate toward them that are nigh... I wait on the door-slab), and Blake's *The Four Zoas,* because nothing exists apart from the body of Albion and Whitman. Both Albion and Whitman transform the world into a community and become the virtual archetypes of "images of symposium, communion, order, friendship and love".[56] The Primal Man myth in Whitman, therefore, apart from the possibility of having been derived from the Hindu sources available to him, and from Emerson and Thoreau, might also have been derived from Whitman's readings of Blake who, in turn, derived it from Hindu sources.

Notes and References

1. Northrop Frye, *Fearful Symmetry: A Study of William Blake* (Princeton: Princeton University Press, 1947), p. 173.
2. *Blake: Complete Writings* (ed.), Geoffrey Keynes (London: Oxford University Press, 1974), p. 583.
3. A.C. Swinburne, *William Blake: A Critical Essay* (London: J.C. Holten, 1968).
4. See Swinburne's essay on William Blake reprinted in *The Complete Works of Swinburne* (1926), ed., Sir Edmund Gosse and Thomas James Wise, VI. pp. 342-46. Swinburne remarked that Blake and Whitman are so much alike that there might be some reason "to preach the transition of souls or transfusion of spirits".

5. S.F. Damon, *William Blake: His Philosophy and Symbols.* (New York, 1947).
6. "A Descriptive Catalogue", in Keynes, *op.cit.,* p. 565.
7. Gay Wilson Allen (ed.), *Walt Whitman: Leaves of Grass* (New York: The New American Library, 1958), p. viii.
8. James E. Miller, Jr. (ed.), *Walt Whitman: Complete Poetry and Selected Prose* (Boston: Riverside Edition, 1959), pp. 449-50.
9. "A Descriptive Catalogue", in Keynes, *op.cit.,* p. 565.
10. Milton O. Perceival, "Blake's Philosophy", in Judith O' Neill, (ed.), *Critics on Blake* (London: George Allen & Unwin Ltd., 1970), pp. 32-3.
11. Malcolm Cowely (ed.), *Walt Whitman: Leaves of Grass* (New Delhi: Allied Publishers, 1959), p. xi.
12. T.S. Eliot wrote in 1920: "His (Blake's) philosophy, like his versions, like his insight, like his technique, was his own". *The Sacred Wood* (London: Methuen, 1920), p. 155.
13. Swinburne, generally appreciative of Whitman, attacked him in an essay, "Whitmania": But Mr. Whitman's Eye is a drunken applewoman, indecently sprawling in the slush and garbage of the guner amid the rotten refuse of her overturned free-stall". See "William Blake: A Critical Essay," in *The Complete Works of Algernon Charles Swinburne* (New York. 1926), Vol. VI, pp. 242-43. T.S. Eliot found the same formal breakdowns in Whitman which he had earlier found in Blake.
14. A.C. Swinburne, *William Blake* (London, 1868), p. 337.
15. Gay Wilson Allen, *The Solitary Singer: A Critical Biography of Walt Whitman* (New York: Macmillan, 1955), p. 392.
16. *Ibid.,* p. 400.
17. Thomas B. Harned (ed.), *The Letters of Anne Gilchrist and Walt Whitman* (New York, 1918), Quoted in Gay Wilson Allen, *op.cit.,* p. 415.
18. Thomas B. Harned (ed.), *op.cit.,* pp. 56-7.
19. *Ibid.*
20. Reprinted in Thomas B. Harned (ed.), *op.cit.,* pp. 3-22.
21. William 1. Fisher, II. Willard Reninger, Ralph Samuelson, K.B.Vaid (eds.), *American Literature of the Nineteenth Century: An Anthology* (New Delhi: Eurasia, 1955), p. 281. See also Gay

Wilson Allen, (ed.), *Walt Whitman: Leaves of Grass:* "He was interested in books and ideas, especially those of deistic Tom Paine whom he knew personally. . .", p. vi.

22. Geoffrey Keynes (ed.), *Blake: Complele Writings,* p. 383.
23. Gay Wilson Allen, *The Solitary Singer: A Critical Biography of Walt Whitman* (New York: Macmillan, 1955). p. 540. The design showed "a triangular capstone, and the location at the base of a small hill with laurel and oak trees".
24. Richard Maurice Bucke. Thomas B. Harned and Horace L. Traubel (eds)., *The Complete Writings of Walt Whitman* (New York, 1902). Vol. III, p. 55.
25. Gay Wilson Allen (ed.), *op.cit.,* p. 141.
26. Gay Wilson Allen (ed.). *Walt Whitman: Leaves of Grass* (New York: New American Library. 1955), p. ix.
27. *English Journal* (College ed.). XXVII, 597-607 (Sept., 1938).
28. Harold W. Blodgett and Sculley Bradley (eds.), *Walt Whitman: Leaves of Grass* (London: University of London Press, 1965), p. xxxi.
29. G. Keynes (ed.), *Blake: Complele Writings,* p. 578.
30. W.J. Wilkins. *Hindu Mythology* (New Delhi: Rupa, 1978), pp. 343-44.
31. R.C. Zaehner (ed.), *The Bhagavadgita* (London: Oxford University Press, 1975), p. 177.
32. W.Y. Evans-Wentz (ed.), *The Tibetan Book of the Dead* (London: Oxford University Press, 1960), p. xiv.
33. Maud Bodkin. *Archetypal Patterns* in *Poetry* (London: Oxford University Press, 1978). p. 2.
34. N. Frye, *Anatomy of Criticism* (Princeton: Princeton University Press, 1973), p. 99.
35. "... he (Whitman) early identified himself with the great 'archetypal' poetry of the past and recognised some obscure relationship between it and the primitive natural forces of the universe", says James E. Miller, Jr., in his *Walt Whitman* (Allahabad: A.H. Wheeler, 1971). p. 42.
36. Both Blake and Whitman identified the Father and the Son. Blake makes Christ say in *Jerusalem:* "I am in you and you in me mutual in love divine." Plate 4 in Geoffrey Keyecs (ed.),

Blake: Complete Writings, p. 622. In the poem "To him that was Crucified" Whitman calls Christ his "comrade" and "dear brother". See Gay Allen (ed.). *Walt Whitman: Leaves of Grass,* p. 305.

37. "You cannot create a very large poem without introducing a more impersonal point of view or splitting it up into various personalities". T.S. Eliot, *The Sacred Wood* (New Delhi: B.I, Publications, 1976), p, 156.
38. For a comparison of Wordsworth and Whitman, see F.O. Matthiessen, *American Renaissance* (Delhi: Oxford University Press, 1973), pp. 613-18.
39. N. Frye, *Anatomy of Criticism* (Princeton: Princeton University Press, 1957), p. 163.
40. "But never will you be able to see Me with this your (natural) eye. A celestial eye I'll give you, 'behold my power as Lord"'. Chapter XI, 8, in RC. Zaehner (ed.), *The Bhagavadgita,* p. 305.
41. N. Frye, *op.cit.,* p. 171.
42. See G. Keynes (cd.), *Blake: Complete Writings,* p. 152.
43. R.C. Zaehner (ed.), *The Bhagavadgita,* Chapter XVIII, 20-2, p. 104.
44. Apart from sense (Tharmas), mind (Luvah), and soul (Urizen), who are within the world of nature, *Ātman* (Self) is a minute part of God himself and as such it does not manifest itself. However, a part of it conjoins to the psychosomatic organism: "In the world of living things a minute part of Me, eternal (still), becomes a living (self), drawing to itself the five senses and the mind which have thcir roots in Nature", See R.C. Zaehner, *op.cit.,* p. 367. This minute part is Blake's Los.
45. W.J. Wilkins, *Hindu Mythology,* pp. 343-44. Frye has also referred to the myth in connection with Blake. See his *Fearful Symmetry,* p. 287.
46. R.C. Zaehner, *op.cit.,* p. 306.
47. James E. Miller, Jr. (ed.), *Walt Whitman: Complete Poetry and Selected Prose,* p. 444.
48. Horace Traubel (ed.), *Re Walt Whitman* (Philadelphia, 1983), p. 24.
49. See the translation of *Laws of Manu* in Lord Teignmouth (ed.), *The Works of Sir William Jones,* Vol. VIII, pp. 92-4.

50. R.C. Zaehner, *The Bhagavadgita,* XVII, 5-6, p. 376.
51. "A Descriptive Catalogue", in G. Keynes (ed.), *Blake: Complete Writings,* p. 580.
52. *Ibid.*
53. *Ibid.*
54. R.C. Zaehner (ed.), *Op.cit.,* XVIII, 42, p. 393.
55. William J. Handy and Max Westbrook (eds.), *Twentieth Century Criticism: The Major Statements* (New Delhi: Light and Life, 1974), p. 242.
56. *Ibid.*

Suggested Reading

Aldridge, A. Owen (ed.), *Comparative Literature: Matter and Method,* Urbana, 1969.

Auerbach, Eric, *Mimesis,* trans. W. Trask, New York: Doubleday Anchor Books, 1953.

Baudkin, Maud, *Archetypal Patterns in Poetry,* New York: Vintage Books, 1958.

Brandt-Corstius, Jan, *Introduction to the Comparative Study of Literature,* New York, 1967.

Brower, Reuben A (ed.), On *Translation,* Cambridge, Mass, 1959 and New York, 1966.

Burke, Kenneth, *The Philosophy of Literary Form,* Baton Rouge, La.: Louisiana State University Press, 1941.

Campbell, Joseph, *Hero With a Thousand Faces,* New York: Pantheon Books, 1949.

Curtius, E.R., *European Literature and the Latin Middle Ages,* trans. W. Trask, London: Routledge & Kegan Paul, 1953.

Demetz, P., Greene, T., and Nelson, L., *The Disciplines of Criticism: Essays in Literary Theory, Interpretation and History,* Festschrift for Rene Wellek, New Haven, 1968.

Durkheim, Emile, *The Elementary Forms of the Religious Life,* trans. Joseph Ward Swain, London: Allen & Unwin, 1915.

Eliade, Mircea, *Cosmos and History: The Myth of the Eternal*

Return, trans. Willard R. Trask, New York: Harper Torchbooks, 1949,1954,1959.

Eliot, T.S., *Selected Essays,* London: Faber, 1951. First edn., 1932.

—, *The Sacred Wood,* First edn., Methuen, 1920.

Fletcher, John, "The Criticism of Comparison: the Approach Through Comparative Literature and Intellectual History", in *Contemporary Criticism,* Stratford-upon-Avon Studies XII, London, 1970.

Frazer, Sir James, *The Golden Bough: A Study in Magic and Religion,* New York: Macmillan & Co., 1922, 1940.

Freud, Sigmund, *Totem and Taboo,* trans. AA. Brill, New York: Moffat, Yard & Co., 1918.

Friederich, Werner P. and Malone, D.H., *Outline of Comparative Literature from Dante Alighieri to Eugene O'Neill,* University of North Carolina Press, 1954.

Frye, Northrop,*Anatomy of Criticism: Four Essays,* New Jersey: Princeton University Press, 1957.

—, *Fables of Identity,* New York: Harcourt, Brace & World Inc., 1963.

Furst, Lilian R., *Romanticism in Perspective: A Comparative Study of the Romantic Movements in England, France and Germany,* London, 1969.

Gennep, Arnold Van, *The Rites of Passage,* trans. Monica B. Viredom & Gabrielle L. Caffee, London: Routledge & Kegan Paul, 1960.

Gifford, Henry, *Comparative Literature,* London, 1969.

Gillies, Alexander, "Some Thoughts on Comparative Literature", in *Yearbook of Comparative and General Literature,* 1 (1952).

Hassan, I.H., "The Problem Influence in Literary History: Notes Towards a Definition", in *Journal of Aesthetics and Art Criticism* 14 (1955).

Holmes, T. Urban, Jun, "Comparative Literature: Past and

Future", in C.G. Coffman (ed.) *Studies in Language and Literature,* Chapel Hill, 1945, pp. 62-73.

Hough, Graham, *All Essay on criticism,* London, 1966. Howarth, H., *Notes On Some Figures Behind T.S. Eliot,* London: Chatto & Windus, 1965.

Hyman, Stanley Edgar, *The Armed Vision: A Study in the Methods of Modern Literary Criticism,* New York, 1948 (new edn. 1955).

Levin, Harry, *Contexts of Criticism,* Cambridge, Mass., 1957.

—, *Refractions: Essays in Comparative Literature,* Oxford, 1966.

—, "Comparing in Literature", *Yearbook of Comparative and General Literature,* 17 (1968).

Levy-Bruhl, Lucien, *Primitive Mentality,* trans. Lilian A. Clare, London: George Allen & Unwin, 1923.

Lewis, C.S., *The Allegory of Love,* London: Oxford University Press, 1938.

Lewis, R.W.B., *The American Adam: Innocence, Tragedy and Tradition in the Nineteenth Century.* Chicago: University of Chicago Press, 1955.

Lovejoy, Arthur O., *The Great Chain of Being: A Study of the History of an Idea,* Cambridge, Mass., 1936.

—, *Essays in History of Ideas,* Baltimore, 1948.

Malinowski, Bronislaw, *Myth in Primitive Psychology,* London: K. Paul, Trench, Trubner, 1926.

Malone, David H., "The 'Comparative' in Comparative Literature", in *Yearbook of Comparative and General Literature* 2 (1954).

Miner, Earl, *The Japanese Tradition in British and American Literature* New Jersey: Princeton University Press, 1958.

Nagendra (ed.), *Comparative Literature,* Delhi: Delhi University Press, 1977.

Pearce, Roy Harvey, *The Continuity of American Poetry,* New Jersey: Princeton University Press, 1961.

Posnett, Hutchison Macaulay, *Comparative Literature*, London, 1886.

Prawer, S.S., *Comparative Literary Studies: An Introduction*, London: Duckworth, 1973.

Praz, Mario, *The Romantic Agony*, trans. A. Davidson, Oxford University Press (Collins), 1933, 1960.

Remak, Henry H.H., "Comparative Literature: Its Definition and Function", in Newton P. Stallknecht and Horst Frenz (eds.), *Comparative Literature: Method and Perspective*. Carbondale, Ill, 1961, pp. 3-37.

Roellinger, EX., Jun., "Two Theories of Poetry as Knowledge", in *Southern Review*, VII (1942), pp. 690-705.

Santayana, George, *Three Philosophical Poets: Lucretius, Dante, Goethe*, New York: Doubleday Anchor (reprint), 1910.

Savory, Theodore, *The Art of Translation*, (new enlarged edition), London, 1968.

Shapiro, Karl (ed.), *Prose Keys to Modern Poetry*, Evanston, Illinois: Row Peterson & Co., 1962.

Singh, Charu Sheel, *The Chariot of Fire* (Blake & Hindu Thought), Salzburg, 1981.

Spitzer, Leo, *Linguistics and Literary History: Essays in Stylistics*, New Jersey, 1948.

Wellek, Rene, *A History of Modern Criticism, 1750-1950*, New Haven, 1955 ff.

—, *Concepts of Criticism*, New Haven, 1963.

—, *Discriminations*, New Havsen, 1970.

—, & Warren, Austin, *Theory of Literature*, (third edition), Harmondsworth, 1963.

Will, J.S., "Comparative Literature: Its Meaning and Scope", in *University of Toronto Quarterly*, VIII (1939), pp. 165-79.

Wilson, Edmund, *Axel's Castle: A Study in the Imaginative Literature of 1870-1930*.

BIBLIOGRAPHIES, JOURNALS AND YEARBOOKS

Baldensperger, Fernand and Friederich, Werner P. *Bibliography of Comparative Literature,* Chapel Hill: University of North Carolina Press, 1950. Continued in Volumes 1-9 of the *Yearbook of Comparative and General Literature; Comparative Literature* (Journal). University of Oregon, Ed. C.H. Beall; *Comparative Literature Studies* (Journal), University of Illinois, Ed. A.O, Aldridge; *Yearbook of Comparative Criticism,* Pennsylvania State University, Ed. J.P. Strelka; *Cassell's Encyclopaedia of Literature,* Ed. S.H. Steiriberg, 2 Vols, Cassell, 1953; J.T. Shipley, *Dictionary of World Literature: Criticism-Forms-Technique,* London: Routledge, 1943, 1953.

Index

C